FORM 125 M

EDUCATION DEPARTMENT

Cop. 1

The Chicago Public Library

March 13, 1972

Received

*Program Budgeting
for
School District Planning*

PROGRAM BUDGETING

FOR

SCHOOL DISTRICT PLANNING

Sue A. Haggart
Editor

Contributors

Stephen M. Barro
Margaret B. Carpenter
James A. Dei Rossi
Sue A. Haggart
Marjorie L. Rapp
Gerald C. Sumner

Educational Technology Publications
Englewood Cliffs, New Jersey 07632

Copyright © 1972 The Rand Corporation.

All rights reserved. No part of this book may be reproduced or transmitted, in any form or by any means, electronic or mechanical, including photocopying, recording, or by any information storage and retrieval system, without permission in writing from The Rand Corporation and the Publisher, Educational Technology Publications, Englewood Cliffs, New Jersey 07632.

Printed in the United States of America.

Library of Congress Catalog Card Number: 76-170027.

International Standard Book Number: 0-87778-026-9.

First Printing

*A Rand Corporation
Research Study*

PREFACE

This book addresses the question, "What is program budgeting?" It explores the potential of program budgeting as a means to more effective allocation of educational resources at the school district level. The term "program budgeting" is used throughout as a matter of expediency more than anything else; the term "Planning-Programming-Budgeting System" (PPBS) may be substituted as dictated by reader preference. We are using the term "program budgeting" to mean that collection of concepts and techniques that assists the educational planner in the determination of how well resources are being used at the present time and in the selection of preferred ways to use resources in the future. Our emphasis is on the applicability of these concepts and techniques of program budgeting to educational planning.

In this book, we develop the idea that program budgeting, despite its title, is more than a nice, neat method of budgeting by program; and that, as such, program budgeting requires more than just concentration on budgeting and accounting procedures. Program budgeting—basically a resource allocation system—stresses the setting of objectives, grouping activities into programs to meet the objectives, identifying the resources required by the programs, and measuring the effectiveness of the programs in meeting the objectives. The purpose of the program budgeting effort is to provide the organized data base for the systematic selection of the preferred course of action. This means that alternative programs are evaluated in terms of their impact on present programs and in terms of their future consequences. This evaluation makes many demands on all levels of the decisionmaking hierarchy of the school district. The nature and extent of these demands are discussed within the conceptual framework of program budgeting.

In Chapter One, the conceptual framework of program budgeting is briefly described in terms of the activities, the components, and the documentation to the program budgeting process. This framework then serves as the guide for discussions in the following chapters. Chapter One also provides the introductory discussion of the need for improved educational planning and of the ways in which program budgeting can meet this need. The emphasis is on the system-analytical aspect of program budgeting and on the role of program budgeting in the decisionmaking process at the school district level.

The structural aspect of program budgeting is the subject of Chapter Two; the concepts and problems of developing a program structure as the means for relating activities and objectives are discussed, and an illustrative program structure for a school district is delineated. This program structure is then used in Chapter Three in the comparison of the traditional budget of a school district to the program budget. The primary purpose of this comparison is to indicate how differences in the budget reflect basic differences in the approach to planning.

The secondary purpose is to develop the technique of the "crosswalk"—the mechanism that makes it possible to translate the data in the program budget into the traditional budget format. This ability, to translate from one format to another, is necessary when the district plans must continue to be presented in terms of the regular appropriation budget categories. It is also helpful, when used with caution and on a temporary basis, in the early stages of implementation of a program budgeting system; it provides a frame of reference and a link with the past in thinking about the merits of new or old programs.

Chapters Four through Nine are concerned with the analytical aspect of program budgeting. The purpose of analysis is to provide the capability to systematically examine the consequences of decisions; the product of analysis is information in the form of the projected cost and the benefit of proposed courses of action. In Chapter Four, the school district is viewed as a system; and in this way the variables that play a part in defining an educational program can be more consistently and more completely identified. This is a logical first step in developing a model of resource utilization within the school district. It forces what might be called an inventory of district activities—resources, their present use, and the educational outcome achieved. This information then becomes the beginning position for considering the cost consequences and the expected benefit of alternatives.

It is generally agreed that the methodology of resource and cost modeling is relatively advanced in comparison with the state of the art in developing models of effectiveness. A great deal of work needs to be done before it is possible to establish valid predictive relationships between the resource characteristics of an educational program and the resulting educational outcome. However, we believe that the analytical effort necessary just to "do" program budgeting will provide a productive context in which to pursue these relationships between input and output.

The discussions of Chapters Five and Six reflect this belief. By encouraging the use of systematic techniques for planning, program budgeting should lead to the expansion and improvement of ways to relate the quantity and quality of an educational product to the resources used to create it. In Chapter Five, the concepts and the techniques of cost analysis are presented, and the major considerations in the development of a cost model are described. The concepts and techniques are then used in an illustrative program cost analysis. Chapter Five is a straightforward exposition that should help in the quest for better information about the resource requirements of an educational program, better than that conveyed by using only the cost per student or cost per student-hour as an indicator of program cost.

In Chapter Six effectiveness is discussed from two points of view: (1) ways in which the effectiveness of various aspects of a school district's programs can be measured and (2) techniques for using these measures. The discussion is intended to suggest promising avenues for further development as program budgeting is implemented in individual districts. We believe that the crux of the problem is not so much to develop new measures but, rather, to assemble information that is scattered throughout the system in such a way that the best use can be made of it. With this in mind, the discussion draws heavily on dimensions of effectiveness that educational planners are currently using.

Evaluating alternatives—being able to systematically choose the preferred course of action—is both the *why* and the *how* of program budgeting for educational planning. Chapter Seven outlines, briefly, the most basic techniques employed in the evaluation of alternatives and discusses some of the considerations in using them in educational decisionmaking. Chapter Eight provides an example of the analysis of an educational program using Project R-3 of the San Jose Unified School District, State of California. The approach in comparing program configuration is to generate equal-cost alternatives and then to compare their effectiveness. Thus, it provides an illustration of many of the problems and limitations of cost-effectiveness analysis in educational planning. Chapter Nine then explores the more specific problems encountered in the evaluation of innovative educational programs. The emphasis is on the nature of the evaluation and on the role of the evaluator. Special attention is given to evaluation within the informational context provided by the implementation of a district budgeting system.

The use of program budgeting to provide a framework for collecting, organizing, and analyzing information about a school district's activities is the subject of the first nine chapters. Its use is not, however, restricted to the resolution of problems within the jurisdiction of the school district; Chapter Ten looks at some ways in which program budgeting can assist decisionmakers and the public by providing insight into problems both within and outside of the school district.

Chapter Eleven discusses some of the considerations in developing a program budgeting system. It outlines some steps that might be taken to ensure that the effort to develop a program budgeting system will not result in just another accounting scheme. In addition to outlining these steps, a discussion of the activity areas involved in designing, implementing, and operating a program budgeting system is provided.

This effort was jointly funded by the U.S. Office of Education, the California State Department of Education, and The Rand Corporation. The results should be of interest to educational planners and administrators concerned with the more effective allocation of resources within their educational system.

Sue A. Haggart
The Rand Corporation

ACKNOWLEDGMENTS

We are indebted to the staff of the San Jose Unified School District of The State of California for technical assistance, for general advice, and for providing the data used in some of the illustrative examples. In particular, we wish to acknowledge the help of James R. Anderson, Associate Superintendent, and William A. Doyle, Supervisor of Compensatory Education. We are also indebted to many of our colleagues at Rand for the comments, the criticisms, and the support they provided during the preparation of this book. We especially wish to thank David Novick, Robert D. Specht, Gene H. Fisher, and Lee D. Attaway.

Finally, we wish to thank The Rand Corporation for the opportunity to do the research supporting our preparation of the material in this book.

LIST OF FIGURES

Figure		Page
1.	The Nature of Program Budgeting	8
2.	The System-Analytical Aspect of Program Budgeting	14
3.	A Segment of One Hierarchy of Educational Objectives	27
4.	Three-Way Categorization of Educational Programs	34
5.	Overall Structure of a Model of a School District	72
6.	School System Decisions, Programs, and Their Implications	74
7.	School System Resource Requirements and Budgets	89
8.	District Operating Staff as a Function of District Size as Measured by Average Daily Attendance	114
9.	Comparison of Five-Year Costs for Base Case and Two Alternatives	122
10.	Examples of Relationships Between Effectiveness and Resources	136
11.	Finding the Effectiveness of Program Elements	138
12.	The "Effectiveness" of a District	140
13.	A Hypothetical Benefit-Cost Relationship	149
14.	The Process of Analysis as Adapted from E.S. Quade	155
15.	Academic Gains	165
16.	Attitude Indicators	166
17.	Primary Objectives of R-3 Components	177
18.	Long-Term Growth in Reading Achievement	179

19.	Long-Term Growth in Reading Achievement for R-3 Program	179
20.	Effects of Reading Achievement Gains on Achievement in Science	179
21.	Effectiveness of Alternatives—First Assumption	181
22.	Effectiveness of Alternatives—Second Assumption	181
23.	Two Measures of Alternatives—First Assumption	183
24.	Two Measures of Effectiveness—Second Assumption	183
25.	The Impact of Features of a Program Budgeting System on Its Design, Implementation, and Operation	223
26.	Schematic of Activity Areas in the Development of a Program Budgeting System	228
27.	Nature of the Program Structure	231
28.	Characteristics of a Program Structure	233
29.	Partial Program Budget for the Department of Health, Education, and Welfare	234
30.	Illustrative Program Structure for a State Department of Education	234
31.	Pearl River Program Structure	235
32.	Programs Organized by What Is to Be Learned and by Other Student-Oriented Objectives	237
33.	Program Budget Example	239
34.	Summary of Traditional Expenditures and Reserves Budget	239
35.	Crosswalk Example	240
36.	Allocation of Students by Septile and Sex Among Groups	248
37.	Use of Curve Fitting to Project Enrollment: A Straight Line	260
38.	Use of Curve Fitting to Project Enrollment: A Growth Curve	260
39.	Error in Projection Related to District Size	262
40.	Enrollment Trends by Zone	262
41.	School District Boundaries and Demographic Areas	264
42.	Error in Projection Related to District Size	266

LIST OF TABLES

Table		Page
1.	Categorization of Activities into Programs According to Their Relationship to Educational Objectives	36
2.	A Possible Categorization of Programs by Type of Student	42
3.	A Possible Categorization of Programs by Level of Instruction	44
4.	A Possible Program Budget Format	47
5.	Crosswalk Example	51
6.	Distribution of Instructional Program Costs	56
7.	Summary Budget of Expenditures and Reserves	62
8.	Program Budget Example	63
9.	Specification of Programs, Vertical Organization of Instruction, and Rules for Assignment of Students for a Hypothetical School District	77
10.	Curriculum Composition by Program	79
11.	Instructional Design: Class Sizes and Resource Inputs	84
12.	School District Configuration: School Enrollment by Program and Level	92
13.	Translating Proposed Actions into Program Alternatives	97
14.	Variables in the Model of a School District	100
15.	Cost Element Structure	107
16.	Five-Year Projection of a Program Showing Cost Element Structure	109

17.	Average Daily Attendance and Operations Staff for Thirteen Hypothetical Districts	113
18.	Total Operations Salaries	115
19.	Cost of Base Case and Two Alternatives	122
20.	Programs Organized by What Is to Be Learned and by Other Student-Oriented Objectives	126
21.	A Breakdown of Socioeconomic Areas	131
22.	Test Results for a Program Element	132
23.	Cost of Options	169
24.	Supporting Cost Details	170
25.	Classroom-Related Cost	171
26.	Student-Related Cost	172
27.	Generation of Equal-Cost Alternatives	174
28.	Some Contributions of a School District Program Budgeting System to the Solution of Various Categories of Educational Problems	207
29.	Some Examples of Issues Categorized by "Scope of Action" and Program Orientation	218
30.	Group Means and Standard Deviations	249

CONTENTS

PREFACE — vii

ACKNOWLEDGMENTS — xiii

LIST OF FIGURES — xv

LIST OF TABLES — xvii

Chapter

I. PROGRAM BUDGETING FOR IMPROVED SCHOOL DISTRICT PLANNING — 3
    Sue A. Haggart
    Introduction — 3
    The Nature of Program Budgeting — 6
    The Uses of Program Budgeting — 10
    The Analytical Aspect of Program Budgeting — 13
    Scope of This Book — 18

II. DEVELOPMENT OF A PROGRAM STRUCTURE — 20
    Stephen M. Barro
    Introduction — 20
    Some Characteristics of a Program Structure — 21
    Formulating Educational Objectives — 23
    A Rationale for Program Categorization — 31
    A Set of Program Categories — 35
    The Complete Program Structure — 43
    Program Budget Formats — 45
    Summation — 48

III.	**THE PROGRAM BUDGET AND THE TRADITIONAL BUDGET**	49
	James A. Dei Rossi	
	Introduction	49
	The Crosswalk	50
	Information from the Program Budget	54
	Differences in the Budgets	57
	An Example	61
IV.	**MODELING RESOURCE UTILIZATION IN A SCHOOL DISTRICT**	67
	Stephen M. Barro	
	Introduction	67
	Resource Allocation Decisions and Alternatives	68
	A Public School System as a System	71
	Major Decision Variables in the System	73
	Curriculum Composition	78
	Resource and Cost Implications of a District Program	86
	System Variables and Program Effectiveness	93
	Issues and Alternatives	95
	Modeling the Program of a School District: A Summary	100
V.	**COST MODELS AND ANALYSIS OF COST**	102
	James A. Dei Rossi	
	Introduction	102
	Cost Analysis Methodology	103
	Developing a Cost Model	104
	Cost Models	117
	Program Cost Analysis	120
VI.	**THE ANALYSIS OF EFFECTIVENESS**	124
	Margaret B. Carpenter and Marjorie L. Rapp	
	Introduction	124
	Effectiveness of Program Elements	125
	Uses of Measures of Effectiveness	131
	Allocating Resources Among Program Elements	141
	Criteria of Effectiveness	142

Relationships Among Program Elements	143
Summary of Program Elements	146
Extra-Institutional Measures of Effectiveness	146
General Principles for Assessing Effectiveness	149

VII. EVALUATING ALTERNATIVES IN SCHOOL
DISTRICT PLANNING   152
    Sue A. Haggart

Introduction	152
Elements of the Analysis	153
The Process of Analysis	154
Characteristics of a "Better" Analysis	156
Some Techniques of Analysis	157

VIII. AN EXAMPLE OF THE ANALYSIS OF AN
EDUCATIONAL PROGRAM   160
    Margaret B. Carpenter and Sue A. Haggart

Introduction	160
Description of Project R-3	160
Generation of Equal-Cost Alternatives	167
Comparing the Effectiveness of Equal-Cost Alternatives	175

IX. EVALUATING INNOVATIVE EDUCATIONAL
PROGRAMS   185
    Marjorie L. Rapp and Gerald C. Sumner

Introduction	185
Three Functions of Evaluation	186
Planning for Evaluating	188
Considerations in the Experimental Design	190
Measuring Achievement	193
Planning for Future Implementation	196
Long-Term and Short-Term Program Assessment	197
Developmental Aspects of Evaluation	198

X. THE USE OF PROGRAM BUDGETING IN
DECISIONMAKING   203
    Margaret B. Carpenter

Introduction	203

	Categorization of Problems in Public Education	205
	Examples of the Use of Program Budgeting in Dealing with Issues	209
	Summary	218
XI.	**CONSIDERATIONS IN DEVELOPING A PROGRAM BUDGETING SYSTEM** *Sue A. Haggart*	220
	Introduction	220
	Problem Areas in Developing a Program Budgeting System	222
	Program Budgeting Educational Effort	224
	Coordination of Development Activities	225
	Developing an Analytical Capability	226
	Activity Areas in Developing the System	227
	Developing the Program Structure	229

Appendix

A.	ALLOCATION OF STUDENTS AMONG GROUPS *Gerald C. Sumner*	242
B.	EVALUATION AS FEEDBACK IN THE PROGRAM DEVELOPMENT CYCLE *Marjorie L. Rapp*	252
C.	PROJECTIONS OF ENROLLMENT *Margaret B. Carpenter*	257
D.	COST-EFFECTIVENESS ANALYSIS FOR EDUCATIONAL PLANNING *Margaret B. Carpenter and Sue A. Haggart*	270

SELECTED BIBLIOGRAPHY	284
INDEX	289

*Program Budgeting
for
School District Planning*

CHAPTER ONE

PROGRAM BUDGETING FOR IMPROVED SCHOOL DISTRICT PLANNING

Sue A. Haggart

Introduction

Many educational administrators are currently involved in efforts to develop a planning-programming-budgeting system (PPBS) for their organizations. These efforts were begun for a variety of reasons. In California, legislative action, through Assembly Bill 61, resulted in the formation of the State Advisory Commission on School District Budgeting and Accounting. The Commission has the responsibility "to recommend to the State Board of Education procedures for implementing program budgeting and accounting for school districts." In Philadelphia, an incoming school board president initiated and supported the development of a program budgeting system as a means of helping him to understand, and react to, the educational and financial crises of his district.

Underlying the specific impetus for these developmental efforts was, perhaps, a recognition that program budgeting—basically a resource allocation system—might provide the way to meet the need for improved educational planning. The need is recognized by the educational community as well as the lay community.

It is not necessary, here, to quote all the data that reveal the increasing size and complexity of the job school district administrators are being asked to do; nor will we give all the details of the financial picture. These areas have been extensively covered in publications of the U.S. Office of Education, in journals of the educational community, in magazines, and in the daily newspapers. Educational administrators are faced with the pressure of increasing enrollment and with the demand for a greater diversity in educational programs. Programs have to be tailored in recognition of the special problems of some groups of students, such as the educationally handicapped student or the minority group student.

The increased cost of maintaining the educational status quo is a fact of life; the same educational resources cost more each year. Resource availability also presents a problem; in some cases, exactly what is needed is not available at any price. That the educational community is being asked to do a better job under a severe financial handicap sums up the situation. The squeeze is on, and the pressure is increasing.

Increasing taxpayer resistance also is being demonstrated. Tax override requests and school bond issues are being defeated with great regularity. Following a recent defeat, the statement was made that the taxpayers might be trying to show their demand for increased state aid to local districts, rather than increased local support. This might be true.

On the other hand, the taxpayers might be asking for some indication of better management of the resources used or evidence of a better product from the educational system. In short, they might be asking for information about what is happening: What is the educational system? What kind of education is being provided for their children? Is there a different, and perhaps better, way of doing business? Alex Mood, a former U.S. Assistant Commissioner of Education, gave a succinct description of this feeling:

> Education is on stage as never before. Results are demanded. Resources cannot be piled upon resources to achieve those

results. The nation must discover more efficient as well as more effective ways to conduct educational operations.*

In a more general sense, the same thoughts were expressed not long ago by thirty acknowledged leaders in their respective fields.** These leaders identified five major challenges facing society in the 1970's. These were: (1) international relations and the dangers of triggering a world war; (2) the deficiencies of our physical environment, particularly in our cities; (3) population control and feeding the world; (4) the need for more, better, and different education; and (5) the human problems associated with advancing technology.

Education has an impact on all of these challenges, on some more than on others. But we are interested in the fourth item. How do you go about planning to meet this challenge? Logically, one must know what he has today before he can plan for *better* education. Planning for *more* education is a problem all the time, not just a challenge for the 1970's. Planning for a *different* education is the most difficult, but certainly the most interesting, challenge. Planning to meet this challenge demands a great deal more information about the educational system as it is today. Answers should be available to these questions: What should the educational system be trying to do? What are the dimensions of the future? What is being bought for the resources being spent? How does what is being bought contribute to the purpose of the educational programs? What, actually, is the effectiveness of current programs? Could another means achieve the same result for, perhaps, a lower cost? Or, at what cost could a greater effectiveness be achieved? In a broader sense, what kind of education will be needed by what type of student five years from now?

Program budgeting has a good chance of being an excellent

---

*Alex Mood, "The Operations Analysis Program of the U.S. Office of Education," in Werner Z. Hirsch *et al., Inventing Education for the Future,* Chandler Publishing Company, San Francisco, 1967, pp. 184-185.
**L.L.L. Golden, "Challenges of the 1970's," *Saturday Review,* March 9, 1968, p. 104.

approach to improved educational planning, if the analytical aspect is given as much emphasis as the accounting aspects. As a resource allocation system that stresses setting objectives,* defining programs to meet these objectives, identifying the resources required, and systematically analyzing and evaluating alternative programs, program budgeting provides a viable framework for determining a better use of scarce educational resources. It is the purpose of this book to explore this potential.

The book will concentrate on the program budgeting process at the school district level. In educational planning there are, at this time, at least three major decisionmaking levels—federal, state, and local. Basically, all levels have the same broad objective of "education"; but each level has different operational objectives, pursues these objectives through different activities, and encounters different resource allocation problems. Each level is different in the decisions that are made, in the information needed to help make the decisions, and in the means of financial control. Because of these differences, the program budgets are different. Thus, three program budgets result: the federal or national program budget for education, the state educational program budget, and the school district program budget. The differences mentioned are reflected in the program structure for each level. The components of the program budgeting *process* are, of course, the same.

The Nature of Program Budgeting

Since this book is not intended as a summary of the literature on program budgeting, it is assumed that the reader is acquainted with many of the current studies of program budgeting in general. In addition to Novick,** other sources listed in the bibliography of selected publications provide an excellent insight into the

---

*Throughout this book, we use the word "objective" in its general sense. This is as opposed to the narrower usage in the educational community that is concerned with the definition of specific "instructional objectives" *within* a given course of instruction.

**David Novick (ed.), *Program Budgeting: Program Analysis and the Federal Budget,* 2nd ed., Harvard University Press, Cambridge, Massachusetts, 1967.

Program Budgeting for Improved School District Planning   7

problems of program budgeting.

For the purpose of this book, the briefest way to describe program budgeting is first to cover the activities involved in the process, next to describe the components of the process, and then to outline the formal documentation of the system. This breakdown is shown in Figure 1.

William Gorham, President of the Urban Institute, described the *activities* involved in the process in the following statement:*

> The Planning-Programming-Budgeting System is a framework for planning—a way of organizing information and analysis in a systematic fashion so that the consequences of particular choices can be seen as clearly as possible. It attempts to do three things:
>
> (1) To display information about the functioning of actual governmental programs so that it is possible to see easily what portion of federal resources is being allocated to particular purposes, what is being accomplished by the programs, and how much they cost;
>
> (2) To analyze the costs of alternative methods of achieving particular objectives so that it is possible to rank the alternatives in terms of their relative costs;
>
> (3) To evaluate the benefits of achieving objectives as comprehensively and quantitatively as possible in order to facilitate the setting of priorities among objectives.

Gorham's statement supports the major contention of this book—that program budgeting is more than a method of budgeting by program. Many activities are involved. These activities are carried on within the various components of the program budgeting process. The results are reported in the documentation demanded by the process.

There are four major components of the program budgeting process. All are essential in the complete system. The first component concerns the *structural aspect*. This involves the

---

*William Gorham, "Notes of a Practitioner," *The Public Interest*, Issue No. 8, Summer 1967, pp. 4-5.

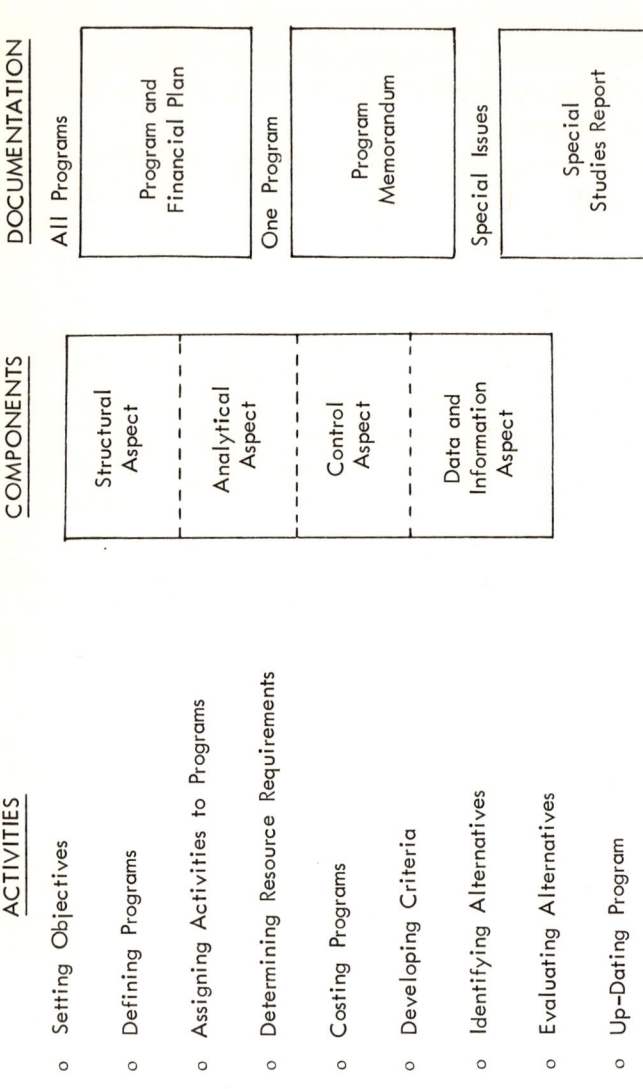

Figure 1

The Nature of Program Budgeting

setting of objectives and the development of a program structure. These are interacting activities. Attempts to identify groups of programs that, either singly or in combination, help to meet objectives will also help to clarify objectives. Conversely, clarification of the objectives will facilitate the task of grouping program elements into programs.

The second major component of program budgeting is the *analytical aspect*. It is within this area that the cost-effectiveness analyses and trade-offs are made. It is in this area also that the generation or identification of alternative ways to meet objectives most often takes place.

The third major component of program budgeting is the *control aspect*. Basically, this involves keeping tabs on how well a new program is being implemented and recording program changes—in other words, progress reporting and control.

The fourth component of a program budgeting system is its *data and information aspect*. The analytical component of program budgeting influences the choice of data. As the successful implementation and utilization of the system progresses, certain data appear that were not evident before. These data then become useful, not so much as an end in themselves, but rather because they support the analytical part of the process.

The implication is that *all* of these activities must be carried out to produce and maintain the program budgeting process. This is true. The program budget produced is rather formally referred to as the *Program and Financial Plan*. This report is a summary of all programs. It displays the expenditure consequences over time—usually five or ten years—of decisions already made. It shows, where possible, the physical dimensions of the programs and the non-dollar resource requirements of the programs. Thus, it is more than just the financial picture of a particular plan.

In addition, for educational planning, data concerning the objectives of the programs, the criteria used for evaluation of effectiveness, and the effectiveness of the programs should be reported in a separate section of the Program and Financial Plan document. The educational achievement of the district's programs should be visible. This visibility is essential if progress is to be realized in determining measures of educational results and in developing input-output relationships within the educational process.

There are two other formal documents that are an integral part of an operational program budgeting system. These are the *Program Memorandum* and the *Special Studies Report.* The Program Memorandum is prepared for each major program—either instructional or support—and contains the recommendations; identifies issues involved, in terms of a selection from among alternatives; and explains the basis for the selection. The Special Studies Report is prepared for individual issues of particular importance and provides the analytical background for recommendations. The Special Studies Report may well encompass more than one program.

The Uses of Program Budgeting

In addition to providing timely information for the program budgeting process, the Program Memorandum and the Special Studies Report also provide convenient vehicles for responding to special requests. In school district planning, these requests could come from the State Board of Education, federal agencies, the local school board, and various citizen committees. Information about school district plans, when organized in support of the program budgeting system, becomes readily available to answer these requests with a minimum of time and effort. This use of program budgeting is a direct benefit to the administrative staff of the school district.

Program budgeting is a way of life—a planning life. It forces explicit consideration of many things not usually thought of as an integral part of the budgeting process. Such things as objectives, the priorities of objectives, and the dimensions of the future take their place along with the usual considerations of fund availability, resource availability, and required expenditures. The result is budgetary documentation that is a part of the decisionmaking process and not just a record of what happened last year, what might happen this year, and a five percent increase for what might happen next year. The program budget becomes, in fact, an instrument for orderly, considered change—the means to achieving improved educational planning.

The analytical effort necessary just to do program budgeting provides a focal point for identifying, developing, evaluating, and implementing educational change. The major output of this effort is an organized information base to aid the decisionmaker in making a more informed decision. The decisionmaker has a framework for identifying alternative ways of meeting objectives, for evaluating the contribution of alternative ways of meeting the objectives, and for analyzing his current mode of operation.

The program budget also aids educational planners by serving as a communication device for both intradistrict and extradistrict communication. The Program and Financial Plan, with its supporting documentation, is a meaningful display mechanism for presenting the magnitude and purpose of school district operations to the school board, to the public in general, and to taxpayers in particular.

For example, an educational program was recently presented as a list of needs that were envisioned for the coming year. These needs were stated in terms of instructional *input,* such as ten master teachers to improve reading, rather than in terms of *output.* Each need had a price tag. That much was all right. What was unknown was, what was this money buying? What was the contribution of this need-list to meeting the objectives of the district? If this particular list of needs was bought for the coming year, what would be the financial implications for the next few years? These questions were not even asked, let alone answered. However, there was one interesting point raised by a member of the school board. He asked, "Is there any place to cut the budget without decreasing the availability of education or the quality of education? Are there any programs that can be deleted?" There was no answer to that question. The answer is not to tell the school board what programs should be deleted but to provide them with information about the effectiveness and the cost of various alternatives so that an informed selection can be made.

For extradistrict communication, the program budget can serve as a common basis for discussion and exchange of ideas with other districts and with state and federal educational agencies. All available knowledge about a particular innovation should be on record, accessible and meaningful to other interested agencies. "On record" does not necessarily mean on file in a state-wide educational data bank, but rather recorded so that all assumptions, problems, results, etc., about an innovation, such as educational television, are together in one package.

Erick Lindman, Professor of Educational Administration, University of California at Los Angeles, noted the requirement for a framework for evaluating educational innovation as follows:*

> Clearly, the evaluation process must be more than a comparison of achievement-test scores, it must recognize the many dimensions of education. During this period of ferment in education, we need, above all, an innovation in the process by which educational practices and innovations are evaluated... Each decisionmaker needs information relevant to the choices he must make.
>
> A review and evaluation system which provides continuously for each decisionmaker the evidence he needs to make his decision would do much to improve education. To some extent such a process functions now, but major improvements are possible and sorely needed. This is the central challenge to school administrators during the current demand for innovations in education.

Developing and maintaining a framework for this evaluation is a major activity of an operational program budgeting system. An indispensable component of this activity is, of course, the data file of student characteristics. Information about the student, including personal and educational data, is prerequisite to the determination of the educational outcome for a given mix of inputs—in short, for the evaluation of innovation.

A system of review and evaluation of innovations should result in less duplication of effort in the educational research area; certainly, if other agencies know what has been tried, under what conditions (in terms of student characteristics as well as resource

---

*Erick Lindman, "Resistance to Innovation in American Education," in Hirsch *et al., op. cit.,* pp. 312-313.

inputs), and with what effectiveness, they are in a better position to make a decision about whether or not to institute some project.

There is another way program budgeting would improve planning. The existence of program budgeting within a district provides a good means for ensuring continuity of administration with a change in district personnel. For example, a new district administrator is provided with some knowledge about the program of the district, about the future expenditure consequences of decisions already made, and about the problems facing him. Thus, he has a good idea of what he has to work with, in terms of resources, in formulating his own alternatives. This is not to say that the new administrator's hands are tied because there is a program budget for five years in the future. This is a popular *misconception* about program budgeting.

The Program and Financial Plan—the program budget—shows the expenditure consequences over time of decisions made today. It is *not* a commitment of funds for five years ahead. It is no more constraining than the traditional budget.

The Analytical Aspect of Program Budgeting

A fully developed planning, programming, and budgeting system comprises more than the program budget and its record of program and financial information; it is, in fact, a system of analysis intended to assist the decisionmaker in choosing among alternative courses of action that involve school district programs. The program budgeting process can be thought of as a special kind of system analysis in which the programs of the district as a whole are the system. This system-analytical side of program budgeting is one of its most valuable features. How the program budgeting process and the system-analytical activities are interwoven can best be shown by sketching the total process (see Figure 2).

Several activities are involved in the program budgeting process. The process itself, in district planning, begins with the statement of objectives and the categorization of district activities, or programs, by objectives. This relatively detailed categorization provides the program structure composed of objectives and programs—P1, P2, to Pn. The program structure is the format for

Figure 2

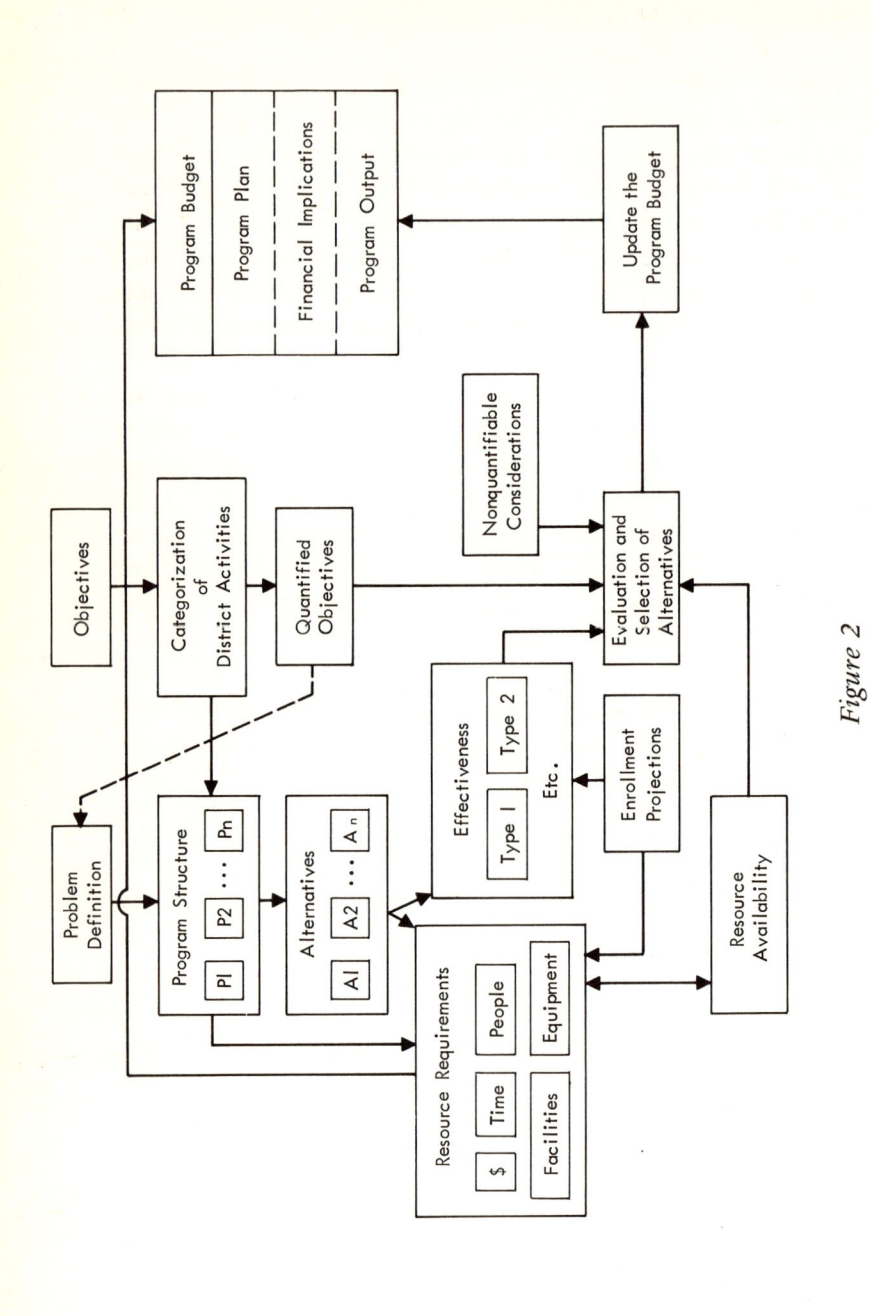

The System-Analytical Aspect of Program Budgeting

the program budget—it is the means of organizing the costs identified with activities contributing to specific programs. It is the display of the expenditure consequences over time of current policies and decisions. One could, of course, stop at this point and have a budget that would be a better communication device than the traditional budget. To stop, however, with what is essentially only a rearrangement of the traditional budget, would be to forego other major advantages of a program budgeting system as an aid to decisionmaking.

Assume that a school district has already developed the mechanics of a program budgeting system and that the cost of each program is known. Suppose, also, that the effectiveness of each program has been assessed, at least qualitatively; that is, the decisionmakers in the district have judged those programs that are more successful and those programs that are less successful. These judgments are based on the decisionmaker's implicit (or explicit) beliefs as to what constitutes success. Making these beliefs explicit, in effect, provides operational and perhaps quantifiable objectives for each of the district programs. The judgments coupled with these objectives allow identification of failing programs. In addition, as time passes, the district will be confronted by other problems or issues. These problems may affect one or more of the programs or may require a rearrangement of the program structure itself.

For simplicity, assume that a problem involves only one program. More often than not, the decisionmaker will have some ideas of possible solutions to the problem; these become alternatives to the existing program, which may be considered the base case for comparison. In some instances, the analyst may propose additional alternatives, with an eye to highlighting the preferred solution; this dialogue between the decisionmaker and the analyst is a pivotal activity in making the most of the program budgeting process.

Next, each alternative is translated into its future resource requirements (in terms of dollars, personnel, facilities, etc.) and into its various aspects of effectiveness. Most of the hard work of analysis occurs in these areas. A great deal of effort should be devoted to the analytical aspect of program budgeting. When the alternatives have been described and are analyzed in terms of their cost and effectiveness, they are evaluated so that the preferred alternative may be chosen. The evaluation of alternatives is not simply a matter of reviewing the results of the cost and effectiveness analyses. Resource requirements must be weighed against resource availability, and estimates of effectiveness against objectives. In addition, there will usually be several aspects of cost (rather than a single cost) and several aspects of effectiveness (rather than a single measure) for each alternative. These multiple measures must be weighed against each other. The evaluation must also account for other factors and constraints which may or may not be quantifiable but are to be thought of as an integral part of the evaluation process.

A possible result of the evaluation of alternatives is that *no* alternative is preferred or attractive. This could occur because none can meet the criteria for effectiveness within available resources, or because the only useful alternative is politically unpalatable. In this case, the procedure must be repeated. In such an effort, the interaction of the decisionmaker and the analyst may lead to the discovery of new alternatives that are more attractive than those originally proposed. This could happen for several reasons, but the most likely one is that both the decisionmaker and the analyst have a better understanding of the problem and a greater knowledge of the capabilities and limitations of different ways to solve the problem. This is one major benefit of the analytical aspect of program budgeting.

On the other hand, and still part of the analytical process, the decisionmaker often needs to revise his objectives because the original goals were unrealistic. Perhaps both the objectives and the alternatives will need revision if a solution is to be found. As Hitch and McKean have stated: "It can in fact be argued that the chief *gain* from systematic analysis is the stimulus that it provides for the invention of better systems."* This iterative aspect of the

---

*C.J. Hitch and R.N. McKean, *The Economics of Defense in the Nuclear Age,* The Rand Corporation, R-346, March 1960, and Harvard University Press, Cambridge, Massachusetts, 1960, p. 187.

analytical process reveals the close interrelationships among the various components of the totality of the program budgeting process.

Generally, most programs will not be subjected to such a detailed analysis because at any given time only a few programs will be problem areas. For most programs, or program elements, the continuation of the current practice will be the preferred alternative or course of action. Once the preferred alternative is selected, the expenditure consequences of the decision are incorporated in the program budget, and the changes in the description of program activities and in the statement of operational program objectives are recorded in the supporting documentation. The result, then, is an up-to-date program budget—organized information about the consequences of choices made through a systematic examination of alternatives.

A discussion of the analytical aspect of program budgeting seems to be a good place to mention the role of the analyst in the program budgeting process. There has been much discussion about whether the analyst makes policy decisions during this process. This is actually too simple a question for a complex matter; certainly anyone who contributes to an analysis concerned with policy decisions takes part in the decisionmaking process in some sense. And the analyst must make many decisions himself—along the way—in translating alternatives into their resource requirements, in assessing the effectiveness of alternatives, in proposing other alternatives, in evaluating alternatives, and so on.

To make these decisions, the analyst needs informed judgment; he must be familiar with the system he is analyzing and with the political and social pressures that shape its immediate and long-range problems. He does not, of course, make final choices, for he has neither the competence nor the responsibility for doing so. But just as surely, the way he shapes the analysis will have some impact on decisions that are made. To enhance or improve his judgment, he must work closely with the decisionmakers that have the experience and the understanding that the analyst lacks. For these reasons, the best (that is, the most influential) analysis is carried out when there is extensive interaction between the analyst and the decisionmaker.

In short, the answer to the question about the role of the analyst is that he should serve as a catalyst in the decisionmaking process. He should provide the informational bridge between the identification of the problem and the delineation of potential solutions, with the choice being made by the decisionmaker responsible for policy determination. As a safeguard, the analyst should make known any and all assumptions made in the analysis at the time the information is presented to the decisionmaker. Nice, neat, unsubstantiated results are dangerous; in the hands of a nonparticipating decisionmaker, or a lazy decisionmaker, such results might be used in a way that gives rise to the belief that the analyst is, in fact, "making the decision."

It is for this very reason that the idea of interaction must be stressed. Interaction and the active participation of all levels of the institution are necessary, not only in the analytical aspect of the program budgeting process but also in developmental and operational phases of a planning-programming-budgeting system.

Scope of This Book

In a planning sense, program budgeting can be thought of as a management tool used by the school district administration to enable the systematic analysis of the district's operation. Within the traditional cost-effectiveness approach, this means that the administration is attempting to maximize the educational outcome for a given level of resources or to minimize the cost to achieve a given level of output. The primary user of the program budgeting system, then, is the district superintendent, who is employed by the school board to manage the resources of the educational system in the district. It is mostly from the superintendent's viewpoint that we will discuss the concepts and techniques of program budgeting for school district planning. This means that more emphasis is placed on the decisionmaking role of the superintendent than on the policymaking role of the school board.

Policy decisions are implied in our suggested definition of program budgeting as a way of life—a way of thinking about where you are going, where you want to go, how to get there, at what cost, and with what benefit. However, consideration of the role of program budgeting in the area of policymaking is beyond the scope of this book. Here we will develop the idea that program budgeting, despite its title, is more than a nice, neat method of budgeting by program, and that, as such, it requires more than just concentration of budgeting and accounting procedures. The nature and extent of these requirements constitute the major portion of this book.

CHAPTER TWO

DEVELOPMENT OF A PROGRAM STRUCTURE

Stephen M. Barro

Introduction

   The structural phase of program budgeting consists of efforts to generate, assemble, and organize information about the resource-using activities of an organization. These efforts are intended to accomplish two purposes: first, to display information in a way that will be meaningful to administrators and directly usable in decisionmaking; second, to provide an information base that will support subsequent efforts at systems analysis. A principal thrust of the literature on program budgeting is that each of these purposes can be accomplished by establishing a classification scheme that groups the organization's activities according to the objective that each activity serves. Within the resulting taxonomic framework, information can be brought together on resource requirements, cost, outputs, and benefits of all the activities carried on by the organization. The array of categories used to represent the activities of the organization and their interrelationships is known as a *program structure.*
   This chapter examines the nature of a program structure and some of the major considerations in developing it for a public

school system. In order to be concrete, the discussion focuses on one particular approach, out of many conceivable approaches, to grouping and arraying school district activities. The rationale behind this approach is set forth, and a proposed set of program categories is presented. This program structure is then used in later sections of the book to illustrate the process of constructing a program budget, certain aspects of cost and effectiveness analysis, and other facets of program budgeting.

One cautionary note is in order. The use of this program structure throughout the book should not mislead the reader regarding its status. The program structure is intended to be *illustrative* only. Although some effort has been made to determine the applicability of these categories to actual school district programs, they have not yet been subjected to the more rigorous testing that would accompany an effort to implement a working program budgeting system in a public school district. Therefore, the categories are provisional. It is anticipated that they will be refined and modified as a result of continuing interaction with school administrators and other persons knowledgeable about public education.

Some Characteristics of a Program Structure

A capsule definition of a program structure is as follows: *A program structure is a classification system that categorizes the activities of an organization according to their relationship to the organization's objectives.* This definition expresses the single most important criterion in formulating program categories: that they be linked to a conception of the purposes of the organization. In the context of program budgeting for a school district, this means that the system used for classifying the district's activities should be derived from a conception of the objectives of primary and secondary education. The problem of identifying such objectives and expressing them in a way that will be useful in developing a program structure will be explored later.

In addition to linking program categories and objectives, a program structure has several other properties:

1. The program structure should embrace *all* the activities of

the organization. In the case of a school district, this means that program categories must provide for instructional activities (both inside and outside the classroom), administrative activities, activities related to operation and maintenance of facilities, and activities related to a variety of ancillary and support functions performed by the school system. The reason for this comprehensiveness is that program budgeting is intended to help administrators in allocating all the resources at their disposal among the district's various programs.

2. The program structure is a hierarchical classification scheme. District activities are grouped into a relatively small number of *programs*; these are subdivided into more narrowly defined *subprograms*; and the subprograms, in turn, are composed of still more narrowly specified *program elements*.* These successive levels correspond to a parallel hierarchy of objectives: broad educational ones at the top and progressively more specific ones at each lower level.

3. The program structure should allow for categorization of activities according to several attributes. Attributes other than relationship to educational objectives may include such things as target population, geographic location, and various descriptors of the process involved in each activity. Classification according to such variables results in a multidimensional program structure. This is an aspect of program categorization that has sometimes been neglected in the literature, but not in practice.** However, it is a particularly important property to bear in mind in developing a program structure for a school system, or for other types of educational institutions, as will become evident later.

4. The program structure should allow for and reflect

---

*This three-level schema corresponds to the general structure prescribed for federal agencies, as described in Bureau of the Budget, Bulletin No. 68-9, Washington, D.C., April 12, 1968, p. 3. However, the schema may be altered as needed to serve the purposes of the school district program budgeting. In particular, additional levels of categorization may be included, as necessary.

**Planning-Programming-Budgeting: Guidance for Program and Financial Plan, U.S. Department of Health, Education, and Welfare, Washington, D.C., April 12, 1967.

differences in how directly activities relate to objectives. In some cases the relationship is clear and direct. For example, instruction in reading contributes to attainment of the objective, "learning to read." However, many district activities make their contributions in much less obvious and direct ways. For instance, supervision of instruction by the principal and provision of electric light in the classrooms also contribute ultimately to "learning to read" and to many other educational objectives. The program structure must be designed to show the nature of the relationship between each type of activity and the postulated educational objectives.

5. The program structure should be made up of categories that remain relatively stable over the years, so that long-range planning can be carried on; but it should also be able to accommodate new activities when necessary. Obviously, these two attributes are somewhat in conflict. A workable compromise may involve (a) setting up the higher-level categories (programs and subprograms) so that they encompass relatively broad ranges of activities—not only the activities actually carried on by the organization at a particular time—while (b) allowing for occasional replacement or realignment of the individual program elements that fall within these categories. Thus, the broad outlines of the program structure will be stable, while program changes will be reflected at the detailed level of the classification system.

Formulating Educational Objectives*

Because the link between program categories and objectives is fundamental, the structural work typically begins with an effort to examine, identify, and formulate objectives. In the present instance, the task is to define a set of objectives for a public school system. The statement of objectives should identify the major categories of benefits or services that the school district undertakes (or is expected) to provide for the community. It should provide a framework within which proposals for alternative ways of providing education can be examined and within which district

*This discussion of educational objectives is based on M.B. Carpenter, *Program Budgeting as a Way to Focus on Objectives in Education*, The Rand Corporation, P-4162, September 1969.

performance can be evaluated. Also, to be of value administratively, the objectives can be associated with particular district activities. There are a number of conceptual and practical difficulties in formulating a set of objectives that meets these requirements.

Expressing Objectives at Appropriate Levels

One source of difficulty is that educational objectives, as they appear in statements by school officials, educational program planners, curriculum specialists, and others, are usually not expressed at a suitable level of detail or in language that facilitates translation into a program structure. Discussions of educational objectives appear to take place at either of two widely separated levels of abstraction. One of these is what may be termed the "philosophical" level. It provides global statements of educational aims, generally in the context of a broader framework of social or governmental goals. Sometimes, discourse at this level focuses on educational benefits for society. It examines the results, and hence the objectives, of education in terms of its contributions to the economy, the social order, the culture, and so forth. An alternative approach emphasizes the contribution of education to the well-being of the individual student. The socially oriented point of view leads to formulation of such objectives as preparation of students for productive roles in the economy, development of good citizens, and production of psychologically sound, socialized individuals. The more individually oriented point of view leads to formulations emphasizing individual fulfillment, along the lines of the often-heard slogan, "helping each individual develop to his full potential." Both types of language are encountered regularly in the statements of educational goals and philosophies issued by local school districts and other education agencies.

At the other end of the scale with respect to level of abstraction, there is widespread interest in development of sets of operationally defined, behavioral objectives for instruction. This interest is associated with current work on curricula and also with evaluation efforts in connection with special-purpose federal and state education programs. It has also been stimulated by the advent of programmed instruction and other developments in educational technology. The objectives defined at this level are detailed and specific. Typically, a statement of an instructional objective identifies a specific terminal behavior to be observed or measured, certain conditions under which the observation or measurement is to take place, and a standard of performance to be attained.* The level of detail is such that a large number of objectives must be written to describe the results that are to be achieved by instruction in a single subject in a single year.

Neither the philosophical objectives nor the behavioral instructional objectives are directly usable in formulating a program structure. The former do not fill the need because they are too abstract, are not operational, and tend to cut across all school activities. It is difficult, for example, to define even in a general way the contribution of specific school activities to such vague objectives as "developing good citizens" or "developing each child to his full potential." On the other hand, the behavioral objectives are *too* specific and *too* detailed. They are pitched at a suitable level for dealing with tactical questions of curriculum composition and instructional design, rather than strategic questions of resource allocation. Also, the behavioral objectives tend to be specifically tied to particular curricula. Alternative curricula that vary widely in the makeup of their specific behavioral objectives might still be aimed at the same educational objective, more broadly defined. Therefore, comparisons between programs at the level of their detailed instructional objectives cannot provide a satisfactory basis for high-level decisionmaking.

Objectives for program budgeting need to be stated at levels of abstraction that lie between the philosophical objectives and the behavioral, instructional objectives. To be useful at the program element level, objectives must be operational. That is, they should be translatable into well-defined measures of effectiveness or performance, such as achievement test scores, attitudinal

---

*Robert F. Mager, *Preparing Instructional Objectives,* Fearon Publishers, Inc., Palo Alto, California, 1962.

indicators, and measures of post-school success.* Objectives at the subprogram and program levels represent aggregations of the program-element level objectives. They need not correspond directly to operationally defined effectiveness or performance measures, as do the lower-level objectives, but they should group the lower-level objectives in ways that are relevant to the larger strategic issues that arise in school district decisionmaking.

To make the discussion of objectives more concrete, consider a hierarchy of educational objectives, ranging from broad, social objectives to specific instructional objectives. A small segment of such a (hypothetical) hierarchy is shown in Figure 3. At its highest level is the very general goal, "to develop good citizens." At level II, an effort is made to give this vague aim some substance by identifying some broad classes of knowledge, attitudes, and skills that are thought to be conducive to developing good citizens. One of these is "to learn the nature of U.S. and other societies." At level III, the latter objective is made somewhat more precise by specifying some relevant subject fields. At the fourth level, still greater specificity is obtained, by taking one of these fields, "learning about the American political system," and translating that into some specific subjects of instruction. Finally, at the lowest level, a small sample is shown of the many behavioral objectives that identify what is to be learned in one of these subjects.

At each level except the highest, there is an implicit assumption that accomplishment of the specified objectives will contribute to attainment of the next higher objective in the hierarchy. Thus, from one point of view, each subordinate objective is a means to a higher-level goal. However, as has already been pointed out, the level I objective is so encompassing that it does not provide any substance on which to base program planning, while the level V objectives reflect details of curriculum design that are below the level of the main areas of interest in program budgeting. The intermediate levels of the hierarchy are

*Questions concerning measures of effectiveness and performance and their uses in program budgeting are discussed in Chapter Six of this book.

I
```
To develop good citizens
```

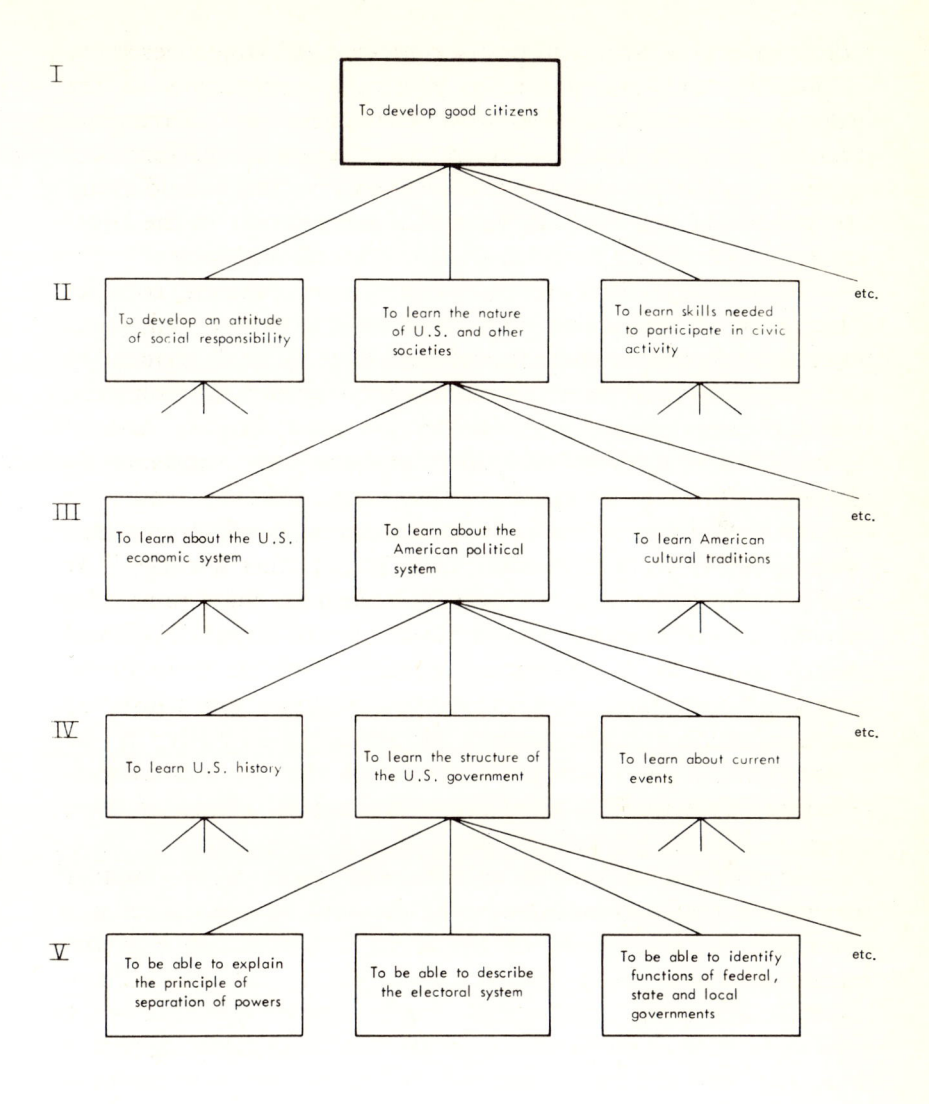

II

| To develop an attitude of social responsibility | To learn the nature of U.S. and other societies | To learn skills needed to participate in civic activity | etc. |

III

| To learn about the U.S. economic system | To learn about the American political system | To learn American cultural traditions | etc. |

IV

| To learn U.S. history | To learn the structure of the U.S. government | To learn about current events | etc. |

V

| To be able to explain the principle of separation of powers | To be able to describe the electoral system | To be able to identify functions of federal, state and local governments | etc. |

Figure 3

A Segment of One Hierarchy of Educational Objectives

the ones that are of value for program categorization. The level IV categories correspond to specific activities, i.e., courses and subject area instruction, carried on in the schools. They also represent the level at which it is reasonable to construct instruments to measure program effectiveness. The level III and level II objectives represent two stages of aggregation, corresponding to the subprograms and programs of the program structure.

Relating Activities to Objectives

Several problems may arise in the attempt to associate activities with objectives. Some of these may be resolved through careful formulation of objectives and appropriate design of program categories. Others have to be dealt with in the analytical phase, rather than the structural phase, of program budgeting.

An obvious and frequently encountered problem is that a single, indivisible activity may contribute to the objectives of two or more programs. For example, so-called core programs, which combine English and social studies at the secondary level, clearly contribute to learning objectives related to each of the two subject areas. Since there is no practicable, nonarbitrary way of deciding which resources used in such a combined activity apply to each objective, it is necessary to represent the activity as a separate program element in the program structure. This has a relatively minor effect as far as the structural aspect of program budgeting is concerned. The main impact is on analytical work, which will inevitably become more complicated because of the need to evaluate an activity in terms of its contributions to several programs.

It should be noted that support activities may also be thought of as activities that contribute to multiple objectives. However, they are treated somewhat differently from the activities considered above and will be discussed later in this chapter.

Another problem is interdependence among objectives and among activities. Even though two objectives may represent different educational benefits to the community, attainment of one may be a means to attainment of the other. As examples, achievement in learning about society probably depends, in part, on prior achievement in acquiring language skills; achievement in solving science problems probably depends on prior achievement in mathematics. In these situations, it might not be thought unreasonable to relate instructional activities in language and mathematics, respectively, to objectives in social studies and science, as well as to the more direct objectives in the two areas of instruction.

The whole set of relationships between district activities and objectives could be characterized by identifying relationships of this kind among the various school district activities in considerable detail. A table could be constructed in which each objective was listed together with all activities that contribute to it. The result would constitute a kind of program structure. It would have the advantage of displaying all of the stated relationships explicitly, but the disadvantage that some activities would be linked to several objectives and hence appear in several program categories. This property would make it difficult to examine the district's distribution of resources among programs and to compare program results with program cost.

In developing this program structure, a simpler approach has been chosen that avoids this difficulty, at the cost of a certain amount of explicitness in relating activities and objectives. The activities that enter frequently into interdependency relationships (language and mathematics instruction, in the foregoing example) have been identified and set apart in the program structure. They are designated as activities contributing to "learning of fundamental intellectual skills," with the implication that the fundamental skills contribute to attainment of other skills. This makes it possible to associate an activity with only one program category, while still acknowledging that certain activities contribute indirectly to attainment of multiple objectives.

However, this approach is a less-than-perfect solution. It does not handle all interdependencies. In some instances, there may be a two-way interaction between activities. For example, although language instruction contributes to the objective of learning about society, studying society also contributes to learning of language skills because of the opportunities it provides for experience in using oral and written language. Where such a two-way relationship exists, it is no longer entirely acceptable to say that one activity is "fundamental." The relationship is a more symmetrical one. It is also a difficult one to represent in a program structure that is to be limited to a single array of activities. The upshot is that some relationships among activities will not be brought out in the program structure but must be dealt with as a part of the analytical process.

A third problem is that a given activity may contribute to different objectives for different students who participate in it. As an example, certain music and art courses may be of value to most students primarily as sources of cultural enrichment and means of nonvocational self-expression, while for other students they may constitute training for future artistic careers. Similarly, certain shop or craft courses may constitute vocational training for some students, while they may provide avocational or recreational skills for others. For this reason, it is important to distinguish among categories of students in the process of associating activities with objectives. The multidimensional approach to development of a program structure, which cross-classifies activities by several attributes, including student type, can provide the flexibility needed to make the necessary distinctions.

Program Categorization as a Two-Way Process

An implication of all the foregoing is that the process of defining objectives and categorizing activities into objective-oriented programs needs to be approached from two directions simultaneously. From one point of view, the process begins with formulation of a set of objectives that are derived from a socially or philosophically based conception of what the schools ought to be doing. Each objective is disaggregated into more operational subobjectives, that are then associated with specific educational activities. But the process can also be viewed as taking the existing set of activities as the starting point. It groups these activities into categories according to apparent similarity of purpose and then assembles the groups into larger program aggregates. Examination of these aggregates then leads to a synthesis of objectives. The former approach is primarily *prescriptive*. It defines programs according to a conception of what the schools ought to be doing. The latter is more *descriptive*. It identifies programs and objectives inductively from relationships among actual, ongoing activities.

In developing a program structure it is important to pursue both approaches and to try to bring them into agreement as much as possible. This means that the categorization process must be an iterative one. Each cycle will involve some regrouping of activities and restatement of objectives in order to reconcile mismatches. The final program structure and statement of objectives will take form only after the process has been repeated several times. Past experience with program budgeting has shown that this process is often valuable in itself, apart from the immediate objective of formulating a program structure, because of the incentive it provides for re-examination of established activities in relation to organizational goals.

A Rationale for Program Categorization

The program structure presented below adheres to the general principles discussed thus far. It also incorporates three additional specifications that give the proposed structure its particular character and distinguish the rationale for program categorization from a number of other approaches that might be selected for educational program budgeting. The specifications are as follows:

1. The proposed program structure is to be linked to a conception of objectives that includes both post-school career and life objectives and subject-oriented learning objectives.
2. Programs are to be grouped into several classes according to how directly they are related to learning in the various subject areas.
3. The program structure will be a three-dimensional one. It will classify activities by type of student and level of education in addition to relationship to subject areas.

These three points are developed in the following paragraphs.

Life Objectives and Learning Objectives

A major premise underlying the program structure is that the school district aims (or should aim) to provide students with the skills they need to function in a variety of life situations. Those situations include career-related activities, family and community involvement, participation in cultural affairs, and other aspects of personal life. Successful performance in each area calls for competence in an array of skills. The learning objectives of the school district correspond to major subject areas in which skills are needed to prepare for each major area of life.

A number of the learning objectives defined from this perspective apply to a basic core of educational activities that districts generally provide for all of their enrolled students. The core consists of activities aimed at providing fundamental intellectual skills and skills related to physical, social, and emotional development that students will need regardless of their career patterns. Activities that fall into this category include virtually all education at the elementary level and a large proportion of secondary education. We have defined learning objectives within this broad domain to correspond to the major subject areas in which basic skills are to be acquired.

Objectives primarily related to preparation for careers may be differentiated according to students' prospective post-school destinations. Some students are preparing to go directly into the job market or into training for specific occupations. Others are preparing for higher education. We have defined learning objectives for the different classes of skills required to prepare for each destination.

Direct and Support Programs

As was pointed out earlier, activities carried on by the school district vary in how directly they are related to learning objectives. Some school activities, including most classroom instruction, are undertaken to promote learning by students in specific subject areas. Other activities, such as operation of libraries, resource

Development of a Program Structure 33

centers, etc., are carried on to promote learning generally, but not learning in specific areas. Still other activities, such as student transportation and health care, are aimed at providing certain services that benefit students, but are only indirectly related to the learning objectives. A fourth cluster of activities provides services to groups in the community other than the regular student population. A fifth and final category consists of activities of an "overhead" or "support" nature that do not have educational end-products of their own but are necessary to provide the setting within which the other activities can take place. Each of these classes of activities is represented in the program structure.

Three-Way Classification of Programs

The subject-oriented learning objectives discussed thus far categorize instructional activities according to *what* is to be learned. However, both educational objectives and instructional activities are likely to be differentiated within a school district to meet the needs of different groups of students; therefore, another dimension of classification is needed to specify who is to learn in each subject area. "Learning by whom" has been accounted for by establishing a set of student type categories that can be used to classify activities according to the groups of children for whom they are provided.

A third dimension of categorization is needed to distinguish activities aimed at students at different levels of the educational system. At the different levels—which may be viewed as different stages of the educational "production process"—activities vary in both resource requirements and performance criteria. Identification of activities by level is needed for program analysis and evaluation and in order to relate the program structure to the organizational structure of the district. Accordingly, we have included a set of level-of-education categories as one element of the program structure.

Inclusion of the student type and educational level dimensions of classification produces a three-way classification system for school district activities. The system may be pictured as a three-dimensional array (see Figure 4) with each set of categories

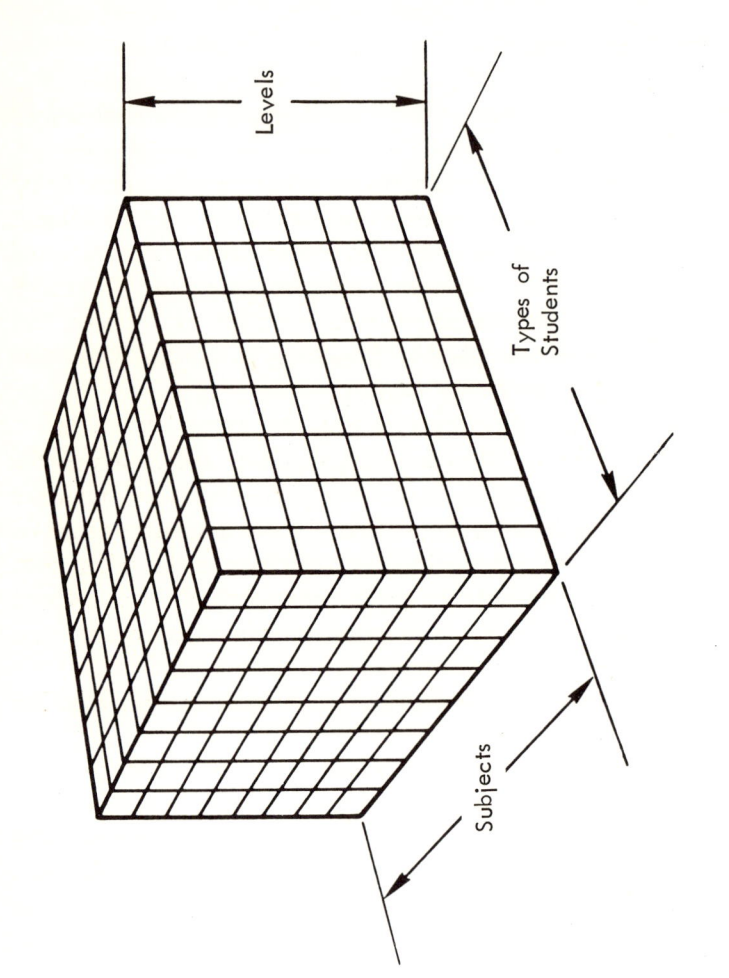

Figure 4

Three-Way Categorization of Educational Programs

Development of a Program Structure

aligned along one axis. The three-dimensional nature of the overall program structure should be kept in mind during the following description of the detailed categories.

A Set of Program Categories

Categorization of Activities According to Subject-Oriented Learning Objectives

Table 1 presents a hierarchy of categories for classifying district activities according to how they relate to a set of subject area objectives. Programs 1 through 5 are direct instructional programs subdivided by subject field. Programs 6, 7, and 8 comprise activities that contribute to instruction as a whole, but not to specific subject areas. The remaining programs contribute to ancillary objectives or have a supportive role.

Only two levels of categorization are shown in the table. These identify a number of broad subject fields within which the school district strives to promote learning. A lower level, which is not shown in the table, would correspond to individual subjects of instruction or other specific organized activities in the schools. In this context, "subject matter" and "instruction" are defined broadly to encompass school activities aimed at emotional and social development and so-called extracurricular activities with objectives related to intellectual, social, emotional, and physical learning.

Among the instructional programs, Program Categories 1 through 3 correspond to the basic core of public education, as defined earlier. They represent the parts of the educational program that are "universal"—applicable to all students regardless of career choices. Categories 4 and 5 comprise activities carried on specifically to prepare students for employment or higher education destinations.

Category 1 is "fundamental intellectual skills." Its main subheadings are "language and communications skills," which includes reading, oral and written language, and related subjects; "quantitative skills," which covers mathematical and related subjects; and—for want of a better title—"study skills," which

Table 1

*Categorization of Activities into Programs According to
Their Relationship to Educational Objectives*

Instructional Programs Aimed at Providing a Basic Education to all Students
1. Learning fundamental intellectual skills
   1.1 Language and communication skills
   1.2 Quantitative and reasoning skills
   1.3 Study skills

2. Learning about the world
   2.1 Learning about the U.S. and other societies
   2.2 Learning about the physical world and living things
   2.3 Learning about literature and the arts
   2.4 Learning knowledge and skills for everyday application

3. Development of the individual physically, socially, and emotionally
   3.1 Physical development
   3.2 Development of means of self-expression
   3.3 Development of interpersonal relationships

Instructional Programs Aimed at Preparing Students for Specific Futures
4. Learning knowledge and skills in preparation for future employment or occupational training
   (classified by occupation)

5. Learning academic subjects to prepare for higher education
   (classified by academic field)

Direct Support of Instructional Programs
6. Assessment, guidance, and counseling

7. Program development and evaluation

8. Instructional resource and media services

Ancillary and Support Programs
9. Auxiliary services to students
   9.1 Health services
   9.2 Transportation
   9.3 Food services

10. Community service programs

11. Operation and maintenance of physical plant and equipment

12. Provision of physical plant and equipment

13. Administration and general support

includes library and reference skills, study methods, information gathering techniques, and other skills often grouped under the heading, "learning how to learn." Category 2 brings together all the subjects with substantive or empirical content about the world. Under its subheadings it comprises the social studies or social sciences, the physical and life sciences, and studies of literature, the arts, and other elements of the culture. The last subheading brings together a large number of school activities aimed at providing students with skills for everyday life, including household skills, shop skills, typing, driving an automobile, and others. The third category brings together a number of school activities with primarily noncognitive objectives, including physical education and related activities, development of artistic and other modes of individual expression, and school subjects and other organized activities aimed broadly at socialization of the individual.

Note that in Program 3 we have identified categories in a much more limited way than we might have if we dealt with the whole range of school objectives from a philosophical point of view. That is, we have interpreted the content of Program 3 in a narrower way than may be suggested by the title, "Development of the Individual Physically, Socially, and Emotionally." This is the result of a deliberate choice. What we have done is to recognize only those categories for which there are specific activities in the schools. Thus, there are no categories, for example, for development of positive attitudes in various realms, or for more "personal" or internal aspects of psychological development, even though the schools may contribute to these ends. The reason is that it is difficult to associate them with specific educational activities.

The whole realm of "affective" objectives of education is one that poses some tricky problems. There is no question that effects on children's attitudes are important end-products of the public schools. On the other hand, influences in the schools that affect attitudes may permeate all the activities to which children are exposed. Therefore, it is probably impossible within the present state of the art to isolate specific activities, much less specific sets of resources, to be identified as programs for attitude formation. A number of activities that do seem to be aimed primarily at affective objectives are brought together in Program 3. However, these do not necessarily encompass either the major portion or the most important of the influences in the schools that affect children's attitudes. Of course, effects on attitudes should enter into educational system analysis, but there does not seem to be a satisfactory way of incorporating them into the program structure. Considerable experimentation with alternative structures is under way in this area, and we may begin to see some breakthroughs in the affective domain.

Programs 4 and 5 comprise activities related to preparation for employment or for higher education, respectively, as has been explained. Two important points to note about these categories are that they are usually relevant only at the secondary level and that a student, say in high school, may be involved in either of these programs while also being involved in some of the universal aspects of education, Programs 1 through 3.

It is suggested that activities in Program 4 be classified according to the occupational field(s) to which they are relevant. A first order subcategorization might involve such broad occupational classes as technical occupations, business and clerical occupations, skilled manual trades, arts, and health-related occupations. The next level of subcategorization would identify the specific subjects or skill areas into which training for the various occupations is organized.

Similarly, it is suggested that activities in Program 5 be categorized by academic field. The rationale is that instruction in Program 5 is offered to prepare students for admission to college and must therefore be oriented to the academic field categories in which college admission requirements are customarily stated. Also, subject field categories may be appropriate ones to describe the secondary school programs that students select to prepare for specific major fields of study in college.

One final point about Programs 4 and 5: In a number of instances, the same subject areas that appeared as subcategories in Programs 1 through 3 will also appear in Programs 4 and 5. For example, instruction in mathematics appears under Program 1, but also under Programs 4 and 5. The distinction is that the mathematics appearing under "fundamental intellectual skills" belongs to the basic, or universal, part of the curriculum prescribed by the district for all of its students, while the mathematics that enters into Programs 4 and 5 varies according to students' anticipated career destinations. There are also cases in which a single course is appropriate both for students preparing for college and for others preparing for occupations. These are situations in which an activity has different objectives for different students, as was discussed earlier. The problem of classification that arises in such instances is resolved by making use of the "type of student" dimension of the program structure.

Program Categories 6, 7, and 8 may be thought of as "instructional support programs" because they include activities that are carried on to advance the learning objectives in general, but that cannot be readily classified by subject. The Assessment, Guidance, and Counseling Program, for example, functions, in part, as a kind of assignment or traffic control mechanism. It includes academic guidance, vocational and college guidance, and personal/psychological counseling. These functions help to assess students and to distribute them among programs according to their abilities and needs. They also attempt to provide remediation for a variety of learning difficulties that frequently are not associated with specific subject areas.

The Program Development and Evaluation category covers work aimed at improving all of the other elements of the instructional program. It encompasses the design and application of evaluation procedures for instructional activities (including special and experimental projects), testing in support of evaluation, curriculum design and development, study and evaluation of educational innovations, and supporting research.

The Resource and Media Services program comprises supporting or centrally performed instructional services. It includes library and audio-visual services; human resource services, such as consultant services that are not related to specific areas; and centrally operated technological services, such as those involved in instructional television or computer-assisted instruction.

Program 9, Auxiliary Services, is self-explanatory. The main subcategories of auxiliary services are health, transportation, and food services. Note that these activities—like the instructional activities—may be differentiated by type of student and by level of education. The Community Services program encompasses a number of services provided by the school district to groups in the community other than the regular student population. Some of the services merely involve the use of district facilities or resources for civic, recreational, or cultural purposes. Others involve district-operated services outside of the normal educational program, such as provision of day care centers, or operation of summer recreation programs.

The last three programs encompass "overhead" activities needed to support all of the "direct" programs. Program 11 contains all activities related to operation and maintenance of school plant and facilities. Program 12 brings together activities needed to acquire and expand plant and facilities (procurement of contractor services for building construction, planning, real estate transactions, financing). Program 13 includes all administrative and general support functions not otherwise accounted for. It does not include administrative activities that fall within the other programs, such as administration of development and evaluation, of auxiliary services, or of specific instructional or instructional support programs.

Categorization by Type of Student

Table 2 presents a set of categories for use in classifying activities by type of student. The categories represent groups of students who are likely to require differentiated educational programs. School districts operating in different environments or with different philosophies may vary in the kinds of programs they offer for special groups of children. The groupings are also likely to change over time. The categories presented here cover most of the segments of the student population for which differentiated programs are generally available in California school districts, and in most other states.

Development of a Program Structure

Table 2 identifies five attributes of students that may provide grounds for assigning them to differentiated programs.

First, in most school systems there will be a "regular," or "standard," or "normal" program in which students will be enrolled, unless they are specifically selected for a special program. Usually the regular program will include the majority of students in a district. However, the regular program may be differentiated internally according to ability levels; or in a more limited way, it may provide remedial programs and other differentiated activities for designated ability or achievement groups.

Second, there may be special programs for groups with specific environmental circumstances or cultural backgrounds. For example, provisions may be made for students who are from low income families, who are members of minority groups, or who live in certain designated "ghetto" areas. These programs may be fully or partially differentiated from the regular program. A district may have a full-scale compensatory program with its own curriculum, a distinct form of school organization, and different teaching methods, or it may modify parts of the curriculum to meet the needs of specific disadvantages, as is done in providing special language instruction for students from non-English speaking homes.

Third, special programs may be carried on for students with certain mental, physical, or emotional handicaps or exceptionalities. Some of these programs are explicitly provided for in the California Education Code. Others may or may not be included among the programs of a given district or may be defined and organized in different ways from one district to another.

Fourth, programs may be differentiated according to students' career choices. The two main groups of categories are programs for students preparing for various higher education majors and programs for students preparing for different vocations or occupations. The reasons for classifying students by career destination have already been discussed.

Fifth, a district may offer programs for adults or others not in the normal school population. Groups that fall under this heading may include persons in continuing education programs,

Table 2

A Possible Categorization of Programs by Type of Student

1. Regular Program (may be differentiated by ability levels)

2. Programs Differentiated by Environmental or Cultural Backgrounds of Students
   A. Culturally disadvantaged
   B. Non-English speaking

3. Programs for Students with Intellectual, Physical, or Emotional Exceptionalities
   A. Educable mentally retarded
   B. Severely mentally retarded
   C. Mentally gifted
   D. Physically handicapped
   E. Emotionally disturbed
   F. Other learning disorders or educational handicaps

4. Programs Differentiated According to Student Career Options and Capacities
   A. Programs for training in different occupations
   B. Programs to prepare for different areas of higher education
   C. General programs

5. Programs for Adults and Others Not in the Normal School Population

0. Programs Not Categorized by Type of Student

former dropouts, persons learning English, and so forth.

Categorization by Level

The third dimension of classification is by level of education. This dimension is needed for a complete program description because instruction at each level (for a given subject category and given student type) may employ different forms of organization, different methods, and different amounts or combinations of resources. The reason for including levels in the program structure is somewhat different from the reasons for the other two forms of classification. The level categories do not, themselves, point to objectives of education. That is, provision of kindergarten education or third grade education, or high school education is not a goal in itself (although the term "a high school education" may be used as shorthand for the whole range of knowledge and skills we normally expect of a high school graduate). Rather, the various levels represent stages in the educational "production" process— the sequence of steps by which objectives are accomplished during the 12 or more years a student is in school.

The levels that appear in the program structure (Table 3) may be school grades, to which students are assigned primarily according to age; or, more generally, they may be a series of age/ability groupings that overlap in age, as in an ungraded or multigraded program. For many purposes the appropriate levels to deal with are the broader strata into which grade levels are grouped: lower and upper grades of elementary education, junior high, and high school education, as shown here, or primary, middle, and secondary education, or other arrangements.

The Complete Program Structure

Each activity of the school district needs to be categorized by all three modes of classification. For example, it is necessary to specify the subject area, type of student, and level in order to fully identify an instructional activity. It seems useful to modify the customary usage of the term "program element" (see Chapter One) to reflect the three-dimensional nature of the program structure. Thus, we may reserve the term to apply to an activity or

Table 3

A Possible Categorization of Programs by Level of Instruction

1. Preschool Programs

2. Kindergarten

3. Elementary Education—Lower Grades
   Grade 1
   Grade 2
   Grade 3

4. Elementary Education—Upper Grades
   Grade 4
   Grade 5
   Grade 6

5. Junior High School Education
   Grade 7
   Grade 8
   Grade 9

6. High School Education
   Grade 10
   Grade 11
   Grade 12

7. Junior College Education
   Grade 13
   Grade 14

0. Programs Not Categorized by Level of Instruction

group of activities at the detailed level of the subject area taxonomy that is cross-classified by type of student and level. By this definition, the following groups of activities would be program elements:

- Activities carried on to teach reading to regular fourth grade students.
- Activities carried on to prepare physically handicapped high school students for employment in skilled trades.
- Activities carried on to guide and counsel educationally handicapped junior high school students.

It may also be desirable at times to use the terms "program" and "subprogram" to refer to aggregates of program elements arrayed along any one or two of the three axes of the classification scheme. Thus, one may want to speak of a program for learning of basic intellectual skills, or a program for the mentally retarded; or, aggregating program elements in two dimensions, one may speak of a physical education program for high school students or a preschool program for the disadvantaged. When using the terminology in this way, it is important to be sure that there is no confusion about what kinds of aggregates of activity are being described.

One other point about the program structure: It should be realized that not all the cells of the three-dimensional program array (see Figure 4) must be filled in. In some instances, one dimension of the program structure may not apply. For example, programs to prepare students for higher education or for employment apply only to secondary education; there are no programs differentiated by career choices in the elementary schools. An "uncategorized activities" item is added to the student and level of instruction program structures as a technical device for indicating when a mode of classification does not apply.

Program Budget Formats

If we look at the three modes of program categories in the context of their intended use to illuminate educational issues, there does not seem to be any natural reason for treating any one dimension as the primary form of program categorization. Each set of categories may be the most important in connection with particular educational issues or situations. For example, if a current issue facing the district has to do with educational provisions for special groups such as disadvantaged, retarded, or gifted students, it would be important to have information on resources and expenditures for these groups. Then, a categorization by student type would be important. If, however, the problem were to decide on plans for constructing new school buildings, classification by level would be important because different buildings are required, say, for primary, middle, and high schools. Or, if the issue at hand had to do with the adequacy of instruction in reading or some other subject, or if it involved a question of balance between vocational and college preparatory programs, categorization by subject area would be most informative.

An advantage of a multidimensional classification scheme is that it provides the flexibility needed to display information in formats appropriate to different situations. The three-way classification of program activities and their resource requirements makes it possible to construct a number of different program budget formats to suit each audience and issue.

A complete program budget format consists of an array of program categories plus a time dimension, which extends several years ahead, plus a set of resource and cost categories. Since the latter two elements will be discussed in a later chapter, the comments made here apply only to the set of program categories. Using the three-way classification system that has been described, it is possible to construct different arrays of categories to emphasize different aspects of a district's program. For example, one way of presenting a program is shown in Table 4. Here, the subject area categories are primary, types of students are the main subcategories, and levels of education are third-order categories. Sometimes, it will not be necessary to show all three sets of categories. For example, an alternate form of presentation, which might be relevant to decisions about school construction, might

Table 4

A Possible Program Budget Format

1. Fundamental Intellectual Skills
    1.1. Regular students
        1.1.1 Early childhood
        1.1.2 Elementary—lower grades
        1.1.3 Elementary—upper grades
        1.1.4 Junior high school
        1.1.5 High school

    1.2 Disadvantaged students
        1.2.1 Early childhood
        1.2.2 Elementary—lower grades

                . . .

    1.3 Physically handicapped
        1.3.1 Early childhood

    1.4 Educable mentally retarded

2. Learning About the World
    2.1 Regular students
        2.1.1 Early childhood

                . . .

    2.2. Disadvantaged students

                . . .

3. Development of the Individual Physically, Socially, and Emotionally

                . . .

etc.

treat educational levels as primary, types of students as secondary, and not show the breakdown by subject at all. Altogether, there are six possible permutations of the three sets of categories for complete arrays plus a variety of condensed or abbreviated formats. For general budget presentations and as a means of communication with the community, an effective presentation may be achieved by presenting separate budget breakdowns according to each of the three sets of categories. This provides a compact summary of how the program array looks when viewed in all three dimensions.

Summation

To sum up, a definition of a program structure has been provided and its characteristics elaborated on in the specific context of school district program budgeting. The key problem of formulating objectives and relating them to activities has been examined at some length. A three-way classification system for school district activities—the result of a particular approach to defining and categorizing school district programs—has been presented. Finally, ways in which the program structure can be translated into a number of program budget formats were briefly discussed. Later chapters of this book will show in more detail how the program categories are used in presenting program and budget information and how they provide a framework for the analytical aspects of the program budgeting process.

CHAPTER THREE

THE PROGRAM BUDGET AND THE TRADITIONAL BUDGET

James A. Dei Rossi

Introduction

In this chapter, differences between the traditional budget and the program budget will be compared and discussed. Throughout the chapter, the term "traditional budget" will be used to designate the budget currently used by school districts in the State of California. A budget may be defined as: A plan of financial operation embodying an estimate of proposed expenditures and the proposed means of financing them. In what follows, however, attention will be restricted primarily to the expenditure side of the budget. Financial questions will be addressed only to the extent that they relate to expenditures.

The goal is to indicate how the difference between the traditional budget and the program budget, as proposed plans, reflect basic differences in the approach to the problem of planning. Planning, as used here, means the formulation, evaluation, and selection among future alternative courses of action. Thus, the question of central concern is not, simply, "What are the differences in the ways the budgets or plans are presented?" but is, rather, "What are the differences and how do these differences reflect differences in approaches to, and techniques of, planning?"

The Crosswalk

Although, as will be pointed out, there are significant differences between the traditional budget and the program budget, it is generally possible to translate the data in the program budget into the traditional budget format, and conversely. The former translation—going from the program budget to the traditional budget format—is essential when planners are required to relate their plans to appropriation budgets or other funding documents not geared to the program structure. The latter translation—going from the traditional budget to the program budget—is sometimes desirable in the early stages of implementing a program budgeting system in order to provide an initial frame of reference and to clarify the relative quantitative importance of various programs and program elements.

As a matter of definition, the term "program" is used in this report to mean the largest group of activities designed to achieve a specified goal. The term "program element" will be used to mean any of the specific activities in a given program. In this usage, for example, the term "program" would be applied to the group of activities performed to "teach fundamental intellectual skills" but not to those subgroups of activities, such as teaching language communication skills or teaching mathematics skills. Examples of program elements in the above program are: reading, writing, mathematics for regular junior high school students, and so on.

The expression of the relationship between the program budget and the traditional budget is generally referred to as a "crosswalk." A crosswalk is basically a tabular array, with the columns showing the traditional budget cost categories and the rows showing the program budget cost categories. Underlying the crosswalk, of course, must be a set of definitions and procedures for allocating the data in a cost category in one budget to a corresponding cost category in the other. The actual level of detail at which the crosswalk translation is performed can vary greatly. Table 5 shows an example of a crosswalk in a very summarized

Table 5

Crosswalk Example
(In $ thousands)

Account Number	Account	Total	Instructional Programs[a]					Noninstructional Programs						
			1	2	3	4	5	Assessment, Guidance, and Counseling 6	Development and Evaluation 7	Instructional Resources and Media 8	Auxiliary Services 9	Community Service 10	Operation and Maintenance 11	Capital Outlay 12	Administration 13
100	Administration	580	---	---	---	---	---	---	50	---	---	---	---	---	530
200	Instruction	15,945	4,410	4,210	2,560	760	630	915	355	215	---	---	---	---	1,890
300	Health	290	---	---	---	---	---	---	---	---	290	---	---	---
500	Transportation	280	---	---	---	---	---	---	---	---	280	---	---	---
600	Operation	1,760	---	---	---	---	---	---	---	---	---	---	1,760	---	---
700	Maintenance	915	---	---	---	---	---	---	---	---	---	---	915	---	---
800	Fixed Charges	1,100	245	235	140	45	35	50	20	10	15	---	165	---	140
	Subtotal	20,870													
900	Food Service	500	---	---	---	---	---	---	---	---	500	---	---	---	---
1100	Community Service	700	---	---	---	---	---	---	---	---	---	700	---	---	---
	Total Current Expense	22,070	4,655	4,455	2,700	805	665	965	425	225	1,085	700	2,840	---	2,560
1200	Capital Outlay[b]	500	---	---	---	---	---	25	---	25	---	---	---	450	---
	Total Current Expense and Capital Outlay	22,570	4,655	4,455	2,700	805	665	990	425	250	1,085	700	2,840	450	2,560
	Percentage of Current Expense[c]	100.0	21.1	20.1	12.2	3.6	3.0	4.5	1.9	1.1	4.9	3.1	12.9		11.6

[a]Instructional Programs:
1. Learning Fundamental Intellectual Skills
2. Learning About the World
3. Development of the Individual Physically, Socially, and Emotionally
4. Learning Knowledge and Skills in Preparation for Future Employment or Occupational Training
5. Learning Academic Subjects to Prepare for Higher Education

[b]Provision of physical plant and equipment.

[c]These are percentages of "Current Expense" excluding "Capital Outlay." This conforms to current practice.

form. The vertical column is the summary form of the traditional budget as currently required by the California State Department of Education. The numbers on the left indicate the accounting code to which each of these categories relate. The horizontal row shows programs such as those described in Chapter Two, on program structure, and as defined above.

The example in Table 5 represents the budget of a hypothetical unified school district. The figures are based on an analysis of actual school district budget data and the example is reasonably typical of actual school district experience. Thus, the results obtained in this crosswalk are similar to the results that would be obtained for many districts.

Although the crosswalk in Table 5 is in summary form, it can be used to illustrate some basic relationships between the traditional budget and the program structure. The procedure in using this example will be to describe how the costs for each of the lines in the summary traditional budget have been allocated to each of the columns representing the programs. It is emphasized, however, that the procedures illustrated in this example are only general guidelines for crosswalking between the traditional budget and the program budget; they are illustrations of the basic logic involved in performing such a crosswalk. They should not be construed as the last word in relating traditional budget accounts to program budget categories.

In Table 5, it can be seen that not all the costs in the 100 Account, (District) Administration, have been allocated to the program column headed Administration; about ten percent of these costs have been allocated to the Development and Evaluation program. Although none of the costs has been allocated to the first five programs, some of the activities included in the 100 Account of the traditional budget are undoubtedly traceable to other specific programs in many districts. However, the most important point illustrated is that the allocation of support costs, such as Administration, should be made to other programs only if it is actually possible to relate the activities or purchases giving rise to these costs to those programs directly. No attempt should be made to allocate or prorate general support costs to other

The Program Budget and the Traditional Budget

programs on the basis of arbitrary, although logical, rules.

The program categorization used in the example is exhaustive; therefore, all costs, allocated or not, appear. Further, the convention of not attempting to allocate indirect costs* has gained acceptance among practitioners of program budgeting because it reduces the danger of unknowingly biasing costs of individual programs. Such biasing can occur because it is generally possible to conceive of more than one logical rule for allocation; and different rules can produce different results for identical circumstances. For example, for many indirect costs it might be equally logical to allocate either on the basis of the number of students or the number of square feet. Programs utilizing facilities on a high density basis will cost more using the first rule than they would using the second, even though the actual total costs involved do not change regardless of the rule used.

Looking next at the 200 Account, Instruction, most of the costs have been allocated to the first five programs, as one would expect, since these are the direct instructional programs. The allocation to Program 6, Assessment, Guidance, and Counseling, includes some teacher time but is mainly the cost of the salaries and material and supplies for the counselors, psychologists, and psychometrists. The Instructional Account costs listed under Program 13, Administration, are the cost of the building administrators (including principals, vice principals, and certificated directors and counselors), except for a portion listed in the column for Development and Evaluation.

The logic associated with this split of 200 Account costs among Administration and other specific programs is the same as that discussed for the 100 Account: If the building administrators actively participate in other activities, the cost of their time should be allocated; however, administration is a necessary function and

---

*Indirect costs are those support costs not directly traceable to specific programs. Thus, the cost of administration services performed by the district superintendent or school principals is generally viewed as indirect and not allocated. In contrast, the services of the supervisor for guidance is a traceable cost and is included in the Assessment, Guidance, and Counseling program in this example.

its cost should not be hidden through artificial allocations.

The next four lines, Health (300 Account), Transportation (500 Account), and Operation and Maintenance (600 and 700 Accounts) require little explanation. The principle underlying the nonallocation of operation and maintenance costs to other programs is the same as that outlined for the administrative costs: Support costs should not be arbitrarily allocated to other programs.

The costs in the 800 Account, Fixed Charges, generally include costs for retirement fund, other employee insurance, insurance for equipment and buildings, rental costs for land and buildings, interest on current loans, and other charges for such things as special assessments. For this example we have assumed that the fixed charges account has costs only for the retirement fund and insurance for employees, buildings, and equipment. All of the employee insurance and retirement costs have been allocated to the specific programs, since these costs can be directly traced to the salaries in each and are, in fact, actual salary costs. The equipment and building insurance costs have all been allocated to operations and maintenance.

Allocation of costs in the accounts for Food Service and Community Service (900 and 1100 Accounts) requires no explanation since the program categories to which they have been allocated are essentially identical to them. The Capital Outlay (1200 Account) cost allocation was based on the same principle as the allocation of administrative costs: If it is possible to relate these costs directly to specific programs, they should be allocated; otherwise, no attempt should be made to allocate on the basis of arbitrary rules.

Information from the Program Budget

There are various kinds of additional information that data organized by program provide to the district planner. First of all, Programs 1 through 5 are what may be called direct instructional programs; i.e., those in which actual classroom instruction takes place. The remaining Programs, 6 through 13, constitute what may be called the support activities for the classroom instruction, although some activities, such as Program 6—Assessment, Guidance, and Counseling—have objectives in their own right.

Using this general distinction, the data indicate that there is an approximate 60-40 split of cost between the direct instructional programs and the support programs. In the traditional budget format, instruction amounted to about 72 percent in the example. The 12 percent difference is due to the fact that individual school building administration costs and the costs of Program 6, Assessment, Guidance, and Counseling, and Program 8, Instructional Resources and Media, have not been included in the instructional program costs. In addition, salary-related costs, such as health insurance, carried under fixed charges in the traditional budget, have been included under the individual programs. This is discussed in greater detail in Chapter Five.

One important question that might be asked about Programs 1 to 5 at this point is: Does the distribution of costs among these programs appear to coincide with basic district philosophy on what should be taught and what emphasis should be placed on each area of instruction? For instance, the percentage distribution of costs for Program 4, Preparation for Employment, is 3.6 percent; and the percentage distribution of costs for Program 5, Preparation for Higher Education, is 3.0 percent. These appear to be startlingly low percentages of the total cost of instructional programs.

To clarify the meaning of these percentages, it is necessary to take a more detailed look at these programs, as shown in Table 6. The first column of this table is a repetition of the percentages shown in Table 5. The second column puts these percentages into better perspective by showing them as they relate to total instructional program cost, i.e., total cost less support cost in Programs 6 to 13. Although this method provides a slightly clearer picture, the reason for the imbalance between the first three programs and the last two is still obscured by the fact that the percentages are aggregated over all levels of instruction.

By disaggregating to three categories of levels—elementary, junior high, and senior high—it can be seen that the reason for these low percentages is that Programs 4 and 5 are only offered in

Table 6

Distribution of Instructional Program Costs
(%)

Instructional Program	Percent of Total Cost	Percent of Instructional Cost	Distribution by Level of Instruction		
			Elementary	Junior High	Senior High
1	21.1	35.2	47.5	34.8	11.0
2	20.0	33.3	30.1	47.1	28.6
3	12.2	20.3	22.4	18.1	14.8
4	3.6	6.0	–	–	25.0
5	3.0	5.2	–	–	20.6
Total	59.9	100.0	100.0	100.0	100.0

senior high, which accounts for only about 25 percent of total enrollment. While costs incurred for Programs 4 and 5 as a percentage of total district costs are quite low, when viewed in proper perspective, that is, by level, the distribution of costs among programs, especially Programs 4 and 5, appears more reasonable. About half of the cost for instruction in senior high is devoted primarily to Preparation for Employment and Preparation for Higher Education (Programs 4 and 5) and the other half to Improving Skills, General Knowledge, and Personal Development (Programs 1, 2, and 3).

We do not have enough information to determine whether or not this 50-50 split does indeed coincide with district policy. For example, we do not know exactly what courses or subjects have been grouped under each program, nor do we know what percentage of the students are college bound. However, even at this level of aggregation, it can be seen how program orientation can permit the analysis of the extent to which district activities correspond to district objectives—in a way that is not possible with the traditional budget.

Differences in the Budgets

The crosswalk is a useful communication device. It helps those familiar with the traditional budget understand the content of the various categories in the program budgeting system. It helps those who must implement a program budgeting system develop a better understanding of current and past activities. Further, it is extremely useful when the program categories cut across organizational units, and it becomes necessary to translate the data back to a form consistent with the organizational structure in order to administer and control district activities. However, many important differences between the program budgeting process and the traditional budgeting process are often obscured by the fact that crosswalk translations are possible. The existence of the crosswalk is sometimes erroneously viewed as an indication that the differences between program budgeting and traditional budgeting are simply differences in format.

As a consequence, a primary aim of the remainder of this chapter is to discuss how the differences between the program budget and the traditional budget are indicative of very important differences in the corresponding budgeting processes. We will describe this difference in terms of the approach, the concepts, and the techniques used for planning. The major differences between the program budget and the traditional budget can be categorized under three headings: (1) differences in content, (2) differences in structure, and (3) differences in time horizon.

Content

The differences in content between the two budgets are due primarily to differences in the completeness of description of the proposed plan. The complete program budget includes a full description of the physical resources required for the implementation of the budget plan. This description includes physical data on equipment, buildings, and other facilities. The traditional budget, although it does allow for capital outlays, ordinarily includes detailed physical resource data only on those resources required for current operation. These include such things as personnel, materials, supplies, and other miscellaneous expenses.

A fully documented program budget for a school district would also contain data on the objectives, enrollment (or some other measure of the expected "target population"), and the key design and operational characteristics of each program. All of these supplemental data are required for the estimation of cost and for use in evaluation and selection among alternatives in a program budgeting context. These are the data from which the program budget itself is constructed. They are not included as an afterthought and should not be viewed as window dressing providing additional, but not intrinsically essential, information.

Analysis for program budgeting must take place in a total operational context. The full implications, both cost and gain, of all resource requirements must be included as part of the planning process. Thus, land, construction, and equipment costs and operational characteristics can be as important in the evaluation of future alternatives as projected current expense.

Structure

There are two distinct types of differences in structure between the traditional budget and the program budget: differences in the presentation of various cost categories and differences in the way the costs in each category are related to the objectives and activities of the school district. The program budget is organized with reference to objectives, as embodied in the various programs and program elements; while the traditional budget related primarily to organizational units and functions. Note that the traditional budget relates primarily, but not exclusively, to organizational units and functions. This means that even though traditional budget detail is given by object class, it is always aggregated organizationally or functionally. As examples, the traditional budget shows the annual cost of such things as Instruction and Administration. The former is a function and the latter is an organizational aggregate; namely, the offices of the district superintendent, his associates, and their staff. In contrast, the program budget shows the cost for programs (such as teaching fundamental intellectual skills) and program elements (such as business mathematics for high school students).

Some of the items in the traditional budget do correspond to some of the items in the program budget. For example, the health service category in the traditional budget might correspond exactly to the health service program in a program budget structure. However, the important point is that the differences in structure are, by far, greater than the similarities.

The importance of this overall difference in structure reflects a difference in the approach to planning in three ways. The first and most obvious is that the data in the program budget are organized to be *directly* responsive to many of the planning requirements of educational planners. Many of the program elements in the program budget correspond directly to various courses and subjects in school curricula. This permits a direct assessment of the implications of many changes in curriculum. This type of direct analysis is not possible with the data used in the development of the traditional budget.

The second way in which the difference in structure affects the relative planning value of each budget is less obvious. The object of the program budget and program budgeting, as previously stated, is to facilitate evaluation by program. Thus, it is logical to begin with objectives that can be translated into program elements designed to meet these objectives and then to determine the resource requirements and cost activities involved in the program elements. This is a radically different analytical approach from that currently used for traditional budgeting, in which primary attention is given to required inputs rather than to desired objectives and the alternative means of attaining them.

The program budget is more than simply a translation of traditional budget line items in some definitionally consistent sense. The process of program budgeting is more than the subsequent analysis of each program and program element based on such allocations. The program budgeting approach must be grounded in analytical techniques making direct and extensive use of program data. Mainly, this means that program descriptors must play an active role in cost analysis and evaluation of alternatives within the program budgeting process. It is from the description of the programs that the resource implications of programs are determined and the cost estimates are derived. And it is on the basis of these same descriptors that each alternative is judged and compared as a means to an objective or objectives.

Time Horizon

The third major difference between the program budget and the traditional budget is characterized by the fact that the program budget shows the resource requirements for a longer time period than the traditional budget. The traditional budget shows the financial impact for a single year; the program budget shows the financial impact over many years. This difference in the time horizon of the budgets indicates another important difference between traditional budgeting and program budgeting: Program budgeting is long-term planning. But let us emphasize at the outset one thing this difference does *not* imply. A longer planning time horizon does not require formal commitment to the plan for longer periods of time. Single-year funding and authorization are in no way incompatible with long-range planning.

However, it is true that current commitments can and often do carry with them a need to follow through. But this is true regardless of the planning time horizon. Instead of increasing the likelihood of creating undesirably restrictive circumstances, longer planning periods can lessen this possibility. By forewarning planners of future commitments implicit in current decisions, long-range planning makes the occurrence of unforeseen requirements less likely. The longer time horizon encourages and, in some cases, requires the planner to examine the future implication of current decisions. In this way, programs with small costs in their initial stages that require significant cost increases for their fruition and continuation can be recognized early.

Extending the planning time horizon also permits the systematic investigation of the *aggregate* cost impacts of pursuing several programs that present no apparent problems when considered singly. Such information may indicate the need to sequence the initiation of various programs to even out the flow of required resources and costs. For example, the combined requirements of follow-up teacher training for a program initiated in the current year, together with the proposed training for a program to be initiated next year, may exceed reasonable limits. In this case, it might be possible to avoid overtaxing district resources by postponing the initiation of the new program by one year. Assuming that training for the first program would then be completed, the training for the new program could be undertaken without causing any excessive financial burden.

An Example

This chapter has been concerned with the major differences between the program budget and the traditional budget and has indicated how these differences reflect differences in approach to the task of planning. A numerical example of these budgets in summary form will illustrate these ideas. Table 7 shows the traditional budget for a hypothetical unified school district with an enrollment of 34,000 and 45 schools. It is the same district used to illustrate the crosswalk.

Using this data as a starting point, Table 8 shows what the five-year budget for the school, arranged with reference to the program structure, might look like, making the following assumptions:

1. The annual rate of increase in enrollment will be four percent per year.
2. There will be an overall inflationary trend of three percent per year.
3. All the characteristics of the district, including (a) the composition of the student body by level (i.e., year of schooling) and capability and (b) the manner and composition of district instructional and support activities will continue unchanged during this five-year period.

This last assumption is somewhat unrealistic, but it makes the extrapolation of district costs for a five-year period a feasible

Table 7

Summary Budget of Expenditures and Reserves

Account Numbers	Description	Dollars in Thousands	Percentage
100	Administration	580	2.6
200	Instruction	15,945	72.2
300	Health	290	1.4
500	Transportation	280	1.3
600	Operations	1,760	8.0
700	Maintenance	915	4.1
800	Fixed Charges	1,100	5.0
	Subtotal	20,870	94.6
900	Food Service	500	3.2
1100	Community Service	700	2.2
	Total Current Expense	22,070	100.0
1200	Capital Outlay	500	
	Total Current Expense and Capital Outlay	22,570	
1400	Transfers	250	
	Total Expenditures	22,820	
	Reserves	3,000	
	Total Expenditures and Reserves	25,820	

Table 8

Program Budget Example

Program Number	Program Description	Year 1	Year 2	Year 3	Year 4	Year 5
		($ thousands)				
1	Learning Intellectual Skills	4,655	4,905	5,265	5,630	6,025
2	Learning About the World	4,445	4,785	5,130	5,484	5,875
3	Developing the Individual	2,700	2,920	3,135	3,350	3,590
4	Preparation for Employment	805	865	930	995	1,070
5	Preparation for Higher Education	665	720	765	820	880
	Subtotal—Direct Instruction	13,270	14,195	15,225	16,280	17,440
6	Assessment, Guidance & Counseling	990	1,035	1,105	1,185	1,275
7	Development & Evaluation	425	455	490	525	560
8	Instructional Resource & Media Services	250	240	260	275	295
	Subtotal—Instructional Support	1,665	1,730	1,855	1,985	2,130
9	Auxiliary Services	1,085	1,185	1,310	1,445	1,595
10	Community Services	700	110	110	115	120
11	Operations & Maintenance	2,840	3,050	3,190	3,480	3,750
12	Capital Outlay	450	725	1,325	1,695	2,195
13	Administration	2,560	2,805	3,010	3,215	3,445
	Total	22,570	23,800	26,025	28,215	30,675

Physical Data			(number of units)			
Students						
Elementary		20,000	20,510	21,510	22,180	23,070
Junior High		7,500	7,780	8,090	8,415	8,750
Senior High		6,500	7,070	7,355	7,650	8,155
Total		34,000	35,360	36,775	38,245	39,775
Teachers		1,260	1,310	1,365	1,416	1,473
Total personnel		1,900	1,975	2,055	2,135	2,220
Schools		45	46	47	49	51
Square feet, in thousands		3,250	3,285	3,320	3,450	3,570

undertaking for purposes of illustration and is generally realistic enough to illustrate the major points.

Year 1 in Table 8 is simply a repetition of the costs shown in Table 7, reorganized by program. The costs for the following years are based on the three preceding assumptions. Since it was assumed that the composition of the student body and the manner of district operation will remain unchanged throughout this time period, the increase in cost shown in this table is attributable entirely to the growth in enrollment and to inflation. Total enrollment increased by 5775 students. As a result, the district found it necessary to add 213 teachers and to increase total personnel by 320. It also became necessary to construct five additional elementary schools, one junior high school, and one senior high school. This resulted in an increase of 320,000 square feet in the total gross building square footage to be operated and maintained by the district.

The data on these physical changes are indicated in the lower section of Table 8. This description is by no means complete and is obviously quite abbreviated. The kind of information on physical resources useful in program budgeting is nonetheless illustrated by these data. Even at the summary level, it can be seen that the program budget—both the dollars and the physical description data—puts the decisionmaker in a more favorable position to undertake the main activities in the program budgeting process, namely, the evaluation and selection of various future courses of action. As an example, with such documentation one can assess, at least from a cost point of view, the long-range implications of such things as:

- Changing the student/teacher ratios in various program areas.
- Changing the teaching staff composition by using teacher aides.
- Allowing the average school size to change by either building more or fewer new schools.
- Shifting the emphasis of activities among programs, e.g., more science and less vocational training.

In addition to the advantage of having data covering a longer time period and having them related directly to programs, it can be seen from this example that the program budgeting approach also facilitates the analysis of alternatives in a total cost context. This is especially useful since a district, as it becomes larger, develops more interrelationships and becomes a more complex entity for analysis. As this occurs, the number and degree of nonobvious secondary cost impacts increase. Therefore, when dealing with any but the simplest of problems, it is usually necessary to analyze costs within the context of total cost requirements in order to insure against omitting (or overstating) any secondary or indirect costs. Further, working within the total context encourages the development of systematic and consistent techniques for structuring (1) relationships between the various activities in the district, and (2) data on the cost, resources, and operating characteristics of the district.

Finally, using total costs also lessens the need to prorate or allocate many indirect costs. In the total cost setting, the indirect costs are set forth along with the direct costs, and the decision-maker sees the full cost and resource implications of his choices over the entire time horizon. For example, by using the total cost approach illustrated in Table 8, there would be no need to prorate either the administrative costs in the 100 Account of the traditional budget nor the costs of the school principals, vice principals, and the supporting staff in order to evaluate proposed alternatives. It is sufficient for most purposes to know, for example, that total clerical costs increase by a certain amount when additional teachers are hired for a specified program. There is generally no real need to know the portion of total clerical help required by that program, or any other specific program, for most evaluation purposes.

It should be noted that there is one category in the program budget format for which there is no corresponding item in the traditional budget: the Program Development and Evaluation category. This, of course, does not mean that there are no activities currently performed at the district level that could be classified as developmental. There is extensive work going on in many districts on the development of improved curriculum design and teaching methods. However, this point does highlight another advantage of the program budgeting approach as compared with the traditional budgeting approach. The level of effort devoted to devising ways of evaluating, developing, and improving various aspects of district-level activity—an explicit consideration in district planning—is made visible.

Visibility of this nature, or more simply, the organization of data to provide information relevant to the decisions that are to be made, is one of the major features of a program budget as contrasted with the traditional budget. The differences in content, in structure, and in time horizon are all reflections of this feature of program budgeting.

In sum, differences between the program budget and the traditional budget are indicative of differences in approach to the task of planning. And, although it is possible to crosswalk between the two types of budgets, it would be erroneous to conclude that the program budget is no more than a rearrangement of the traditional budget.

CHAPTER FOUR

MODELING RESOURCE UTILIZATION IN A SCHOOL DISTRICT

Stephen M. Barro

Introduction

   The purpose of the analytical part of program budgeting is to provide a school district with the capability to systematically examine the consequences of decisions about its educational programs. The product of analysis is information, in the form of projected costs and benefits of proposed courses of action. Most of the work that goes into analysis has to do with developing methods for making consistent estimates of resource requirements and educational results of alternative district programs, so that these may be evaluated, compared, and presented to those with the responsibility to choose.

   The concept of *modeling* is central to the analytical effort. Models are the principal tools used in estimating program consequences. By developing generalized models of its activities, a district can acquire the capacity to look at wide ranges of alternatives rather than merely a few. The model provides a guarantee that the alternatives have been examined *consistently*.

Neither of these is available with *ad hoc* methods of program analysis.

A *model,* in this context, consists of a set of quantitative relationships among variables that enter into the determination of program benefits and cost. The set of relationships is structured so that a description of the school district, either as it is or as it might be, can be translated into estimates of the resources needed to operate the district in the specified manner, or of the educational results that are likely to be forthcoming. When such models have been developed, the analyst is in a position to formulate a description of the district at some future date, and then to vary any of the characteristics in the description and observe the consequences. Thus, the models may be said to *simulate* the operation of the district under a variety of conditions.

As a practical matter, models of school district resource utilization and cost need to be sharply distinguished from models of educational results or benefits. The two classes of models differ in complexity, the kinds of data and techniques they require, and the feasibility of operational use in school districts in the near future. The methodology of resource and cost modeling is relatively advanced as a result of much work in other fields and is available for application to school district planning. The methodology of "effectiveness" modeling is relatively undeveloped both in education and in other fields. In education, in particular, conceptual advances and considerable empirical research will be required before it is possible to establish valid predictive relationships between program characteristics and educational results. Therefore, much of this chapter focuses on the more developed area of resource and cost modeling. However, an effort is made to show how effectiveness modeling fits into the picture and to indicate some of the special problems needing resolution before effectiveness models can be made operational.

Resource Allocation Decisions and Alternatives

Analytical modeling of the district is intended to aid school officials in making resource allocation decisions that may be defined as choices among alternative uses and deployments of economic resources. This takes in a broad area, since the term "resources" embraces such diverse items as school buildings, instructional materials, the labor of all types of personnel in the educational system, and even, for some purposes, the time children spend in school. Resource allocation questions arise in a great many concrete forms:

- What size schools to build and how many of them.
- Whether to adopt a compensatory program for disadvantaged students.
- Whether to spend additional instructional time on reading.
- Whether to invest in educational television or other technological aids.
- Whether to adopt team teaching methods, or ungraded schools, or to provide teaching aides in the classroom.
- Whether to use bussing as a means of achieving school integration.
- Whether to spend the money needed to reduce class size.

All of these are problems requiring choices among alternative uses of resources. It is understood, of course, that one alternative is always to do nothing or to continue doing things the same way as before.

An alternative to an existing program is another program with certain differences in its specifications. The differences may be quantitative; for example, the two programs may differ in average class size. The differences may also involve discrete differences; for example, one program may call for building two elementary schools enrolling 500 students each, and the other may require one school enrolling 1000. Differences may also be qualitative: One program may call for graded schools and the other for ungraded schools. Typically, alternatives for resolving an issue might differ in a number of program characteristics. Of two programs designed, say, to improve education for the disadvantaged, one may call for more teachers, fewer paraprofessionals, different instructional equipment, and less classroom space than the other to serve the same number of pupils. The job of the analyst is to translate the specifications of each relevant alternative into the cost and effectiveness information needed by the decisionmaker.

Two important considerations in selecting a set of variables to represent educational programs are generality and compactness. "Generality" needs to be understood in two senses. First, the set of variables must be flexible enough to characterize a great many ways of organizing and operating a school district. It is especially important that it be able to accommodate novel or innovative forms of education so that the analytical framework itself does not inhibit imaginative responses to issues. Second, the set of variables should be applicable to many different kinds of school districts. This universality can probably only be achieved in part, since some issues and circumstances are inherently local. However, it is worth working for, because a generalized representation of district programs is a prerequisite for development of broadly applicable tools of cost and effectiveness analysis.

"Compactness" means that programs can be described with an analytically manageable number of variables. It is important because a school district is intrinsically a complicated system. A large number of interdependent variables would be needed to provide a really complete, or true-to-life description of its activities. Given this complexity, and at the same time, the need to develop a broadly applicable analytical framework within which a reasonably concise set of constructs and categories may be applied to many districts and many kinds of resource allocation questions, it is fortunate that it seems possible to aggregate data and eliminate much detail without losing information that is essential to decisionmaking. This is important simply in terms of the effort required, if we are to analyze and compare numerous program alternatives and if analyses are to encompass a multi-year planning period. An important aspect of the "art" of model building is to select appropriate levels of detail for representing each aspect of the educational program.

A Public School System as a System

Although aggregation and simplification make the problem more manageable, there are still many variables that must be taken into account in constructing a model of resource allocation in a school district. Figure 5 identifies the major classes of variables that enter into such a model and presents a very general picture of their interaction. It shows that certain externally determined magnitudes, such as projected enrollment in the district and certain specifications of the educational program established by school district managers, combine to determine levels of educational activity, resource requirements, financial requirements shown in the budget, and educational output or effectiveness.

Three kinds of variables are represented by the boxes in this figure. First, there are certain magnitudes that are "given" from the point of view of the district planner. The most important one of these is the projected enrollment for the district, which the educational planner must try to estimate, but over which the district has practically no control, since education must be provided for all children within its bounds. Another "given" is the existing physical plant of the district, which was shaped by decisions made in the past, but which must be considered fixed in the context of current planning (except, of course, that there is the option to abandon parts of it). Other variables that are "given" include certain externally determined constants that enter into determination of program costs, such as some of the prices that the district must pay for the resources it purchases. Incidentally, the price of educational manpower—teachers' salaries—does not fall into this category. All of these magnitudes are known as *predetermined variables*, signifying that they are determined before, and are independent of, any decisions taken by the district. The predetermined variables are set off by dashed lines in Figure 5 to show that they are determined independently of current decisions.

The second category of variables with which we are concerned are the variables controlled by the school district decision-maker. These are the *decision variables* or *policy variables* in the system. They are of central interest in program analysis, since they

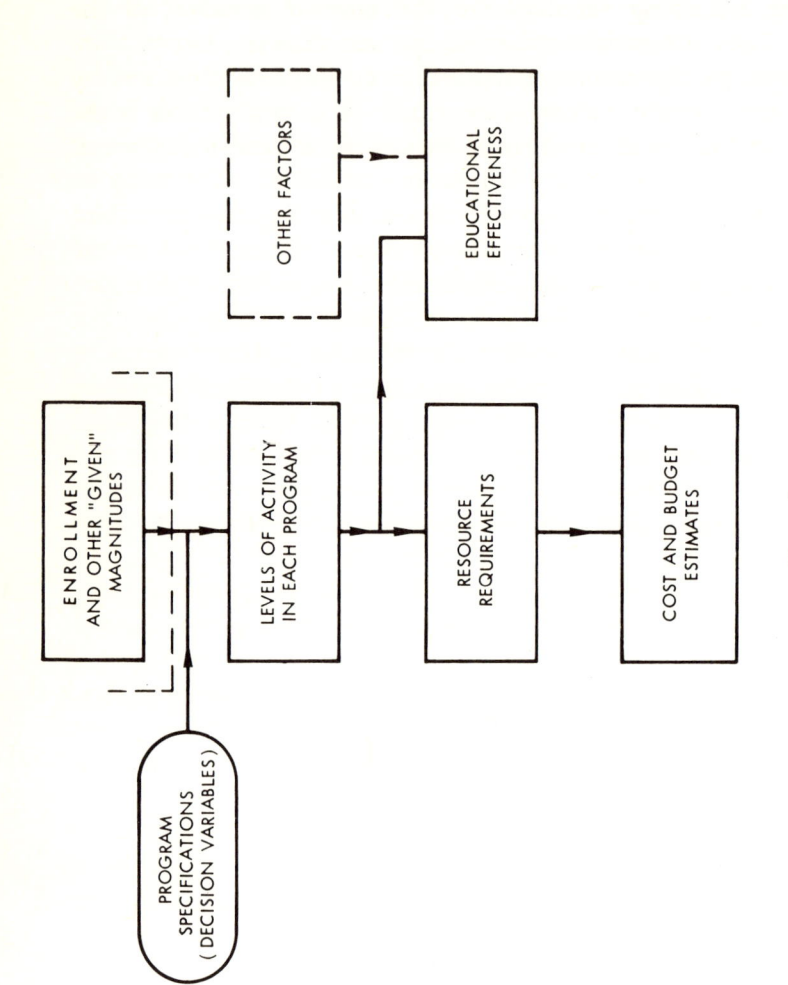

Figure 5

Overall Structure of a Model of a School District

are the variables that district administrators can manipulate and that are the subject of controversy in debates over educational issues. They are represented by oval figures in the diagrams.

The remaining variables are the *internal variables* of the system. They are variables that no one sets directly, but that are determined by the choices embodied in decision variables and by the "givens" of the system. An example of such a variable is the number of third grade teachers in the system, a number that is not decided directly but that emerges as a result of there being so many third graders enrolled and of our deciding to teach third graders certain subjects in a certain way. The elements of the district budget, which are determined by almost the entire constellation of given conditions and decisions taken about the district and its programs, constitute one set of internal variables. Another set of internal variables represents the effectiveness, or "educational output," of the district. In a sense, educational effectiveness and the district budget are the end-points of the system. As such, they may be designated *target variables* to set them apart from other internal variables that perform an intermediate role.

In terms of these variables, the purpose of the systems-analytical aspect of educational program budgeting is to understand how changes in the decision variables affect the target variables subject to given values of variables that are predetermined. Or, in simpler terms, how do choices about the district and its program affect educational and financial outcomes under given conditions?

Major Decision Variables in the System

Figure 6 provides a more detailed representation of the relationship between the educational programs and resource requirements of a school district. The figure shows how a number of decision variables define the district's instructional and other programs, and how this set of specifications then determines levels of program activity and resource requirements. In the following pages, we will examine in some detail the principal variables that enter into the system, and we will attempt to lay out the logic of

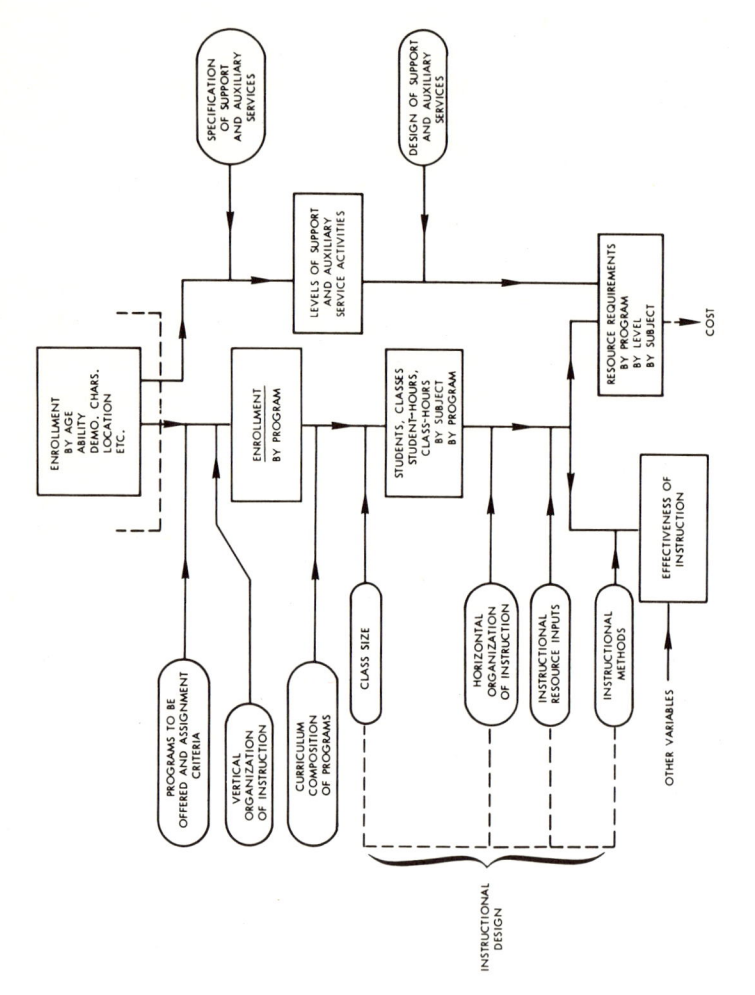

Figure 6

School System Decisions, Programs, and Their Implications

the relationships among them.

*Selection of Programs, Vertical Organization of the
Schools, and Assignments of Students to Programs*

The starting point for determination of resources associated with instructional programs is the district's projected enrollment. A discussion of some of the problems of projecting enrollment is contained in Appendix C. In this section we will skip over the question of how enrollment can be projected, and simply assume that we have year-by-year estimates of numbers of students to be enrolled in the system. Assume that the projections include information on future enrollment by age and by a number of other characteristics that might be relevant to program planning, such as prevalence of exceptionalities, certain demographic variables, and residence location within the district. These projections provide the data according to which students may be assigned to various programs.

Usually, a school district will provide different educational programs to different subgroups of the school population. One dimension of this differentiation is the vertical organization of instruction. Students are grouped vertically into grades or into other age/achievement groups, which in turn are usually combined into several broad levels. These may consist of elementary, junior high school, and high school levels; primary, middle, and secondary levels; or other arrangements. A second dimension of differentiation, as was shown in the program structure in Chapter Two, represents specialization of instruction for students identified by certain significant characteristics. Four broad grounds for program differentiation are identified: ability or achievement; mental, physical, or emotional handicaps or exceptionalities; disadvantageous extra-school environments; and different student options with respect to career goals.

Thus, a school system may be pictured as offering an array of programs to groups of students differentiated by age or grade and by these four kinds of characteristics. But not every public school system provides the same programs or defines them in the same way. One type of decision to be made by a school district is what specific programs are to be offered and by what criteria or specific rules students are to be assigned to one program or the other.

Table 9 shows how such a set of program specifications might be represented for a hypothetical district. Each row represents a category of students for which the educational program is fully or partially differentiated from the regular instruction program. The columns represent the different levels of instruction. For illustration, these are shown as the most common groupings—preschool, kindergarten, lower and upper grade elementary, junior high school, high school, and junior college. All 16 grade levels or any other form of vertical organization, such as the set of overlapping age-group levels that might be found in a system of ungraded elementary or secondary schools, could be shown in the same way.

Entries in the cells of the matrix specify conditions under which a child is assigned to each program. For example, in order to be admitted to the preschool program for disadvantaged, a child might have to fall in a specified age group, his family may have to have an income below some maximum level or, perhaps, he must reside in a designated "ghetto" area of the city. To be in a gifted program, one may have to have certain measured ability or achievement levels and meet certain personality criteria. Assignments to some of the other programs for exceptionalities may be based on medical or psychological diagnosis. Sometimes the criteria to be applied by the district are specified in full or in part in the state education code. Vertical progression through a program is often semi-automatic, i.e., the main qualification for entering the third grade of the regular program is having completed the second grade. However, there are many possibilities for crossovers, for which criteria also need to be spelled out, although they are not shown in the diagram. In connection with some of the programs for remedial exceptionalities, crossovers to the standard program are a main indicator of effectiveness.

Referring back to the overall system diagram, once the district has specified the programs it will operate, including the vertical organization of instruction, and the rules to be used in assigning students to programs, it becomes possible to translate the projections of enrollment by student characteristics into projec-

Table 9

Specification of Programs, Vertical Organization of Instruction, and Rules for Assignment of Students for a Hypothetical School District

PROGRAM	PRESCHOOL	KINDER-GARTEN	GRADES 1-3	GRADES 4-6	GRADES 7-9	GRADES 10-12	GRADES 13, 14
REGULAR STUDENTS		AGE					H.S. GRAD OR TEST
DISADVANTAGED	AGE, INCOME, LOCATION, DEMOG.						H.S. GRAD, INCOME, DEMOG.
GIFTED				ABILITY, ACHIEVE., PERSONALITY			
PHYSICALLY HANDICAPPED		MEDICAL DIAGNOSIS					
EDUCATIONALLY HANDICAPPED		ACHIEVE., PERSONALITY, PSYCH.					
EDUCABLE MENTALLY RETARDED		ABILITY PSYCH. TEST	← GRADE DISTINCTIONS DO NOT APPLY →				
OCCUPATIONAL TRAINING OPTIONS					STUDENT CHOICES, GUIDANCE		
COLLEGE PREPARATION OPTIONS						STUDENT CHOICES, GUIDANCE	

tions of enrollment by program.

Curriculum Composition

An important reason for differentiating programs for different groups and levels, from the point of view of resource planning, is that, in general, they involve different kinds or different mixes of instruction, which have different resource requirements and costs per student. First of all, the curriculum may be different for each program. To find out what the resource implications are of having so many students in each program, it is necessary to define what activities and what resources each program comprises. Part of this definition is a specification of curriculum composition. This consists of an itemization of the subjects or courses of instruction to be included in the program for each level and type of student and a statement of the amount of time allotted for each subject. For example, the curriculum composition for regular fourth grade elementary students could be described by stating that X class-hours per year are spent on language, Y class-hours on mathematics, Z class-hours on learning about society, and so forth. The subject categories among which instructional time is allotted should, of course, correspond to those shown in the subject-oriented program structure of Table 10.

There are several problems of measurement to be resolved in specifying curriculum composition. If instruction is departmentalized, as it usually is in high schools and junior high schools, it is relatively easy to specify the curriculum composition because we can count the number of students enrolled in each subject and the number of hours spent, and produce a set of figures representing the amount of activity in each area of instruction. The natural unit of measurement is student-hours spent in each subject per week, per month or per school year. In elementary schools, which frequently operate nearly self-contained classrooms, the same kind of distribution of effort among subjects could be obtained by estimating amounts of time allocated to different subject activities within the individual classroom. One way of doing this would be to rely on the nominal or prescribed curriculum, which, in many

Table 10

Curriculum Composition by Program
(In class hours per year)

Programs by Subject Area	Regular K	1-3	4-5	7-9	10-12	Disadvantaged Pre	K	1-3	4-6	7-9	10-12	Gifted 4-6	7-9	10-12	Educationally Handicapped 1-3	4-6	7-9	10-12	EMR 1-6	7-12
Intellectual skills																				
Language and communication skills																				
Reading			180																	
Written language			75																	
Oral language			60																	
Quantitative skills			120																	
Learning about the world																				
U.S. and other societies			150																	
The physical world and living things			60																	
Literature and the arts			—																	
Skills for everyday life			—																	
Physical, social, and emotional development																				
Physical education			60																	
Self-expression			120																	
Occupational skills																				
Total	540	900	1080	1260	1260															

districts, specifies a time allocation.

In some cases it may not be feasible to describe a district's curriculum by a time distribution, as, for example, where instructional activities are highly individualized or organized in an interdisciplinary manner. This need not interfere with the resource and cost analysis process, but it is likely to pose difficulties in relating educational resources to outputs.

A method of representing curriculum composition is shown in Table 10. In this table, programs by type of student and by level are shown across the top, and subjects are arrayed vertically. The entries in the table represent instructional time (in class-hours per school year) allotted to each subject within each program. The entries in the bottom row indicate the total time spent in school during the school year by students in each program. These entries subsume certain policy variables related to the overall operating posture of the district, such as the number of school days per year and the hours of daily attendance for students in different programs and levels. The illustrative entries in one column of the table show a hypothetical curriculum in upper-grade elementary school. Students attend school six hours per day, 180 days per year, for a total of 1080 hours per year. About one-fourth of the time, 255 hours, is used for lunch and recess and is included in the total. Although these activities are not specifically set forth in the table, they cannot be ignored, since they are resource-using activities. The remainder is distributed, as indicated, among the various areas of instruction.

Given this kind of quantitative specification of curriculum composition, it is then possible to carry out the next translation shown in Figure 6, which is to convert enrollment into student-hours by subject and by program.

Instructional Design:
Instructional Resource Inputs

The variables in the system that have the most direct relationship to resource requirements and cost, and perhaps to instructional effectiveness, are those included in what we shall refer to as *instructional design*. We use this term broadly to

Modeling Resource Utilization in a School District 81

comprise all the variables that describe *how* instruction is provided. Specifically, instructional design includes the horizontal organization of instruction, specifications of class sizes, specifications of resource inputs in each area of instruction, and specifications of instructional methods. These variables are closely linked, which is why we apply to them the blanket term "instructional design." A program alternative that affects the method of instruction often calls for coordinated changes in a number of the instructional design variables.

Horizontal organization refers to the set of specifications that tells us how students at a given level of instruction are assigned to groups or classes and how the groups are assigned to teachers and classrooms for instruction in different subjects. Some possibilities for alternative forms of horizontal organization include self-contained classrooms, full or partial departmentalization, team teaching or other flexible grouping arrangements, and so forth. The important variable, group size, or class size, tells us how many students are exposed as a unit to each form of instruction. This, obviously, is a central variable in any kind of resource analysis, since it acts as a "scale factor" with respect to many of the specifications of resource inputs.

Decisions about the organization of instruction may have a bearing on both educational effectiveness and cost. However, the effects of organizational arrangements on resource requirements and cost are accounted for by the class size specifications and the variables that express instructional resource inputs. Therefore, we do not have to define a variable specifically representing a "form of horizontal organization" to do resource analysis. However, a form of organization may need to enter explicitly into efforts to relate program specifications to effectiveness.

Resource input specifications define the number of units of resources or resource services associated with a unit of each form of instruction. For example, they tell us that the services of a teacher and, perhaps, a teaching aide are required during each class-hour of first grade reading, that so many dollars of instructional materials are consumed per student in art instruction in the fifth grade, and that the services of instructional equipment worth Y dollars are required for teaching a high school chemistry class. An important thing to note about these resource ratios is that the denominators are different for different categories of resources. That is, requirements for teachers are related to the number of class-hours; requirements for equipment may be related to the number of classes, regardless of how many hours they meet; requirements for materials may be related to the number of student-hours; and requirements for textbooks may be related to the number of students, regardless of either class size or the number of hours of class meetings. Therefore, as indicated in Figure 6, the class size and curriculum composition specifications are transformed to generate indexes of instructional activity in all of these units of measurement—students, classes, student-hours, and class-hours.

The question of the appropriate level of aggregation of data, mentioned earlier, arises here because it is possible to distinguish a great many different kinds of instructional resources. We could identify many categories of teachers, based on their qualifications, specialties, length of experience, and proficiency. In principle, both cost and effectiveness of instruction would be affected by a district's choices among these different types of teachers. Similarly, we could distinguish many types of materials, various categories of classroom equipment, different kinds of classrooms, and so on. If we did, the arrays of numbers needed to describe a program would become unmanageably large, and computations based on them would be slow, cumbersome, and costly. Keeping in mind that the purpose of the system model is to contribute to long-range planning, which calls for a capability to assess *relative* results of alternative programs, there is little to be gained by elaborating resource detail beyond that required to represent major groupings of similar resources. For instructional personnel, for example, it may be sufficient to distinguish among, say, regular elementary teachers, regular secondary teachers, specialized teachers, and paraprofessionals. For most purposes, average salary levels within each group will lead to adequate representations of program cost unless there is a deliberate policy of assigning more qualified or more experienced teachers to specific programs, levels, or subjects. For other inputs it may be sufficient to characterize requirements for materials and equipment only by dollar values of consumption or inventories per student or per class. However, for some problems it may be desirable to identify classes of equipment, such as audio-visual, science, and music.

Once resource categories are defined, instructional resource inputs can be represented in a tabular form (see Table 11). This table shows the resource input ratios associated with one particular program, which happens to be the regular program at the high school level. Subjects of instruction are arrayed vertically. The columns provide space for entering class size and resource requirements for each subject. The resources shown include several categories of teachers, materials, and textbooks, several classes of equipment, and different types of instructional rooms. This particular set of categories is only suggestive and may or may not be the most useful for a particular district. Entries in the table are resource input ratios in the appropriate units—for example, one teacher man-hour per class-hour and $20 for textbooks per student for instruction in English.

Note that in some cases there will be more than one set of resource input specifications for a subject, as is shown in Table 11 for a hypothetical high school chemistry course. The reason is that there are two forms of instruction, classroom and laboratory work, each of which has a different class size and different requirements for teachers, materials, and other resources. In contrast, when describing resource requirements of self-contained elementary classrooms, it is not necessary to have specifications for each subject because the basic set of resources—one teacher and one classroom per class—applies across the board. Thus, a single set of specifications can be used to provide an aggregative description of resource requirements for a typical elementary program. Individual subject specifications would be needed only where special resources, such as specialized teachers or facilities, are involved.

A table similar to Table 11 would be needed for each program and level. However, this would not constitute as large a set of numbers as it might seem because some aggregation is

Table 11
Instructional Design
Class Sizes and Resource Inputs (Regular Programs—Grades 10-12)

Selected Subjects of Instruction	Class Size	Teachers (hrs./class-hr.) Regular Elementary	Teachers Regular Secondary	Specialists	Paraprofessionals	Materials ($/student/yr.)	Textbooks ($/student)	Equipment ($/class) Audio-visual	Equipment Science	Equipment Other	Facilities (hrs./class yr.) Elementary Classrooms	Facilities Secondary Classrooms	Facilities Special Subject Rooms	Facilities Auditorium, Gym, Cafeteria
Language and communication skills														
English	30		1				20					1		
Creative writing	18		1				12					1		
...														
The physical world and living things														
Chemistry—classroom	30		1			3	8		3,000			1		
Chemistry—laboratory	60		1		2	15	5		10,000				1	
...														
Literature and the arts														
Music appreciation	100			1	1	2	5			1,500			1	
...														
Physical development														
Physical education	120		1											1
...														

possible; and there is considerable duplication of courses or subjects among programs, which permits their resource specifications to be handled by cross-referencing.

Instructional Support Programs and Auxiliary Services

By a more or less parallel sequence of steps, the activities and resources involved in instructional support programs, such as guidance and instructional resource services, and auxiliary programs, such as transportation, health, and food service, can be specified. For most of these programs, the required sets of variables will be simpler than those needed to define instructional programs. The description of the guidance program, for example, could begin by specifying the type of services to be provided to different types and levels of students, in terms of average numbers of sessions with guidance personnel, numbers of psychological tests to be administered, etc. These specifications can then be translated into requirements for personnel and other guidance program resources. A commonly used shortcut, which may suffice for some purposes, is to specify guidance requirements in terms of staffing ratios, e.g., one guidance counselor for each 300 students.

If transportation is taken as an example of an auxiliary service program, it can be seen that the process is similar. The service may be specified by stating what categories of students are to be transported to and from school. They may be identified by student type, grade level, and distance from school. When these specifications are applied to the enrollment projections, they yield a set of absolute levels of program activity—so many children to be transported to and from school each day. The program design, which describes how transportation is provided, is then specified. If a bus system is used, the program design will include resource input specifications, such as the number of buses and bus drivers required per student. These can then be used to translate the estimates of activity levels into resource requirements, just as was done for the instructional programs. The other instructional support and auxiliary service programs are handled similarly.

Resource and Cost Implications of a District Program

Referring once more to Figure 6, it can be seen that once the district's programs and the distribution of students among them, the curriculum composition of each program, and certain aspects of instructional design have been specified, and once specifications for the instructional support and auxiliary programs have been provided, essentially all that is necessary to determine resource requirements of the district's direct programs has been done. A standard set of variables that can be used to describe a district's program has been identified. This provides the basis for systematic calculations of a program's resource implications, and, ultimately, for examination of the costs of the many alternatives and variations that are likely to be compared in system-analytical studies.

With the system variables thus far defined, it is simpler to "add up" the requirements for each kind of resource—teacher man-hours, dollars of materials and equipment, and numbers of classroom hours—across programs, subjects, educational levels, and types of students. Formally, each set of variables represented by the boxes in Figure 6 can be identified as a matrix of factors that enters into determination of resource requirements.* The total requirement for a given kind of resource, say regular teacher man-hours, is given by a summation that looks like this:

$$R_K = \sum_{\text{Student types}} \sum_{\text{Levels}} \sum_{\text{Subjects}} \frac{E_{SL}}{C_{SLJ}} \cdot h_{SLJ} \cdot r_{SLJK}$$

---

*The mathematical process for translating these arrays of program descriptors into resources is matrix multiplication. The result of the multiplication is a set of numbers representing requirements for each category of resource.

Where E_{SL} = enrollment of students of type S at level L,
C_{SLJ} = class size in subject J for students of type S at level L,
h_{SLJ} = class-hours per year spent in subject J by students of type S and level L (curriculum composition),
r_{SLJK} = amount of resources of type K required per class-hour of instruction in subject J for students of type S and level L.
R_K = total requirement for resource K per year by all instructional programs.

This is a summation—over each type of student, each level of education, and each subject of instruction—of requirements for a particular kind of resource, which in this case is assumed to be teacher man-hours. The variables that enter into this expression are the enrollment in each program and level; class size (an element of instructional design); the number of class-hours per year spent in a subject by students in a given program (the curriculum composition variable); and the amount of resources—in this case the number of teacher man-hours required per class-hour (a resource input specification). These combine to give the total requirement for teacher man-hours for all programs.

This is a relatively simple form of resource requirement calculation, since it assumes that all resource requirements can be related to instructional activity as measured in class-hours. If the computation were being done for instructional materials, for example, it would be likely to include some factors related to class-hours, some to student-hours, and, perhaps, some to the number of students in each subject. This would complicate the form of the equation.

This summation represents precisely the kind of computation that has to be performed over and over again in adding up the budget for any school district. It symbolizes some of the most tedious and repetitive aspects of budget-making. The reason that it pays to be formal and symbolic and reasonably rigorous in defining these variables is that this will help to make these operations routine and suitable for automation. The intent, however, is not to reduce the burden of arithmetic on a district's administrative staff. Rather, it is to create a new capability to examine the costs of program alternatives—to look at many variations and permutations that would be useful to assess in planning a program, but would not be feasible to compute by hand.

Translating Resource Requirements into a Budget

Figure 7 shows how program specifications translate into requirements for specific resource purchases and, ultimately, into the financial requirements that appear in the program budget. It is a continuation of Figure 6, taking up with "resource requirements" where the previous diagram left off. Figure 7 shows that each resource requirement implies certain purchases of goods or services. For example, a requirement for a certain number of teacher man-hours implies the hiring of so many teachers. In this case, the translation factor is simply a utilization rate which represents the number of hours of classroom teaching obtained in a year from a regular, full-time teacher.

Resource requirements have been divided into three categories requiring different treatment. Personnel resources, including teachers, cannot be translated into personnel expenditures until a salary schedule has been specified. The district has a certain amount of control over its salary structure, as opposed to the situation it faces with respect to other resources for which the prices paid may generally be assumed to be externally determined. Figure 7 suggests that the district's decisions about salary policy are likely to have a feedback effect on effectiveness, via an effect on the quality of the teaching staff.

Other current resources—primarily materials, supplies, and other consumables—translate directly into expenditures because the prices paid are constants given from outside.

The translation process for capital items—buildings and

Figure 7

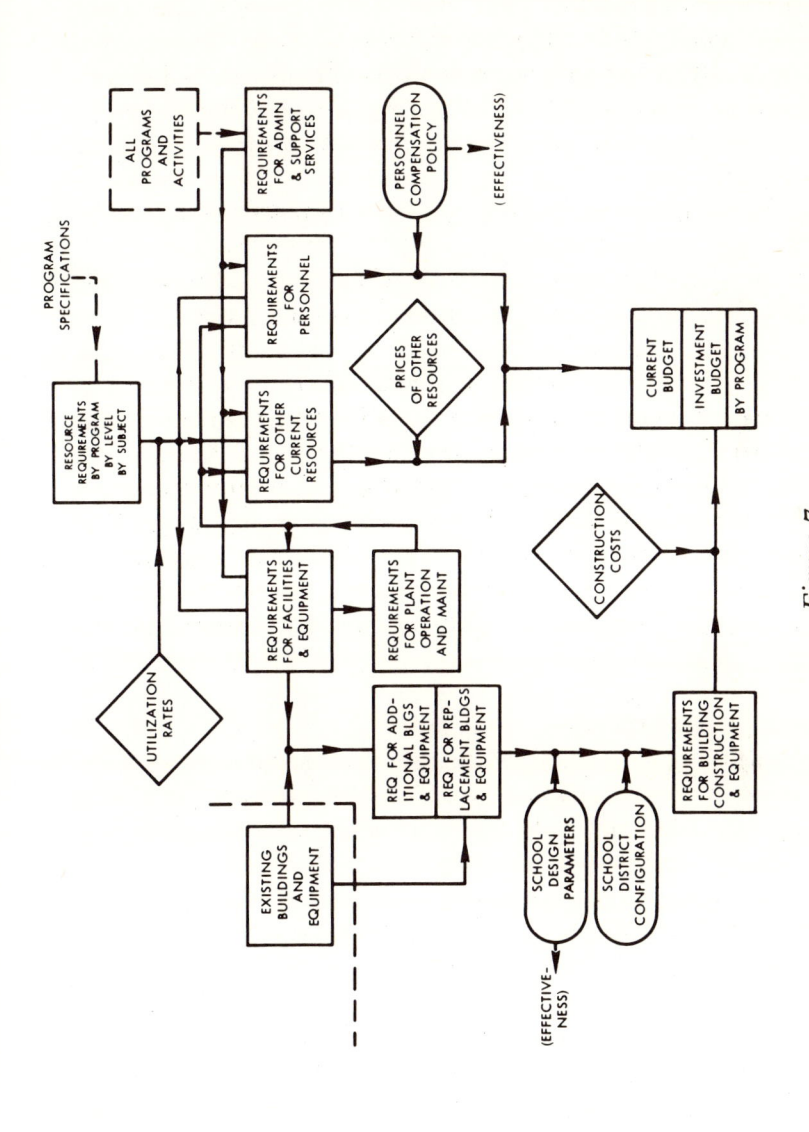

School System Resource Requirements and Budgets

equipment—is a little more complicated. The requirement for new capital investment is obtained by comparing a program's requirements for facilities and equipment with the pre-existing stock. The requirement for new building construction or equipment procurement is the difference between the two. Also, there are requirements for replacement of outdated buildings or worn out or obsolete equipment.

In deciding how to provide additions to physical capital, the district has certain decisions to make. With respect to the construction of a school, given that it will accommodate a certain number of students and that it will house certain programs, there is latitude for considerable variation in design characteristics. Should the school, for example, conform to minimum state requirements for square footage or should it be built on a more ample scale? Should it have a flexible floor plan, extra office space, additional special-purpose rooms, air conditioning, or other features? In principle, these decisions about the quality of physical plant have a feedback effect on program effectiveness somewhat analogous to the effect of decisions about teacher quality. Of course, these decisions about building design have a direct impact on construction cost.

District Configuration

Another decision problem for the district has to do with the shape of the district's physical system as a whole rather than with the design of individual buildings. This is the decision about how many schools to build, what size schools to build, where to locate them, and what programs to house in each building. Some major economic and educational issues are embodied in this last set of decisions: Shall the district have more small schools or fewer large schools? The latter may call for more pupil transportation but may also permit lower operating and administrative costs. Certain educational advantages may also attach to either size of school—perhaps more individual attention in the small school but greater opportunity for specialized programs in the large school. This decision is strongly interrelated with the decision about what programs to house in each building. Shall there be K-6 elementary schools or shall the range of levels in a school be restricted to K-3 in some and 4-6 in others? Or shall there be primary and middle schools on a K-4, 5-8 basis? Or, referring to another dimension of program differentiation, shall classes for exceptional children be held in regular school buildings, or shall there be special schools for the educationally or physically handicapped, retarded, or gifted?

All of these decisions not only affect the specifications of new capital construction and enter into capital cost, but they have important interactions with some of the variables bearing on program effectiveness. For example, decisions about school size and about the division of levels of instruction among schools set certain limits for what can be done with the horizontal organization of the schools. These interrelationships among decision variables represent another of the complications of the effectiveness side that make effectiveness analysis a significantly more difficult undertaking than resource and cost analysis.

Some aspects of district configuration are difficult to represent in a general way because they depend so much on characteristics of a particular community. These are mainly the factors that have to do with locations of the schools; but interpreted broadly, the locational factor takes in many important elements of the interaction between school system and community, including aspects of racial and social integration, community identification with the schools, and so forth. The more tangible elements of district configuration—number and size of schools and identification of programs housed in each—can be represented as in Table 12. Programs are shown across the top of the table and individual school buildings are listed down the side. Entries in the table show the number of students in each program that attend each school. The first column shows total enrollment in each school.

Support Programs

A final set of items in the network shown in Figure 7 represents the generation of support program resource requirements. We show two representative categories of support pro-

Table 12

School District Configuration
School Enrollment by Program and Level

School Buildings	Total	Regular K	Regular 1-3	Regular 4-6	Regular 7-9	Regular 10-12	Disadvantaged Pre	Disadvantaged K	Disadvantaged 1-3	Disadvantaged 4-6	Disadvantaged 7-9	Disadvantaged 10-12	Gifted 4-6	Gifted 7-9	Gifted 10-12	Educationally Handicapped 1-3	Educationally Handicapped 4-6	Educationally Handicapped 7-9	Educationally Handicapped 10-12	EMR 1-6	EMR 7-12
Elementary Buildings																					
1	750	120	340	290																	
2	680	190	490																		
3	820			450					285				85								
.	.																				
N_e	.																				
Secondary Buildings																					
1	1500				920	1500					430	800			100			90	100		60
2	2300																				
.	.																				
N_a	.																				
Special Buildings																					
1	250						120	130													
.	.																				
N_b																					

grams: Plant Operation and Maintenance, and Administration and General Support. The requirement for plant operation and maintenance services is a demand derived from the characteristics of the physical plant and, perhaps, from some explicit district policy about the level or quality of maintenance, which, however, is not depicted in the figure. The operation and maintenance activity, in turn, has its own requirements for personnel, other current resources, and facilities and equipment. In the same way, the other main support program, Administration and General Support, imposes requirements for each type of resource—for personnel, for other current resources (office supplies, transportation, etc.), and for facilities and equipment (e.g., the district administration building). In principle, the level of administrative and support services is a function of practically all of the other programs and activities, but there is no point in cluttering the diagram with the corresponding web of lines.

The District's Program Budget

Finally, application of the appropriate prices or cost factors to current and capital purchases produces estimates of the elements of the district's current and capital budget. As the diagram should make clear, the budget amounts are determined by a large interrelated set of program and resource decisions. Since all the program specifications and resource requirements were expressed in program terms, the budget is a program budget. It is precisely the type of program budget that was presented in Chapter Three.

System Variables and Program Effectiveness

One aspect of the educational system that emerges from this discussion, which bears strongly on the question of what can be done by program analysis, is that it is considerably easier to specify the decision variables in the educational system that determine program costs than the larger set of variables needed to account for program effectiveness. This can easily be seen if we refer back to Figure 6. At the point where all the variables needed to determine program resource requirements had been specified, some of the specifications needed to account for program effectiveness were still missing. At least the following additional elements are needed:

First, the method used for instruction in each subject. So far, instructional methods have been accounted for only to the extent that they are reflected in resource inputs. That is, one method may call for smaller classes or more materials or more instructional equipment than another. However, there are many variations in method that may be chosen within fixed resource limits, or that make a difference in the impact of instruction that is not measured by variations in resource requirements. For example, a teacher in a classroom may provide instruction by lecturing, by class discussion, by administering individual reading and written work, by organizing group activities, or other means. These methods may vary greatly in effectiveness for given students and subject matter, but may produce only minor variations in resource requirements. Therefore, one of the additional specifications that would be needed to appraise program effectiveness is a description of instructional method. This could be quantified, at least partly, in terms of the mode of communication or interaction taking place in the classroom. The time devoted to each form of communication could be specified, along with the transmitter and receiver of information, and the active or passive role of each participant in the classroom. But "instructional method" is a difficult construct to specify concisely or quantitatively or to measure, and it is not obvious that anything would be gained by this sort of approach.

Second, we would have to specify the content of each subject. Thus far, content has been specified only to the extent of identifying the amount of instructional time devoted to each of a number of broad subject categories. But the effectiveness of instruction in terms of what is achieved and, more important, in terms of its value in the outside world depends on what, specifically, is taught in each course or subject. However, quantitative specification of the program in terms of the specific topics to be included does not seem feasible. This is also true of a more tangible aspect of the specification of content, namely, description of instruction in terms of specific textbooks and other instructional materials.

Third, many qualitative factors that affect educational outcomes would need to be specified. Among them are information on resource quality, especially the quality of teachers; information on intangibles in the school system, such as morale and quality of administration; information on other aspects of the community environment; and, most important, further information on the students themselves, including information on their backgrounds, educational histories, and past school achievement, which are needed to define the baseline from which instructional effectiveness of the school system can be measured.

The degree of difficulty in identifying all of these attributes of a school system, and even more important, in discovering the relationships between all of these variables and the educational outcomes, is so obvious as to make clear why effectiveness analysis is a much less developed art than cost analysis and why it is likely to remain so for a long time.

Issues and Alternatives

One of the benefits of modeling a school system in this way is that it permits us to translate proposals for educational change into well-defined alternatives whose consequences can be systematically assessed. We can demonstrate this by showing how suggestions about a particular issue lead to specific, analyzable program alternatives.

Suppose that we are interested in exploring the consequences of proposals for resolving an educational issue and that the necessary techniques of cost and effectiveness analysis exist and are available. A first step is to translate the proposed ways of coping with the issue into precisely specified alternatives to which the analytical tools may be applied. This means that each proposal must be described in terms of a set of changes in decision variables from the values that characterize the existing program.

To show concretely how proposed responses to an issue lead to specific program alternatives, let us consider a specific current issue in education: the question of how to raise reading achievement levels. Proposed courses of action include the following:

- Spend more instructional time on reading.
- Teach reading in smaller classes.
- Use better instructional materials.
- Employ reading specialists.
- Adopt improved instructional methods.
- Teach reading on a more individualized basis.
- Employ technological aids.
- Start to teach reading at an earlier age.
- Provide special reading instruction for children with language disadvantages.

These proposals can be represented in terms of the system variables we have defined. Table 13 relates the proposals to the system characteristics. Some of the proposals are relatively clear-cut. They can be related to specific changes in the values of specific system characteristics. For example, the suggestion to use better instructional materials would be reflected in a change in the materials category of instructional resource inputs. However, most of these proposals are not so well-defined or they involve changes in a number of different variables. To illustrate, the proposal to teach reading in smaller classes seems simple, but in a system with largely self-contained elementary classrooms there is the question of whether smaller classes are to be provided for all instruction or only for instruction in reading. One method of providing smaller classes for reading is to stagger arrival and departure times of students so that one-half of the class may have reading at the beginning of the school day and the other half at the end. Thus, the class size for reading instruction would be cut in half. However, this alternative involves changes in curriculum composition (i.e., more total time for reading) and length of the school day, in addition to the changes in class size for reading. Similarly, the apparently simple change in the amount of time devoted to reading instruction is not completely specified unless statements are made about how the increased time will be provided. Either total instructional time will have to be increased or specific

Table 13

Translating Proposed Actions into Program Alternatives

Program Characteristics

Instructional Design

Proposed Actions to Improve Reading Achievement	Programs and Vertical Organization	Curriculum Composition	Class Sizes	Horizontal Organization	Resource Inputs	Methods	Subject Content
More Instruction time		X					
Smaller Classes		?	X				
Better materials					X		?
Use reading specialists					X		
Improved methods			?	?	?	X	?
More individualization				?	?	X	
Technological aids			?	?	X	?	
Start reading at an earlier age	X						
Provide special reading instruction for the disadvantaged	X	?					

subjects of instruction will have to be eliminated.

The suggestion calling for use of reading specialists requires further specification. Are these specialists to teach reading classes? If so, the change can be represented as an increment to instructional resources. Or, are they to work with teachers? If so, then the change appears as an increase in the human resources available in the instructional resources support program. The proposals having to do with improved teaching methods, in general, or greater individualization in particular, would be reflected mainly in the instructional design variables that affect "output" but not cost. However, one way of promoting individualization would be to reduce class size or provide more personnel. Obviously, the term "improved methods" is so broad that it might cover a whole series of changes. In any event, proposed new methods need to be specified in enough detail so that any resource impacts will be identified. The use of methods involving technological aids may imply changes in a large number of program specifications, including horizontal organization, resource inputs, and instructional methods. In particular, specifications of the technological medium itself, as it affects resource inputs at the classroom, school, and central district levels, must be stated in detail. Finally, the suggestions about reading at an earlier age and special reading for the disadvantaged involve changes in programs and criteria for pupil assignment. Early instruction in reading implies the establishment of a new program at the preschool level or reorientation of existing curricula in preschool and kindergarten. Reading programs for groups with special language disadvantages call for establishment of differentiated programs for those categories of students, perhaps including the changes involved in providing reading instruction at an earlier age.

By being explicit and quantitative about what is meant by each proposal for change, we can improve the quality of debate on the reading issue in several respects. For one thing, well-defined changes in program specifications, corresponding to each proposal for action, can be translated into financial increments with the aid of a resource and cost model. This would permit participants in the debate to understand the financial implications of each program. But more important, when alternatives are specified explicitly, it becomes possible to set up comparisons that fully reflect available choices and that are especially informative to decisionmakers. For example, it becomes possible to set up a series of equal cost alternatives, among which decisionmakers may choose strictly on the basis of their judgment about educational results.

To show how this could be done for the reading issue, suppose that a district is considering three possible approaches to improving reading in elementary school: (1) providing a certain package of special reading materials for each elementary class; (2) reducing class size across the board; or (3) employing reading specialists to teach in the classroom a certain number of hours per week. Beginning with the third approach, the analyst can produce a cost estimate of what it would cost to have reading specialists in each elementary classroom, say, for two hours each week. Then, turning to the second alternative, he would construct an equal cost case by determining what reduction in class size could be obtained for the same number of dollars. Suppose that this turned out to be a reduction in average class size from 30 to 28. Suppose, finally, that the first approach, providing a package of special reading materials, is less expensive than either of these possibilities—say it costs only one-half as much. An alternative that almost suggests itself is a combination of two approaches. For example, for the same money that would be required to provide reading specialists two hours per week in each class or to reduce class size from 30 to 28, it might be possible to provide the package of reading materials for each classroom and to reduce class size by a smaller amount, say from 30 to 29. Thus, three equal cost alternatives have been formulated. The advantage of doing this is that the educational decisionmaker is now free to choose among them on the basis of his professional judgment about their educational merits. He does not have to worry about relative cost because the cost has been equalized for all three alternatives. The analyst may then construct similar equal cost alternatives for several different levels of total expenditure, so that the decisionmaker can see what can be done for different amounts of spending on reading improvement.

Modeling the Program of a School District: A Summary

In sum, a school district can be described by a model that includes the variables shown in Table 14. A particular program for a school district is defined by assigning values to all of these variables. An alternative to a given program is created by changing the values of one or more of the decision variables.

As noted, not all the decision variables enter into the estimates of system cost. Those that are identified in Table 14 constitute a sufficient set of inputs for estimation of cost. All the variables listed in the table enter in some way into determination of effectiveness. In terms of this array of variables, the role of analytical techniques may be stated very simply: The function of resource analysis is to translate the values of predetermined variables plus specified values of decision variables into estimates of resource requirements and costs. Effectiveness analysis has a parallel function to that of cost analysis, but one that is further

Table 14

Variables in the Model of a School District

Predetermined Variables	Decision Variables	Internal Variables
Projected enrollment	Programs and assignment criteria[a]	Enrollment by program
Existing physical plant	Vertical organization[a]	Levels of instructional activities
Prices and other constants	Curriculum composition[a]	Levels of support and auxiliary activities
	Class size[a]	Resource requirements
	Horizontal organization	Levels of overhead activities
	Instructional resource inputs[a]	
	Instructional methods	
	Subject content	**Target Variables**
	Salary schedule[a]	Budget estimates
	Building design[a]	Effectiveness estimates
	District configuration[a]	

[a] Variables necessary for determining program cost.

from realization. It is to translate the variables into estimates of educational achievement and overall educational effectiveness.

The next step in resource analysis is to make some of the relationships among the variables mathematically explicit. It has been shown that in some cases the mathematical statements consist of accounting-type summations. In other cases it will be appropriate to derive statistical expressions that relate resource requirements to the program characteristics. Chapter Five discusses some of the analytical techniques that are needed to derive these relationships and to assemble the individual mathematical statements into a complete resource and cost model.

CHAPTER FIVE

COST MODELS AND ANALYSIS OF COST

James A. Dei Rossi

Introduction

In the broadest sense, the analytical goal of program budgeting is to serve as an aid in the formulation, analysis, and selection of future alternative courses of action. The analytical procedures used in specific instances can take various forms depending on the criteria established, the resources and time available for analysis, the amount of uncertainty associated with each alternative, and so on. However, the basic concept of comparing costs incurred to prospective gains is common to all procedures. Such comparisons provide information for selection among proposed alternatives.

Cost analysis can be thought of as encompassing those activities by which cost and program data are compiled, analyzed, and used to estimate and project future cost. Except for the simplest of cases, adequate cost comparisons must be based on the "total cost" of each alternative. If this is not done, the full cost and resource implications of each alternative will not be shown, which may, in turn, bias the comparisons.

The specification of the time period over which the cost is

calculated also plays an important part in determining what constitutes total cost for decisionmaking purposes in program budgeting. Since program budgeting involves multi-year planning, total cost must include costs for the entire planning time horizon. On the other hand, since program budgeting decisons are decisions about the future, only costs to be incurred in the future should be included in cost comparisons. Costs incurred in the past are "sunk costs" and not relevant, since they cannot be affected by current decisions.

The monetary cost is often an imperfect measure of cost for the purpose of evaluating alternatives. In some cases, there may be a physical constraint not reflected in the monetary cost. For example, consider a situation where there is sufficient money available for two special programs, but the limited availability of qualified teachers precludes the possibility of pursuing both programs. In this case, the monetary cost will normally fail to reflect that fact. Because of this type of situation, it is important that a full description of the resources needed to implement the plan represented by the budget be included in the description of the plan. Such data are useful in helping the planner keep in touch with the physical realities underlying the monetary representation of cost. This in turn will aid in identifying any constraints not reflected in the dollar cost.

Cost Analysis Methodology

The many tasks involved in cost analysis highlight the need to develop a systematic and comprehensive methodology for estimating and analyzing the total cost of proposed alternatives for program budgeting. The focal point of this methodology is ordinarily a cost model. The tasks required to design and develop a cost model generally encompass those required to perform the needed cost analysis for program budgeting. The cost model, in turn, plays an important role in the analysis of alternatives, by providing a way to assess the cost impact of various program characteristics in a total cost setting.

Developing a Cost Model

There are two major considerations in the development of a cost model: the structuring of the cost data and the development of estimating relationships. The discussion of these considerations will be followed by a discussion of the characteristics of a well-designed model and the use of the model. This will show how the model serves as a device for integrating the cost structure, the estimating relationships, and data on the district and its activities that enable the district planner to estimate the cost of the various future courses of action open to him.

Structuring the Cost Data

One of the first tasks to be performed in conducting a cost analysis or in developing a cost model is that of defining and listing all the major categories of resources required by the district. Such categories serve to delineate the segments of total cost that are to be given separate treatment in the analysis. These categories are generally referred to as *cost elements.* The complete list of cost elements comprise what may be called the *cost element structure.*

Each of the cost elements must be carefully defined to insure against omitting or double counting. Careful definition of each cost element also helps to insure consistency. For example, when salaries are used as a cost element, it is essential that questions are clarified regarding such things as whether or not vacation and insurance are included in salaries.

This type of definition clarity is especially important when it is necessary to use data from several sources. Accounting practices change over time, and the only way to be sure that the data base is appropriate and used correctly is to know the exact content of the various categories in the data. Only when this is known can the data for each of the categories be combined in a manner that is definitionally and logically consistent.

The task of developing the cost element structure should logically begin with an appraisal of the distinguishing operational characteristics of the alternatives to be analyzed. For example, in meeting the growth needs of the district, basic operational concepts could be distinguished on the basis of the degree of accessibility of new schools to students and the manner in which accessibility is to be provided. Schools can be made accessible by being small and numerous or by providing student transportation to larger and fewer schools. In the former case, transportation costs will be less, but building costs will probably be greater because of the duplication of many central facilities.

There are also many possible variations on these two basic concepts: smaller schools could be provided for general classroom use and transportation could be provided to centrally located special purpose facilities. It is recognized that in many situations numerous noncost factors play an important, if not the dominant, role in the analysis and selection among all the various conceivable alternatives of this type. We are not implying here that one alternative is preferable to any of the others. The important point is that the appraisal of alternatives in terms of the above kinds of distinguishing operational characteristics can provide important information for developing a cost element structure; that is, it can provide information for determining, in a general way, (1) what general classes of resources are required and (2) what the expected relative cost importance of each of these resource categories is. These are two very important considerations in determining what the appropriate cost elements in the cost element structure should be.

Cost elements should be chosen to correspond as closely to the major classes of resources required as possible. In this way, the cost element structure can facilitate the tasks of evaluation and selection by highlighting the physical resource requirements underlying each alternative. The second desirable characteristic of a cost element is that the resource category represented by it should be a relatively important cost item in a quantitative sense.

This last point illustrates an important principle in cost analysis for program budgeting. Since the basic orientation is on the development of cost estimates to be used in selecting among alternatives, the basic goal is to provide a reasonable degree of accuracy rather than absolute precision. What constitutes reasonable accuracy depends to some degree on the particular circumstances; for example, one expects greater accuracy for plans requiring little change from the present situation than when the plan embodies many innovations. Similarly, greater accuracy is expected for next year's cost than for the cost to be incurred five years hence. In any event, uncertainties about enrollment levels, types of students enrolled, teacher turnover rates, absenteeism, and so on make the attainment of absolute accuracy an unrealistic goal.

It should be emphasized that we are discussing cost estimation only as it relates to planning. We do not mean to imply that cost accuracy does not play an important role in various administrative and control functions of district operation. What we are trying to convey is the concept that the appropriate degree of accuracy in estimating future cost can vary depending on the circumstances.

For example, for any specific cost element the appropriate amount of effort expended on achieving accuracy depends greatly on the relative quantitative importance of that cost element. A 50 percent error in a cost element constituting only one or two percent of the total is of less importance than, say, a 10 percent error in one constituting 30 or 40 percent of the total.

To illustrate the main points that have been made about structuring cost data, examine the cost structure for one year of an illustrative program. Table 15 shows the cost structure and the cost element detail for a typical program in a program budget.

This structure is in summary form. Much of the detail required for the analysis of specific programs or program elements is not presented. For example, the full analysis of instructional programs might require that certificated salaries be designated by teacher types, i.e., regular teacher, special teacher, part-time teacher, and so on. Similarly, the analysis of the requirements of the library, or other centers, for instructional aids might require some detailed knowledge of the specific items of equipment for which costs are presented.

However, the cost element structure shown in Table 15 is a reasonably typical cost element structure for a school district budget and illustrates the main points of this chapter:

1. The cost elements in the structure correspond to the

Table 15

Cost Element Structure

Item	Thousands of Dollars	Percent of Total
Salaries[a]		
Supervisory/Administrative		
Certificated	1,740	7.7
Classified	115	.5
Subtotal	1,855	8.2
Operational/Instructional		
Certificated	13,860	61.4
Classified	3,150	14.0
Subtotal	17,010	75.4
Materials, Supplies, and Other	1,730	7.7
Contract Services	855	3.8
Procurement, Rental, and Repairs		
Land	60	.1
Buildings	625	2.8
Equipment	435	2.0
Subtotal	1,120	4.9
Total	22,570	100.0

[a]Includes sabbatical, sick leave, payroll tax, and health insurance.

major categories of resources required in the district; namely, personnel (salaries), materials and supplies, land, buildings, and equipment.

2. A greater amount of detail is shown for salaries than for any other cost element because of the large relative importance of salaries. Total salaries amount to almost 85 percent of the total annual budget.

3. The content of the salary cost element is defined. It can be seen from the footnote on Table 15 that salary-related cost, ordinarily included in "Fixed Charges" or shown as separate line items in the traditional budget detail, is included in the salary cost element.

4. Contract Services and Procurement, Rental, and Repair are shown as separate line items even though they are not extremely large cost items in this particular budget. This is done because under certain circumstances these categories can provide information on operating characteristics useful for planning and evaluation. For example, a large repair or replacement cost might indicate that the district is paying a large operating cost penalty for postponing the acquisition of new buildings or equipment. Such information could be used to demonstrate, for example, that the rejection of a bond issue is not a tax-saving course of action in a total cost sense.

Table 16 shows the estimated five-year cost for the Assessment, Guidance, and Counseling program of a hypothetical school district. Cost details are shown by cost element. This table illustrates how the cost element structure can be used to show cost detail by program for a program budget.

Estimating Relationships

Having discussed some of the main issues involved in developing a cost element structure, we now turn to the topic of estimating relationships for various cost elements. The emphasis here will be on showing how estimating relationships can provide a basis for developing cost estimates from specific data about the district and its various programs. Our purpose is to describe, in a general way, the basic analytical procedures and concepts impor-

Table 16

Five-Year Projection of a Program Showing Cost Element Structure
(In $ thousands)

Item	\	\	Year	\	\
	1	2	3	4	5
Assessment, Guidance, and Counseling Salaries					
Supervisory/Administrative					
Certificated	20	22	23	23	26
Classified	--	--	--	--	--
Subtotal	20	22	23	24	26
Operational/Instructional					
Certificated	800	835	890	955	1,030
Classified	35	40	45	50	55
Subtotal	835	875	935	1,005	1,085
Materials, Supplies, etc.	105	108	111	114	117
Contract Services	5	6	8	8	9
Procurement, Rental, and Repairs					
Land	--	--	--	--	--
Buildings	--	--	--	--	--
Equipment	25	24	28	34	38
Subtotal	25	24	28	34	38
Total	990	1,035	1,105	1,185	1,275

tant in the development of such relationships.

There are many ways in which estimating relationships used in cost analysis and cost modeling can be categorized and grouped. The primary basis used here for distinguishing among the various types will be whether the relationships are used to estimate the unit cost of each resource or to estimate the number of units required. Relationships for estimating unit costs are usually referred to as cost-estimating relationships (CERs). Cost-estimating relationships are the basic tool for relating resource characteristics, as specified by program requirements, to resource cost. Program-determined resource characteristics useful for cost-estimating are generally those characteristics describing either the physical attributes or the performance capabilities of the resource.

Some estimating relationships can be derived directly from descriptions of proposed alternatives. For example, the assumed student-teacher ratio in each of the programs or program elements is a necessary part of any complete description of future district operation. Total teacher requirements for each program or program element can be obtained by dividing each of the student-teacher ratios into the corresponding number of students. This is an example of a relationship indicating the required number of units of a resource (in this case, teacher) derived directly from the description of the proposed plan.

Other relationships are determined by the interaction between the characteristics of the proposed plan and existing or future conditions. For example, the future utility cost for a district will be determined by the interaction of such things as weather, building construction, and the rate of utilization. This type of interaction is indirectly determined by the description of future district plans. It may also be estimated, in some cases, by a careful examination and analysis of empirical data on past experience.

However, before getting into the question of how data on past experience can be used to derive estimating relationships to estimate future district cost, consider the following example. Suppose it is necessary to estimate playground area investment cost, excluding the cost of land and equipment, for various

Cost Models and Analysis of Cost   111

proposed alternatives for a district. In this case, the appropriate unit for measuring the amount of playground required could be the number of square feet per student. The characteristics used as a basis for estimating cost per unit might be the type of surface to be provided, e.g., concrete, asphalt, grass, or dirt. In this case, the CER would simply be the cost per square foot for different types of surfaces. This CER could then be used to estimate total playground area investment cost for each alternative by referring to the description of each alternative, by specifying the number of square feet required per student, and by referring to the enrollment data indicating the expected number of students.

The estimating problem posed by this example was, of course, simplified by being narrowly defined. Nonetheless, this does illustrate that three distinct activities must be performed in order to determine program costs:

1. Appropriate units of measurement for each of the types of required resources must be determined.
2. CERs indicating the cost per unit as a function of the characteristics of the unit must be developed.
3. Relationships indicating the required number of units of each resource must be established.

To illustrate these points and to indicate how past data can be used to derive estimating relationships, consider the following example: Assume a unified district with an average daily attendance (ADA) of 20,000 students that is projected to increase at the rate of 10 percent per year over the next five years. Suppose that it is necessary to estimate the salary cost for the next five years for Operations—i.e., salaries in the 600 Account of the traditional budget, including salaries for custodians, gardeners, warehousemen, and required supervisory and clerical help.

The task is begun by examining the current situation. This reveals that the current staff is 100—two supervisors, 10 clerical, and 88 custodians, gardeners, and warehousemen. Since most of this staff is quite homogeneous, the total number of persons required without distinction as to type of position held will be taken as the unit of measure. As a consequence, an average salary figure can serve as the basis for the cost-estimating relationships.

Examining the average salary for this staff for the current year and for several past years, it is found that the current average salary is $6700 and that the change in average salary for the last three years has been almost constant at about five percent. As a result of these findings, the following can be set up as the CER:

$$S = 6700 (1 + .05)^t$$

where S =   average salary,
        t =   time variable, that is, zero for the current year, 1 for the next year, 2 for the following year, and so on.

This CER will have the effect of increasing estimated average salary at the rate of five percent per year.

Now that the units of measure and a CER for estimating unit cost have been established, the number of persons or units required for each of the next five years must be determined. To do this, hypothesize that staff requirements for Operations depend mainly on the size of the district. Various measures of district size are the number of buildings, the total square footage in these buildings, and the number of acres of land used by the district. However, one statistic that is readily available, and could be expected to have a very consistent relationship to the various measures of district size, is ADA. Therefore, it can be further hypothesized that ADA is an appropriate measure of size for estimating total Operations staff requirements.

The questions now are: How can this hypothesis be verified? How can it be used as a basis for estimating Operations staffing requirements? To verify this hypothesis, data will be required. One way to gather such data might be to contact other districts of various sizes to find out what their staffing experience has been. Another way is to check the past records of this district. However, assume that past ADA in this district has been fairly stable so that it does not reveal much about how changes in ADA affect

Cost Models and Analysis of Cost

Table 17

Average Daily Attendance and Operations Staff for Thirteen Hypothetical Districts

District Number	Average Daily Attendance	Operations Staff
1	11,715	64
2	2,825	14
3	16,710	103
4	10,125	43
5	635	10
6	28,525	118
7	30,375	149
8	7,160	31
9	5,240	24
10	62,755	342
11	2,435	14
12	10,700	67
13	17,875	82

Operations staff requirements. Data obtained from other districts are shown in Table 17. (Data are for illustrative purposes only.) The range of ADA is from 635 to 62,755 and the range of staff is from 10 to 342. Thus, this sample exhibits a wide range of variation and, therefore, should be useful.

Using these data, the reasonableness of the hypothesis can be checked by plotting these numbers as shown in Figure 8. The fact that the points fall pretty much along a straight line indicates that the hypothesis will be useful and that the relationship between size, as measured by ADA, and staff requirements for Operations is linear. Using these data and the method of least squares, a line representing this linear relationship can be estimated. (The method of least squares is a standard statistical technique for estimating that selects the line that minimizes the sum of the squared

Figure 8

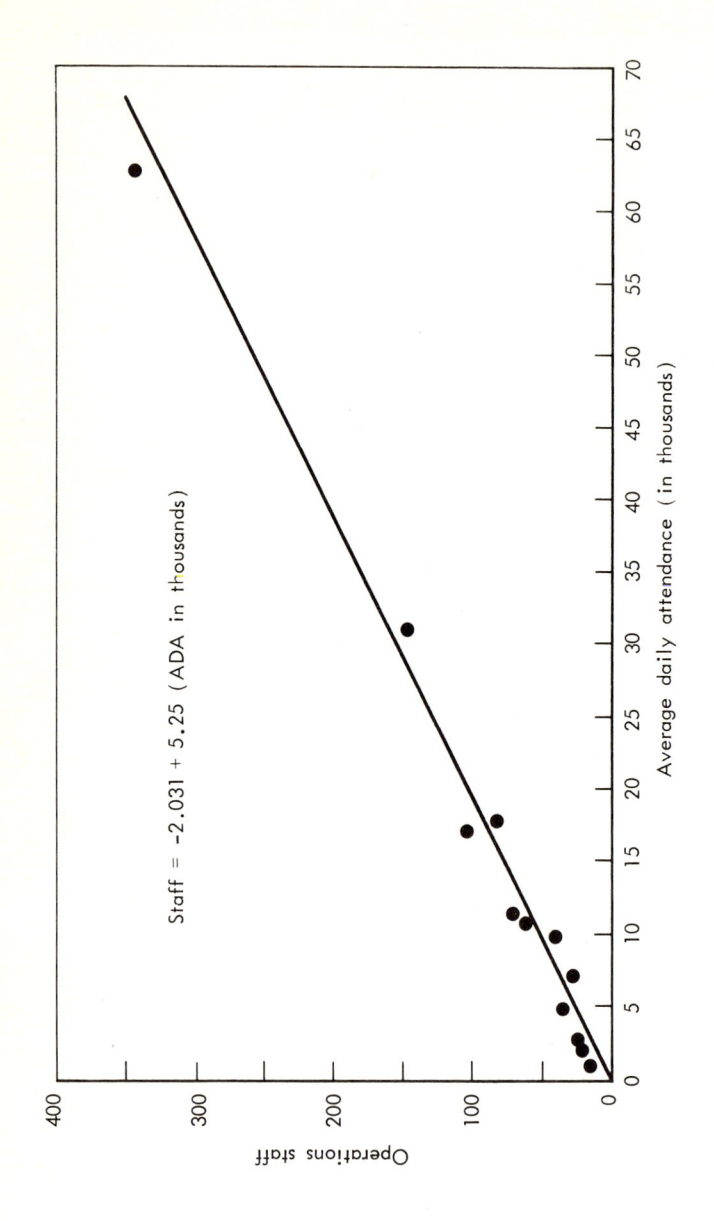

District Operating Staff as a Function of District Size as Measured by Average Daily Attendance

Table 18

Total Operations Salaries[a]

		Year				
Item	Current	1	2	3	4	5
Projected ADA, No.	20,000	22,000	24,200	26,620	29,280	32,200
Average salary, $	6,700	7,035	7,385	7,755	8,143	8,550
Estimated Staff, No.	100	114	125	138	152	168
Total salary, $ thousands	670.0	802.0	923.1	1,071.1	1,237.7	1,436.4

[a]As estimated from projected enrollments, average salaries, and staff requirement.

distances from each of the observed points to the line.*) The results indicate that, on the average, Operations staff requirements increase by 5-1/4 positions for each 1000-student increase in ADA. This is indicated in Figure 8 by the fact that the coefficient for ADA, in thousands, is 5.25.

It is now possible to estimate total Operations salaries for each year of the next five years on the basis of ADA projections by combining the relationship between ADA and Operations staff requirements and the CER. These results are shown in Table 18. It can be seen that a ten percent increase in ADA for each of the next five years will increase total ADA to 32,200 in the fifth year. The CER indicates that the average salary will increase to $8550 by that year; and the estimating relationship for staff requirements indicates that, when ADA reaches 32,200, staff requirements will increase to 168. On the basis of these results, total annual salary cost for Operations is estimated to more than double during the

*A clear and complete discussion of statistical techniques for estimating relationships between variables is contained in M. Ezekiel and K. Fox, *Methods of Correlation and Regression Analysis*, John Wiley & Sons, New York, 1963.

next five years: increasing from $670,000 in the current year to $1,436,400 in the fifth year.

Obviously, these results, although empirically derived, are based on several assumptions and judgments. It was assumed that the average salary was sufficiently representative to be used for estimating future changes in average salaries. Also, the average district experience of several districts was used to estimate the staff requirements of this district. However, one advantage of the type of approach outlined for estimating future costs is that it does force these kinds of assumptions to be made explicit.

Further, since estimating relationships were derived and used for this analysis, it is also possible to test the sensitivity of these results to the underlying assumptions. For example, it is possible to vary the rate of change in average salary; in place of five percent, numbers ranging from, for example, three to seven percent could be used. Similarly, the rate of change in staff requirements could be varied, as could the projected rate of change in ADA.

This kind of analysis plays an important role in cost analysis for program budgeting and is called "sensitivity analysis." It allows the analyst and decisionmaker to test for the relative importance of the various assumptions made. If the results are especially sensitive to one or more of these assumptions or judgments, it may be decided to scrutinize the basis for the assumption more carefully, or it may simply serve as an indicator of the quantitative implications of the various kinds of uncertainty inherent in projecting future costs for long-range planning.

Since sensitivity analysis can provide a means of testing the importance of various assumptions to the *relative* cost position of different alternatives, it can be particularly useful in the evaluation of alternatives. For instance, it is possible to examine questions such as: (1) Would alternative A still appear preferable to alternative B, from a cost point of view, if the following assumptions were changed? or (2) For what *range* of values in the various estimating relationships will alternative A remain preferable to alternative B?

Cost Models

Structuring of the cost data and the development of estimating relationships are two important tasks that must be performed in order to develop operational cost models for use in program budgeting. Cost models may be viewed as devices for estimating the costs of future alternatives by translating the descriptions of the alternatives, in terms of specific performance capabilities, into resource requirements and costs. This translation is accomplished through the use of estimating relationships for each cost element and of rules for aggregating the input requirements calculated with these relationships.

The development of a cost model appropriate for a specific application requires a good understanding of the uses to which it must be put. It is usually necessary to experiment with various forms of the model before a satisfactory result can be obtained. The fact that each model must be tailored to the needs to be served highlights the fact that model building is as much an art as it is a science. Formal rules are of limited value. Experience, skill, and imagination are always necessary, and important, ingredients. Therefore, it is essential to review the nature of cost models, discuss the basic goals of cost modeling, and describe the characteristics of a well-designed model. These ideas can do more to give useful insight into what cost models are and how they can, and should, be used in program budgeting than a "how to build a model" discussion.

A model is basically a representation of some aspect of the real world. The representation generally takes the form of a series of relationships (some empirical and some definitional) among existing conditions, various actions to be taken, and resulting outcomes. Simplification is accomplished by giving detailed attention to factors of greatest significance to the decisions to be made (i.e., choices among possible alternative courses of action) and by aggregating, or disregarding, the remaining less significant factors.

Models vary greatly in degree of formality, level of mathematical sophistication, and degree of automation. These aspects of the model are largely determined by the following considerations: (1) the complexity of what is being represented by the model; (2) how frequently the model is to be used; (3) the precision with which the real world relationships contained in the model are known; and (4) the accuracy required to provide adequate information on cost questions for the decisionmaker.

The role of the cost model in cost analysis for program budgeting is to provide the planners and decisionmakers with a tool for calculating total and incremental cost for each proposed alternative. To be useful for this purpose the cost model should: (1) permit the calculation of cost with a reasonable amount of ease and (2) be responsive to the key differences characterizing the proposed alternatives.

Ease of calculation is a desirable characteristic in a cost model, since it is often necessary to estimate the cost for many variations of key alternatives. Ease of calculation insures reasonably fast response time and reduces the possibility of clerical errors. In the case of large models, ease of calculation requires some degree of automation through the use of electronic data processing equipment. However, *total* automation is not always desirable or feasible. There are often parts of cost models where human discretion is required. Further, it is always necessary to insure against errors in internal logic as the model is developed or modified. Thus, it is customary and desirable for the models to make use of a combination of automated and non-automated calculations. Modeling should not necessarily be equated with automation.

The responsiveness of the model to the cost implications of a wide range of alternatives is derived mainly from the types of variables included in the estimating relationships contained in the model. The explicit analysis of the cost impact of a characteristic distinguishing a proposed alternative requires the inclusion of a variable representing that characteristic. Thus, the more variables included, the more responsive the model becomes to a wider range of situations.

Although the primary keys to responsiveness are the variables and relationships in the model, this responsiveness is also affected by the level of disaggregation at which various costs are consid-

Cost Models and Analysis of Cost   119

ered, as reflected in the cost structure. For example, a model that aggregates over differences in teacher type by using a single average salary as a basis for estimating future salary costs would not be responsive to the cost impacts of alternatives that required significant changes in the composition of the teaching staff. On the other hand, if there are not going to be any alternatives that require changes in staff composition, the level of aggregation indicated by the use of an average salary figure might be sufficiently responsive.

Besides showing how the level of aggregation affects the responsiveness of the cost model, this example also demonstrates the important roles experience and judgment play in model building and cost analysis. There are no general rules that can eliminate the need for discretion in selecting the appropriate level of aggregation. The uses of the model and the types of alternatives to be analyzed must be considered. These *ad hoc* considerations, together with considerations of resources and time available for the development of the model, are the primary determinants of the appropriate level of disaggregation.

The following points should be made about cost models, cost structures and cost-estimating relationships in cost analysis, and cost-estimating for program budgeting:

1. The role of cost models in program budgeting is to provide planners and decisionmakers with estimated costs which can be used in conjunction with effectiveness data for choosing among future alternatives. To accomplish this, techniques must be employed that: (a) permit the calculation of total cost with reasonable ease and (b) are responsive to the cost impacts of a wide range of different program characteristics.

2. Ease of calculation generally requires some degree of automation through the use of electronic data processing equipment. Total automation, however, is not usually a reasonable goal, especially in situations where the uses and needs of the model will be continually changing. Continual change is, in practice, more the rule than the exception. Thus, modeling should not be equated with automation.

3. Responsiveness is achieved by including variables in the

model that characterize the major differences among the various alternatives and by the selection of a suitable level of disaggregation. The level of disaggregation is reflected in the cost element structure. The elements in this structure should correspond to the categories of physical resources required, and separate elements should be shown only for categories that: (a) are relatively important in a quantitative sense or (b) reveal information about operational characteristics.

4. Inclusion of variables characterizing the major differences among various alternatives permits the development of cost estimates from program data. However, this requires that three distinct steps be taken to insure that the relationships containing these variables can, in fact, be used to build up total cost from program data: (1) the unit of measurement, in physical terms, of the item for which cost is to be estimated must be carefully specified; (2) cost-per-unit estimating relationships must be developed; and (3) relationships for determining the number of units required and for aggregating unit costs must be determined.

Program Cost Analysis

The use of total cost to compare alternatives is usually accomplished by establishing a "base case" total cost from which the "incremental cost" of each alternative can be calculated. The base case cost is the future cost of current programs, unchanged except for the effects of irreversible past decisions and unavoidable future changes. The incremental cost of each proposed alternative is simply the difference between total cost of the base case and of that alternative.

Thus, there are two steps in the cost analysis of the programs. First, a base case is established by estimating future total district cost for the entire planning time horizon, making allowances only for existing commitments and other unavoidable changes such as enrollment growth and inflation. Second, total cost is again calculated for each alternative, incorporating the cost impacts of the change or changes embodied in the proposed alternatives. The difference between the total cost of each alternative and of the base case is the incremental cost of the alternative and is the measure of cost appropriate for making cost comparisons among alternatives. For example, using the school district five-year budget shown in Table 19, the total cost of the base case can be represented as a stream of cost through time as shown in Figure 9 by the solid line.

Assume that one alternative to the base case is to introduce smaller class sizes and that a second is to postpone the construction of the new school buildings. The cost consequences of each of these two alternatives over time is also shown in Figure 9 by the dashed lines. The total five-year cost for the base case is $131.3 million, and the cost for Alternatives 1 and 2 is $147.4 million and $131.5 million, respectively. Disregarding the differences in the time patterns of the flows,* the incremental cost of Alternative 1 is $16.1 million and the incremental cost of Alternative 2 is less than $0.2 million.

The difference between the base case and Alternative 2 is negligible; and because of the many uncertainties associated with long-range planning, this small difference, in itself, would not be the basis of decision. The selection of the preferred alternative requires the analysis of the effectiveness and other social and political considerations, as well as cost.

In addition, a minor change in the underlying assumptions could possibly change the relative positions. For example, if the

*In general, the time pattern of costs and gains is, of course, of importance to decisionmakers and planners. The basic issues involved are ones of time preference and uncertainty. In theory, it is possible to make explicit allowance for these considerations through the use of a "discount rate" which can be used to calculate a single "present value" figure for each alternative. A full description of the issues involved is beyond the scope of this discussion. Extensive discussions of the use of discounting in the evaluation of alternatives are continued in: C.J. Hitch and R.N. McKean, *The Economics of Defense in the Nuclear Age,* The Rand Corporation, R-346, 1960, also published by Harvard University Press, Cambridge, Massachusetts, 1960, pp. 205-218; R.N. McKean, *Efficiency in Government Through Systems Analysis,* John Wiley & Sons, Inc., New York, 1958, pp. 74-95; and W.J. Baumol, Testimony Given Before the Subcommittee on Economy in Government of the Joint Economic Committee, Congress of the United States, 90th Cong., 1st Sess., September 1967, pp. 152-179.

Table 19

*Cost of Base Case and Two Alternatives
(In $ thousands)*

	\multicolumn{6}{c}{Years}
	1	2	3	4	5	Total
Base	22,570	23,570	26,025	28,215	30,675	131,285
Alternative 1	23,700	25,725	28,990	32,419	36,578	147,412
Alternative 2	22,170	23,300	25,325	29,090	31,575	131,460

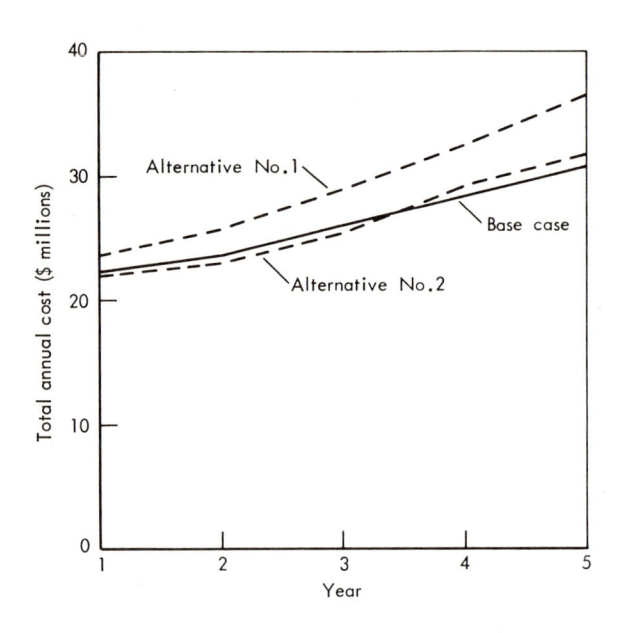

Figure 9

*Comparison of Five-Year Costs for
Base Case and Two Alternatives*

economy appeared to be at the peak of a business cycle in the second year, we might assume a five percent rate of inflation for the first year and assume it would decline to two percent by the fifth year. This alone would be enough to reverse the relative cost positions of the base case and the second alternative.

The purpose here is to briefly illustrate the use of the cost model. The cost model serves as the core of a decisionmaking framework for the systematic evaluation of alternative courses of action. Its main advantage is to facilitate the asking of "what-if" questions about the effect of changes in objectives, programs, activities, resource availability, etc., within the educational system. By facilitating the process, the model allows the decisionmaker to examine, rapidly and routinely, many variations in alternatives.

CHAPTER SIX

THE ANALYSIS OF EFFECTIVENESS

Margaret B. Carpenter and Marjorie L. Rapp

Introduction

Rational planning for better education requires that the analysis of effectiveness of educational systems be as rigorously developed as the analysis of the resources they require. By encouraging the use of systematic techniques for planning, program budgeting should lead to the expansion and improvement of ways to relate the quantity and quality of the educational product to the resources used to create it. Program budgeting would thus encourage some freedom from the tyranny of the budget, because it supplies decisionmakers with defensible criteria other than cost, often a dominant factor in decisionmaking.

These criteria can be grouped under the general term "effectiveness." As opposed to cost, which is a measure of the resources that go into a program element, effectiveness assesses what comes out. Effectiveness is sometimes measured in terms of performance, like the number of students served in the cafeteria daily, but it can also have very broad and qualitative interpretations. For example, the general satisfaction of the community with the school system is an extremely important aspect of the

The Analysis of Effectiveness

school's effectiveness.

Throughout this chapter, effectiveness will be discussed from two points of view: (1) ways in which the effectiveness of various aspects of a school district's program can be measured and (2) analytical techniques for using these measures. The discussions are intended to suggest promising avenues for further development as program budgeting systems are implemented in individual districts.

Effectiveness of Program Elements

The effectiveness of a program element is an assessment of how much the program element has contributed to the attainment of its objective. For example, the elements in the primary programs largely aim to develop the skills, knowledge, and understanding of the students. To assess their effectiveness, then, the extent of this development must be assessed—the extent of change, not just the end result.

An integral part of the design of a program budgeting system is the choice of dimensions of the effectiveness of program elements—the ways in which program elements will be assessed and the format in which assessments will be displayed. This will ensure that needed information will be readily available for decisionmaking. The discussion to follow draws heavily on dimensions of effectiveness that educators are already using, or at least those that are readily available. Although some new measures, particularly criterion-referenced tests, would be useful and need to be developed, the crux of the problem is to assemble information that is scattered throughout the system in such a way that the best use may be made of it. For example, a district-wide testing program would go a long way toward providing many of the needed effectiveness measures. However, the intention is not to present new ideas about tests themselves, but rather, to propose a way to construct a program that will allow systematic, consistent use of test results.

A study of the program structure outlined in Table 20 indicates that all the elements of Program 1 and Program 2 through 2C deal with academic subjects to which all students in the public schools are exposed. Therefore, measures of student

Table 20

*Programs Organized by What Is to Be Learned and
by Other Student-Oriented Objectives**

1. Learning Fundamental Intellectual Skills
    A. Language and communication skills
    B. Quantitative and reasoning skills
    C. Study skills
2. Learning About the World
    A. Learning about U.S. and other societies
    B. Learning about the physical world and living things
    C. Learning about literature and the arts
    D. Learning knowledge and skills for everyday application
3. Development of the Individual Physically, Socially, and Emotionally
    A. Physical development
    B. Development of means of self-expression
    C. Development of interpersonal relationships
4. Learning Knowledge and Skills in Preparation for Future Employment or Occupational Training
    (classified by occupation)
5. Learning Academic Subjects to Prepare for Higher Education
    (classified by academic subject)
6. Assessment, Guidance, and Counseling Services
7. Program Development and Evaluation
8. Instructional Resources and Media Services
9. Auxiliary Services to Students
    A. Health services
    B. Transportation
    C. Food services
10. Community Services
0. All Others

*This structure was developed by S.M. Barro, M.B. Carpenter, S.A. Haggart, and M.L. Rapp.

The Analysis of Effectiveness

achievement in these subjects will be a major component of the testing program.

There are several ways to measure academic success. At the bottom of the hierarchy are teacher-made tests, for which it is difficult to obtain assessments of reliability, even though they may be excellent tools for the diagnosis of learning problems. The next order includes district-constructed tests, given to all students in a specific course. The third and last level is the standardized achievement test.

Most standardized tests are of the paper-and-pencil variety and largely measure a student's verbal skills in reading and writing. But there are other kinds of performance that need to be measured. For example, in oral English, one of the communication skills, a different kind of measure of student behavior is needed to assess the success of the program element. In most classrooms, teachers are aware of whether or not their students use good, grammatical English, and most of them would readily agree on a standard for determining this.

Rather than to go through a laborious process of constructing rating scales or checklists, a simple test of the students' spoken English should be constructed for district-wide use to provide an objective measure.

Thus, in order to assess the success of a program element, its goals must be specified so that the right assessment measures can be chosen. For example, if the goal of a foreign language program element is to be able to converse fluently, there must be a means of assessing this; if it is translation, that is what is assessed; and if it is reading ability, the effectiveness measure must be directed toward assessing that ability. The same kind of reasoning applies to the assessment of a program element to develop such things as library, reference, and study skills.

It is usually true, however, that a particular program element seems to have multiple objectives. Two cases can arise. Either the objectives are really different and incommensurate, or they form a hierarchy with a single, assessable objective at the summit. Because it is more convenient to deal with a single measure than with a set of measures, it is always desirable to combine or eliminate multiple objectives whenever possible. Several methods for doing this have been suggested in Quade,* as follows:

- Eliminate any objective that is important only as a means to another objective.
- Eliminate any objective that will be unaffected by a choice among alternatives.
- Find a higher-level objective to which all of the competing objectives are means.

For illustration, each method will be applied to an artificial set of three objectives for a program element in foreign language. These objectives might be (1) to be able to give the English equivalents of a certain number of words in a written list; (2) to be able to translate text of a given level of difficulty; and (3) to be able to converse at a given level of complexity. It is evident that objective (1) can be eliminated by the first method because it may be considered important only as a means to attaining the second objective. On the other hand, it is clear that neither of the other two objectives is important *only* as a means to the other.

Because the second method for combining objectives is keyed to the consideration of alternatives, it may or may not be useful, depending upon the alternatives. If, for example, one is trying to decide whether to buy a set of audio tapes or to use a televised lesson in teaching conversational skills, the second objective, to attain skills in translation of written text, may largely be ignored. But if the alternatives involve varying allocations of money or other general resources for the entire program element, the effects of these allocations on both objectives must be assessed.

However, in designing the program budgeting system, it is good *not* to have such specific alternatives in mind. Therefore, a way to assess the effectiveness of the entire program element is to define a higher-level objective to which each of the separate objectives is a means. The trick is to find a higher-level objective that is defensible, that is assessable, and whose relation to the

*E.S. Quade (ed.), *Analysis for Military Decisions,* The Rand Corporation, R-387, November 1964, pp. 159-160.

The Analysis of Effectiveness

lower-order objectives can be quantified. An objective such as "to have a given level of mastery of this particular foreign language" says nothing about how such mastery is to be judged nor how much an understanding of the spoken form is to count toward that mastery in relation to an understanding of the written form. Programs with composite objectives such as these will have to be separated into their components for a rigorous analysis of the program itself. However, to provide a general measure for comparison of one such program with another, a weighted average of the measures of the separate objectives may be used. The weightings must represent the judgment of the user (teacher, administrator, or superintendent) as to the *value* of the separate objectives relative to one another. Such value judgments should always be made explicit (not buried in the single measure) so that dissenters may provide their own weightings to derive new measures for comparison.

Most, if not all, program elements have multiple objectives that are incommensurable. Core programs that aim to develop mastery of more than one subject, to teach problem-solving, and to perform other functions are outstanding examples. Courses in English that strive for an appreciation of English literature, the development of skills in writing and composition, and the development of speaking abilities are also difficult to handle. Even in a single subject, achievement tests now in use provide a single measure representing the attainment of a combination of objectives. This measure may or may not adequately account for the value structure of the users of the test results.

Measures provided by criterion-referenced tests exhibit the same problems, even though they are more direct measures of the effectiveness of a particular program than are achievement (norm-referenced) tests. If, however, the student is being taught specific, well-defined tasks that he will subsequently perform (as in vocational training programs tailored to fill job openings in local businesses), the need for value judgments can be minimized by tying the weightings directly to such factors as frequency of task performance, criticality of task, and the like. Such situations arise relatively infrequently in elementary and secondary education.

*Other Considerations in
Definitions of Effectiveness*

The achievement of an individual student depends to a large extent on his ability and on the socioeconomic environment in which he lives. These important variables cannot be controlled by the school district and therefore should be treated as part of the definition of a program element. In other words, the effectiveness measures of academic programs for students of differing mental capabilities or socioeconomic environments are not comparable; they do not measure the same kind of effectiveness of efforts put forth by the school system.

These differences could be accounted for by grouping students by socioeconomic and ability levels. The students could be assigned to several ability levels on the basis of intelligence tests (although these and other currently available measures of presumably inherent attributes are largely achievement measures).

The problem is simplified if the socioeconomic status of the population of the district is homogeneous, because relatively few measures will be needed for the ability levels the district encompasses. On the other hand, if it is heterogeneous, measures for each of the strata within it will be needed, if the success of a program element carried out under what amounts to different circumstances is to be assessed. Eastmond* describes techniques for defining socioeconomic areas. The resulting breakdown might look something like that presented in Table 21.

Many districts already group students in this way, more or less by the use of tracks, but these groupings are often more indicative of student ability vis-a-vis the individual school population than vis-a-vis the district as a whole. The result is that tracks having the same designation may represent different capabilities in different schools.**

---

*Jefferson Eastmond, *Quality Measurement Project, Final Report,* New York State Department of Education, Division of Research, 1962.

**The possibility of the adverse effect of such groupings on teachers' *expectations* for their students has recently been pointed out. There is no reason why records of students' S.E.S. and ability levels could not be maintained in central administration for *evaluation* only and be inaccessible to individual teachers.

Table 21

A Breakdown of Socioeconomic Areas

Area	S.E.S.[a] (Scaled from 1 [high] to 5)	Classroom Type[b]
1	1	H, X, Y, Z
2	3	H, X, Y, Z
3	4	X, Y, Z
4	2	H, X, Y, Z
5	5	X, Y, Z

[a]Socioeconomic status.

[b]H signifies honors classes; X, above average; Y, average; and Z, below average.

Criterion-referenced tests are closely tied to curricula that are likely to be designed to meet the needs of students as individuals or in groups of relatively homogeneous capabilities. Thus, the tests for one student or group may be different from those for another, and the need for stratifying the student population before making comparisons more obvious. The extent of stratification desirable will, of course, depend on the level of the problem being addressed—whether it involves comparisons among districts, schools, or classrooms with similar student populations.

Uses of Measures of Effectiveness

Once it is decided to group test results by student ability and socioeconomic environments (and pretests have been used to make sure that the results measure actual achievement), the results might be displayed in the manner shown in Table 22. Comparison of the class mean with the overall mean reveals immediately how each class in the program element is achieving relative to the others, while the variability within the class indicates how meaningful the class average is. Those classes or schools that are achieving below their fellows are potential problem areas. They

Table 22

Test Results for a Program Element[a]

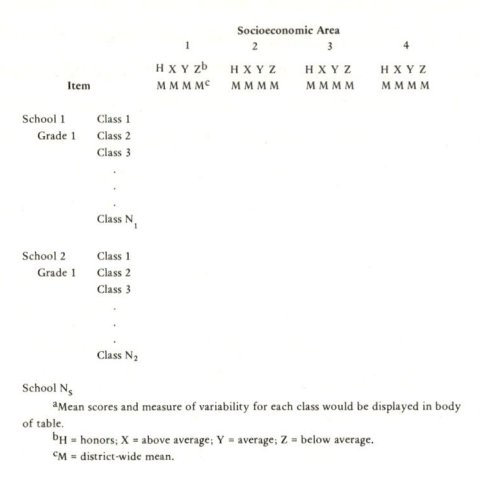

		Socioeconomic Area			
		1	2	3	4
Item		H X Y Z[b] M M M M[c]	H X Y Z M M M M	H X Y Z M M M M	H X Y Z M M M M
School 1 Grade 1	Class 1 Class 2 Class 3 . . Class N₁				
School 2 Grade 1	Class 1 Class 2 Class 3 . . Class N₂				
School N_s					

[a] Mean scores and measure of variability for each class would be displayed in body of table.
[b] H = honors; X = above average; Y = average; Z = below average.
[c] M = district-wide mean.

signal that the instruction may be less effective than it should be—that there may be something within the school or classroom that impedes learning.

However, it may be that the district would like to put more effort into the education of students in poorer socioeconomic environments in order to raise their achievement to levels comparable to those of students in better circumstances. (After all, in the outside world, students will compete across socioeconomic lines.) To this end, test results could also be displayed without the socioeconomic groupings; such a display would delete the area columns but would retain the breakdown by ability because it is not reasonable to expect the same achievement from youngsters of below-average ability as from youngsters who are well above average. Then the weakest parts of the program element would stand out and attention could be concentrated on them.

Achievement (norm-referenced) tests are valuable because they provide measures of a student's attainment relative to a population of students similar to him in general ways. Since he will be judged in relation to this population throughout his academic career and, to some extent, as an adult, such measures are useful in assessing the effectiveness of school programs. Criterion-referenced tests, however, have advantages over norm-referenced tests. For one thing, they are more direct measures of the effectiveness of a program element because they are derived from its specific objectives. Therefore, they provide detailed information that can assist administrators and teachers in continuously improving the program by making use of different materials or methods or by adapting program objectives to student capabilities.

Another advantage is that criterion-referenced tests can measure a wider range of behaviors because they can be tailored to particular schools or even classrooms. For example, skills in using a dictionary can be tested by direct observation without the intervention of a paper-and-pencil test. This is not possible with norm-referenced tests, which must be usable in any classroom in the country.

The use of criterion-referenced tests is relatively new. There seems to be no reason, however, why a criterion-referenced testing program cannot be designed for a particular district by use of judicious samplings of classrooms, students, and test items. Such samples can also be used to assess the reliability of the full gamut of criterion-referenced tests that would be administered by the classroom teacher as an integral part of instruction.

Test results have uses as assessments of effectiveness other than for comparisons of program elements in different schools or classrooms. After the testing program has been in operation for a year or two, information on whether classes participating in the program element are improving or deteriorating can be gathered by comparing present with past results. This information can temper judgments about problem classrooms or schools, or can point to areas where problems may develop in the future.

However, the most valuable use of these measures is probably in comparing alternative ways to conduct the program element within a given school or class. Criterion-referenced tests are of particular value in these applications. Because alternatives in this case can be very similar, analysis of resource requirements and effectiveness promises to be a great help in choosing among them.

The Development of Cost-Effectiveness Relationships

Measures of effectiveness of program elements are of little aid in making decisions unless they can be related to the resources that go into those elements. The public schools offer an outstanding opportunity to find out whether relationships between resources and effectiveness in educational programs can be developed. Ideally, they should assign an effectiveness indicator (or a range of effectiveness) corresponding to the provision of varying amounts of each major resource and be sufficiently refined to permit discrimination among the effects of major independent variables. If such relationships can be discovered, program budgeting and other techniques of system analysis offer hope of finding ways to both more and better education.

There is a tremendous body of literature describing research in education that, carefully culled and organized, might supply or at least suggest some resource-effectiveness relationships. A search of this literature is a logical step in determining whether useful relationships have already been documented and what has been left out of previous research. But the controversy over the Coleman report* suggests that the educational community is far from agreeing on what characteristics of school systems, including the student, are dominant in determining educational effectiveness, let alone what the nature of the relationships is.

The American public schools are being pressured from all directions at the same time that the demand for education of increased availability and quality is growing. The only way out of this situation is through more effective use of resources. To discover how resources may be used more effectively will require systematic research on the relationship between cost and effective-

---

*James S. Coleman *et al.*, *Equality of Educational Opportunity*, Office of Education, U.S. Department of Health, Education, and Welfare, Washington, D.C., 1966; and James S. Coleman, *The Evaluation of Educational Opportunity*, The Rand Corporation, P-3911, August 1968.

ness within the public schools. The schools should provide the medium for research and, at the same time, the channel for implementation of successful research.

Analysts like to talk about the relationship between resources and effectiveness as though it looked like Figure 10A, but in most areas of education the relationship probably looks more like Figure 10B. (The shaded area means that we do not really know where "good" leaves off and "poor" begins.) It is probable that in many areas of education we may never be able to express the relationships between resources and effectiveness in such an aesthetically pleasing and mathematically tractable way as the top figure. (Whether the use of criterion-referenced tests will supply measures more closely related to resource requirements remains to be seen.) Education is not unique in this regard. In almost every field of public endeavor, the really important questions are embedded in gray areas.

But this does not mean that systematic, rigorous analysis of effectiveness in education is either impossible or inappropriate. On the contrary, what it means is that often it will not be possible to get away with letting neat mathematical tools do the thinking.

The logic with which the criteria of effectiveness have been formulated, assessed, and combined will carry the burden for decisionmaking (as it really should anyway, even when precise mathematical tools are applicable).

Additionally, it is important to warn against a misuse of measures of effectiveness—misuse by overuse, to be specific. Frequently, several different ways to accomplish some task will differ in effectiveness by only a few percent. When this happens, the small differences should *never* be the deciding factor in the selection of the preferred alternative. This is because the measures of effectiveness will never be that accurate. Other considerations should be used to make the choice.

The Effectiveness of Nonprimary Program Elements

To this point, the primary programs (Programs 1 through 5, Table 20) have been the chief concern. Other major programs, such as Auxiliary Services to Students, have ends different from

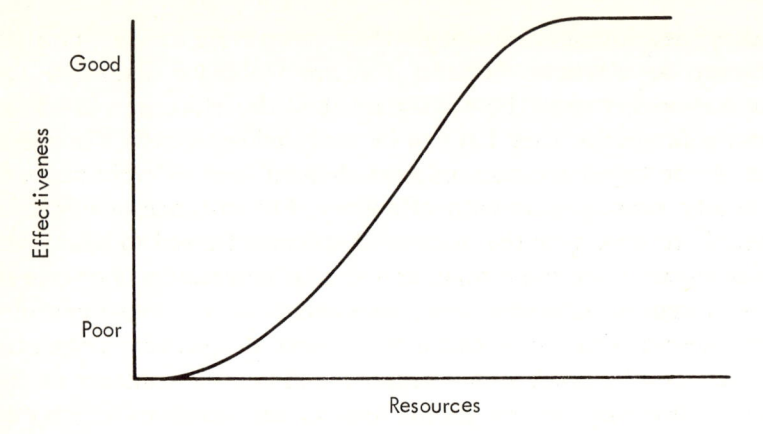

A. A well-behaved relationship

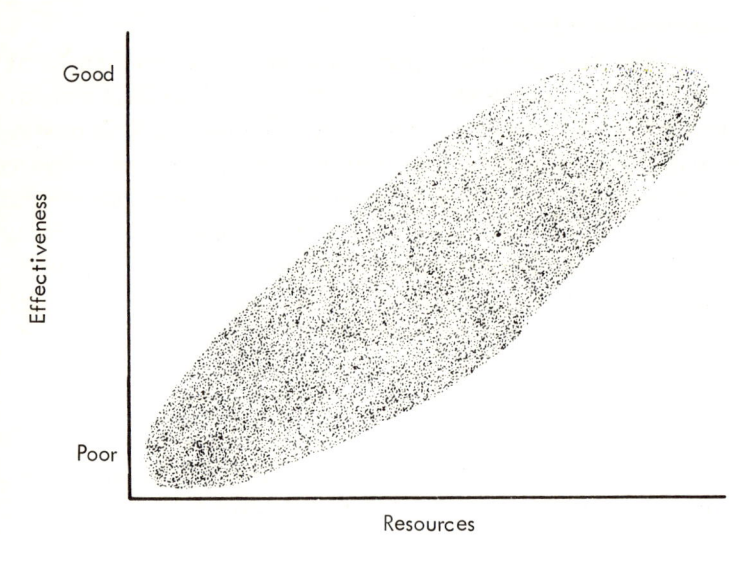

B. A relationship for an educational system (?)

Figure 10

Examples of Relationships Between Effectiveness and Resources

The Analysis of Effectiveness 137

student development—although they contribute to the primary programs as a whole. Because it is impossible to determine the relationship between these programs and the effectiveness of the primary programs, they have to be analyzed separately. For some, such as the transportation program element, cost-effectiveness can be nearly synonymous with efficiency. For instance, it might be desirable to maximize the number of students bussed to school per dollar within reasonable time, and similar constraints. For others, such as central administration, assessments may have to consider such diverse aspects as the effectiveness of primary programs, teacher morale, community support, number of students in the district, diversity of programs, and so on. Analysis related to specific aspects of central administration is possible, but an overall assessment is probably impossible.

District-Wide Effectiveness

Thus far, the discussion has been on the effectiveness of a program element in a classroom or school. If the effectiveness of the element in the district as a whole can be assessed, it is possible, in principle, to determine an optimal allocation of resources among classrooms and schools. Assume the district has grouped students into classes of a given level of scholastic capability and within a given socioeconomic area. For this category of students, i, the district may be thought of as conducting a set of M program elements.

$$P(1_i), P(2_i), \ldots P(M_i).$$

Each element is conducted by a group of N_j classes; N_j classes in which the jth program element is taught could be denoted by

$$C(j_i,1), C(j_i,2), \ldots C(_i,N_j),$$

as shown in Figure 11. (The first number in the parentheses refers to the program element; the second to the class in which it is conducted.) One way to find the district-wide effectiveness of the jth element for the ith level of student classification,

Figure 11

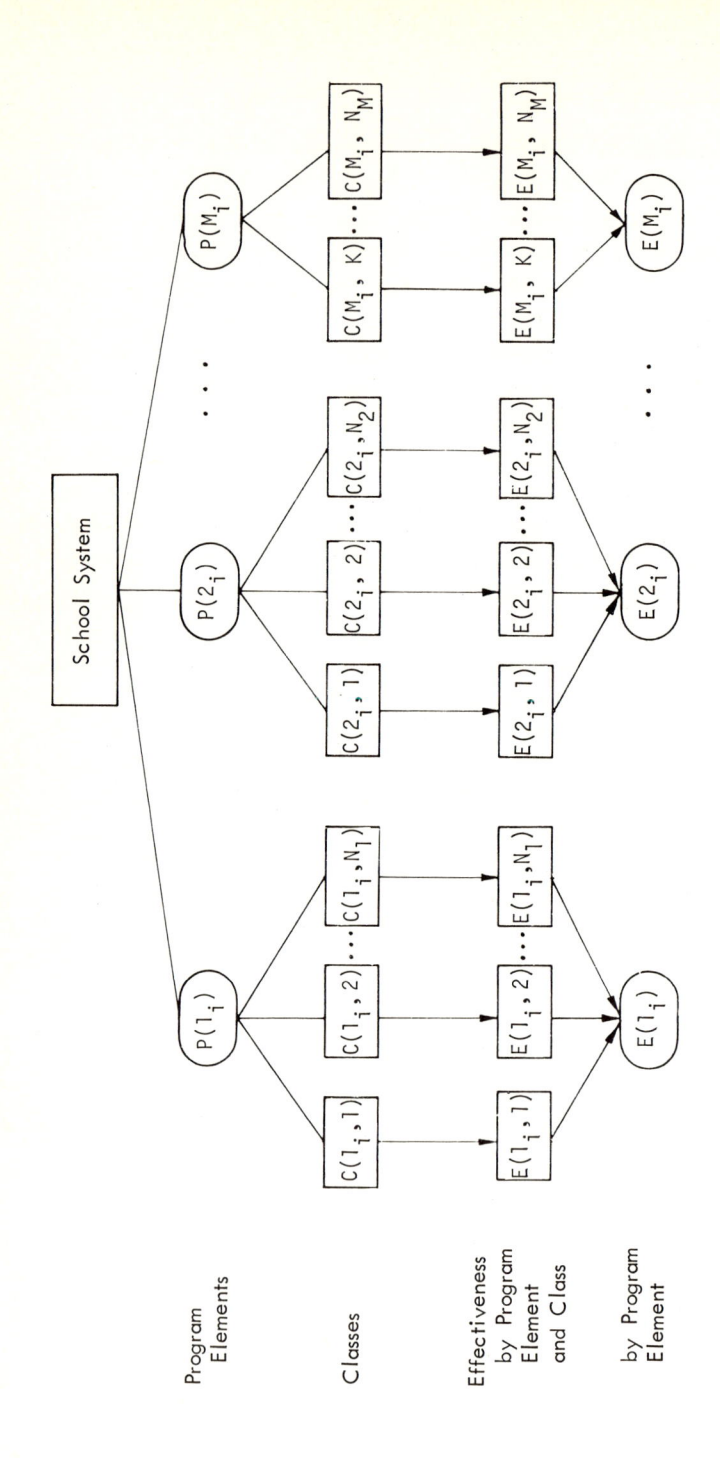

Finding the Effectiveness of Program Elements

$$E(j_i),$$

is to average the measures of effectiveness of that element in each class,

$$\frac{1}{N_j} \cdot \sum_k E(j_i,k).$$

This is permissible because the objective of the program element and the average scholastic capability and socioeconomic environment of the students in each class are the same so that the same kind of student achievement is being measured. The numbers could be combined in other ways, of course. If the classes differ markedly in size, it might be desirable to weight the contribution of each class to the average by its size.

Then it would be possible to find, in principle, an allocation to each class that maximizes the district average for that element, given a fixed budget for each program element. (Techniques for such optimization are discussed in Hitch and McKean.)* The phrase "in principle" is used for three reasons. First, before the determination of efficient allocation can be made, the relationship of the effectiveness of each program element to the resources that go into it needs to be known, and such relationships are not now available. Second, in some cases, depending upon the relationships involved, so-called efficient allocation might result in some schools getting no money at all, a socially unacceptable solution unless students can be accommodated in some other way. Third, the district-wide mean is not necessarily an acceptable standard of performance for the program element. In the outside world students will compete outside of the district and across lines of socioeconomic status and ability, and the district may wish to adjust its effort accordingly. This point will be discussed later.

---

*Charles J. Hitch and Roland N. McKean, *The Economics of Defense in the Nuclear Age,* The Rand Corporation, R-346, March 1960, pp. 361-405.

Figure 12

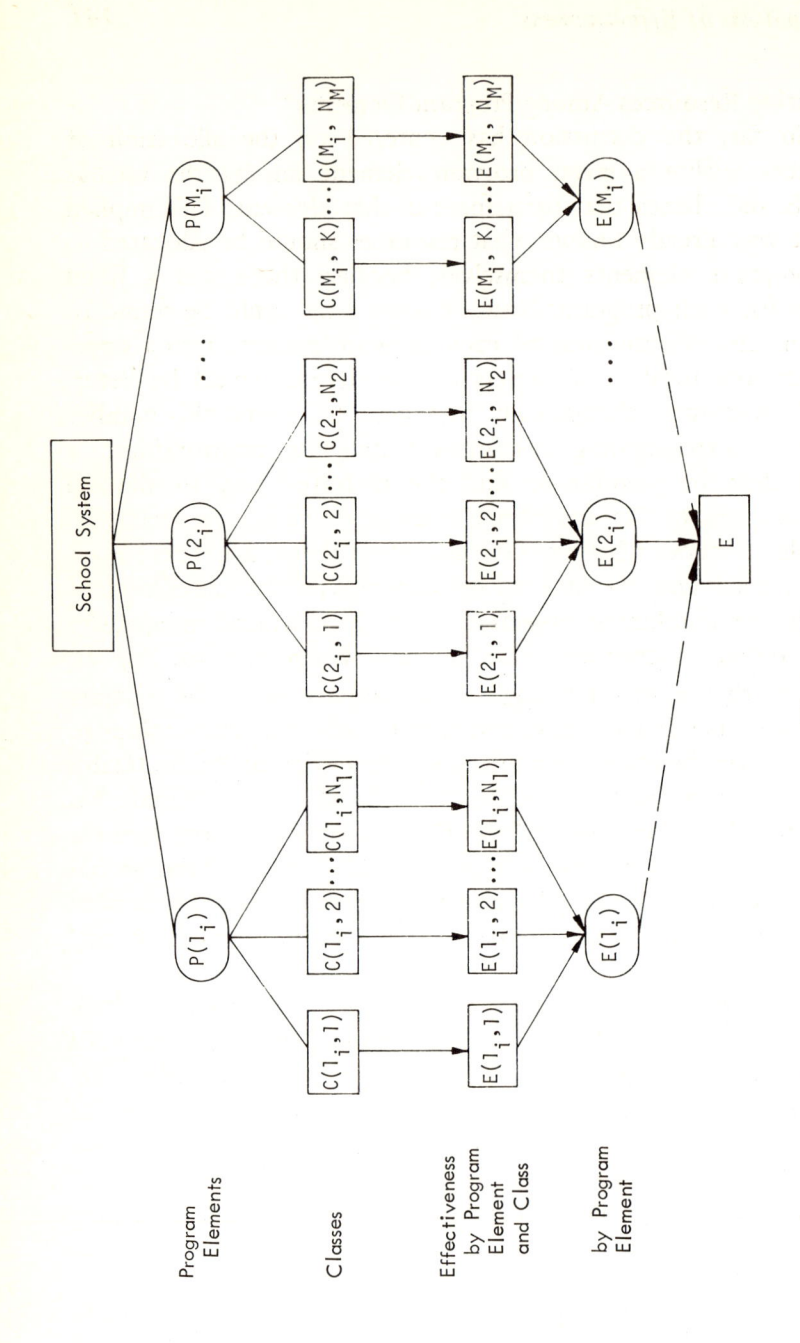

The "Effectiveness" of a District

Allocating Resources Among Program Elements*

So far, the discussion has centered on the allocation of resources *within* a given program element among the various schools and classes that participate in that element. This implied that it was already known what resources should be allocated to the program elements themselves, because there was a fixed budget for each program. Now, if some way could be found to combine the effectiveness of each program element into a single number, the total effectiveness of the district could be determined, as shown schematically in Figure 12. Given this number and the corresponding resource-effectiveness relationships, it would then be possible to find the preferred way to allocate resources *among* the program elements. Obviously, it would be valuable to know what the best allocation would be. There is no cut-and-dried way to find it, because this is the same kind of problem in combining objectives that we discussed previously. Some public institutions have actually been able to find an objective that is broad enough to encompass all of the separate objectives, that is assessable, and that has obvious relationships to the separate objectives. For example, the Office of Public Health Service in the Department of Health, Education, and Welfare has converted the effectiveness of all of their diverse programs into the number of days a person is in good health, and by doing so has learned much about the relative effectiveness of their programs in these terms. There seems to be no such measure for educational programs.

Lacking such a measure, the only way to assess the overall effectiveness of the school district in terms of the effectiveness of its program elements is to inject weightings reflecting value judgments. It still will be impossible to find the *best* allocation of resources among program elements because there are as yet no clear relationships between resources and effectiveness.

Nevertheless, explicit weightings can be invaluable in helping

---

*In what follows, program elements are assumed to be differentiated by student ability and socioeconomic environment, as well as by subject.

administrators and other decisionmakers to decide how to allocate resources among programs and program elements. This can result in a better alignment with the decisionmakers' judgment as to the proper emphasis for the particular student population and community. For example, in poorer neighborhoods, reading and vocational education might be more heavily emphasized than in neighborhoods that are more well-to-do.

In addition, the data made available by the program budgeting system will suggest *how* resources may be shifted from one program to another. Such shifts will be necessary if a fixed overall budgetary level must be maintained and if a desired improvement in the effectiveness of a program demands additional resources. For example, if additional emphasis is needed in the reading program, there should be data that show how much money can be saved by cutting down, say, certain extracurricular activities and then estimate what this money can buy in terms of increased resources devoted to reading.

Criteria of Effectiveness

To attack problems of resource allocation, decisionmakers must have an idea of whether a program element is doing well or poorly. Again, this is a consequence of the lack of clear relationships between resources and effectiveness, as well as the lack of an overall measure of district effectiveness that does not depend on value judgments. How can reasonable criteria of effectiveness be specified? (The term "criterion" is used in its strict dictionary sense—a standard of judging.) If achievement tests are being used, to set the standard that every child in the district must achieve at or above grade level in every subject is unreasonable. And until better measures for predicting potential are developed and more is learned about individual styles of learning, it is impossible to set a standard of every child achieving in accordance with his potential—although this is a goal to strive for. A district will need to specify a definition of success for its various program elements some place short of these goals.

It should be noted that the use of criterion-referenced tests will not *ipso facto* solve this problem. Setting the objectives that each student or class should master is, in fact, even more demanding than determining desirable achievement levels on norm-referenced tests. Certainly, such objectives should reflect similar judgments both of the students' capabilities and of what they should be able to do relative to their peers.

At present, criteria for achievement in both reading and writing English can probably best be determined from some kind of standardized test administered district-wide. The rationale to follow is immediately applicable to these subjects and can ultimately be extended to any program element whose objectives are measurable by a standardized achievement test.

It is natural to establish the several criteria for success on the basis of the socioeconomic strata of the district and the levels of scholastic ability of the students that have been discussed previously. These criteria (which can only be established on the basis of subjective judgment, at present) might be expressed in general terms, such as "at grade level minus six months for below-average classes in socioeconomic area 4."

It is important to point out that this kind of stratification of criteria for success should be a temporary measure. It facilitates the compilation of realistic current base-line data to which future achievement can be compared. But the ultimate goal, at the least, should be for every child to achieve in accordance with his ability. This would mean that in time, as more is known about teaching people of differing backgrounds and cultures, and programs have been devised to fit their needs, the effectiveness of the program elements would be assessed only in relation to ability levels.

As with effectiveness, the overuse of criteria should be avoided. If some alternative way to conduct a program element falls short of meeting a criterion by only a small amount, the small difference should *never* be the deciding factor in the selection of the preferred alternative, as noted above and re-emphasized here.

Relationships Among Program Elements

Each program and program element competes for resources with all others. To some extent, this competition is offset by the interdependence among programs. Resources devoted to reading, for example, are not really taken away from any other academic course, because students must be able to read to perform well in other subjects. In fact, because the effectiveness of other academic programs depends to an appreciable extent on the reading program, they actually make joint use of the resources put into the reading program. To take full account of the effects of joint use of resources, much more needs to be known about the relationships between resources used in one program element and changes in the effectiveness of one or more others.

As an example, Program 6, Assessment, Guidance, and Counseling, will be discussed in some detail. Up to now, the discussion has been about group measures of effectiveness, using the classroom as a unit. But the real concern is with the individual, so another measure needs to be added—progress in relation to an estimate of ability. Though every school system tries to do this job, it needs to be done more rigorously and systematically than it has been done in the past.

The basic assumption that underlies the kind of program to be proposed is that the first years of schooling play a critical role in determining a youngster's success in current and future programs. It would be worthwhile to test the proposition that heavier expenditures in diagnosis, guidance, and counseling in the lower grades would result in a lowered requirement for expenditures and in more effective programs in the later grades. This is one of the alternatives which can be methodically examined in a program budgeting system.

To simplify the discussion, the special problems of any deviant group will not be considered beyond proposing that they be identified early so that they may benefit from the special programs that are provided. Also, for the sake of argument, it will be assumed that there will be sufficient funds and personnel to carry out the program described.

Four steps for enhancing an individual's progress need to be considered: identification, placement, diagnosis, and appraisal. It is axiomatic that the sooner a problem is identified, the sooner steps can be taken to remedy it. At the end of kindergarten, a group-intelligence test will be administered. The youngsters at both ends of the distribution will be given an individual intelligence test. Thus, from the very outset, the group that can profit from enriched or accelerated curricula and the group where achievement problems are most likely to be encountered will be identified so that they can be placed in appropriate classes.

Since even the best assessment measures can only be considered indicators rather than absolutes, especially in the early years, and since youngsters in the early grades are subject to wide variations in performance in a relatively short time span, it will be necessary to keep a constant monitor on their progress in relation to their ability. This means careful observations by teachers in an attempt to confirm or contradict test findings. If a contradiction is consistently found, the child will be retested and, if necessary, given a complete psychological examination.

During the course of the first year, any child that is having difficulty learning to read will immediately be given a diagnostic reading test, on the basis of which appropriate action will be taken. At the end of the year, a reading achievement test can be administered. This kind of continuous diagnosis, the immediate implementation of remedial programs, and frequent checking of progress, if carried out rigorously during the early school years, might go far toward eliminating the problem of the youngster who, in high school, is still reading at an elementary level and consequently failing in all academic subjects.

Although a program such as this is expensive, school districts are already evaluating achievement in several subject areas, and with the current tendency for school boards and the general public to increasingly ask what they are getting for their money, pressures for evaluation will probably increase. Systematic use of evaluation of achievement in the guidance and counseling program would put these scores to another valuable use.

Such a program could pay off in decreased dropout and grade-repetition rates and in large savings in the later years because fewer special classes would be required. If students are achieving more closely to their potentials, the effectiveness of the program might be reflected in fewer disciplinary referrals and better attendance—indications that attitudes are improving. Counselors would have more time to work on other problems with students because they would be spending less time on discipline cases.

Guidance *per se* does not necessarily lend itself to immediate measurement. Rather, the results of individual guidance given in the early years would be reflected in the group results for all the primary program elements in later years. If the concentration of resources in early years is indeed an effective solution to achievement problems, as the years pass an increasing number of academic programs should be meeting the criteria specified for success.

Summary of Program Elements

The effectiveness of the primary program elements may be measured in many ways; which measuring instrument is selected depends on which is best suited to answering the questions at hand. Both norm-referenced (achievement) and criterion-referenced tests are useful in certain applications. These measures supply criteria to which all decisions about the educational system are ultimately referred and which stand at the top of a hierarchy of objectives, each level of which is a means to the one above. Most decisions within the school system will be concerned with subobjectives in the hierarchy. Each of these must be consistent with the primary objectives in the paths above it. Usually, consistency can be established only by judgments based on the value structure of the decisionmaker. Additionally, decisions may be concerned with any aspect of the system, may involve actions to be taken in the community or by other educational entities, or may require a restructuring of the system itself. The possibility that a given decision will influence the effectiveness of a primary program should always be analyzed with care. Whatever influence may be exerted should be spelled out and presented as a dominant constraint in the choice of a course of action.

Extra-Institutional Measures of Effectiveness

The measures so far considered are all internal in that they are related solely to objectives that may be attained and measured within the school system. However, if the primary programs themselves are considered, in contrast to their elements, it can readily be seen that additional ways to assess effectiveness are needed. Because the objectives of the primary programs reach beyond the boundaries of the schools, extra-institutional assessments are needed to determine how well they are being attained. These kinds of assessments relate directly to the "product" of the school districts.

For example, the effectiveness of the program to provide academic preparation for higher education, Program 5, might be assessed by following after high school all youngsters who pursued this program to determine how many entered college, to analyze the courses they took, and to measure success or failure. This information would then be used to improve the elements in this program.

Because this would be a difficult and expensive task, it may be desirable to substitute some simpler methods of judging the effectiveness of this program. Except for the junior colleges, most colleges require candidates for admission to take the Scholastic Aptitude Test (SAT) for which they have cutoff points on the test, tailored to their own experience with what is required for their students to successfully complete a curriculum. It would be entirely feasible to construct a table that would show the SAT scores necessary for admission to different kinds of colleges. General groupings would suffice—such as Ivy League, state colleges and an average of a dozen or so good private institutions. A comparison of the results of the senior classes on the SAT with this table would indicate how many of the students will qualify for college entrance. This, coupled with a similar analysis of grade-point averages, would be a relatively good indicator of program effectiveness.

It is possible to construct measures of the effectiveness of education that are even more highly aggregated. For example, in an economically advanced country such as the United States, it has been shown that the amount of lifetime earnings that an individual may expect is positively correlated with the number of years of formal education that he has completed. If it is granted that the value of education to an economy is measured by the amount of individual income that it will make possible, then it might be said that a measure of the economic effectiveness of education is the increase in lifetime earnings that the individual can expect. This measure has been used and discussed in several papers on the economics of education, such as those by Becker, Weisbrod, and Hirsch.* The benefit of each additional year of education is taken to be the amount of increase in income in dollars. It is often implied that if this increase is greater (or less) than the cost of those additional years of education, the education is (or is not) worth the expense.

This kind of analysis measures both the resources and the results of education in dollars. Economists call it cost-benefit analysis, and because the benefit is a measure of the economic value of education as a whole, it is, in that sense, more comprehensive than assessments of effectiveness, which are often related to specific activities within the educational establishment.

It would certainly be useful if it were possible to assign a dollar value to years of education, because this would shape decisions about the length of education that is economically beneficial to the society. It might be possible to show, for example, whether the addition of a junior college in the district could be economically justified. Plotted against years of education completed, the benefit-minus-cost curve might look something like Figure 13. Note that benefit *minus* cost was used, although it would have been possible to combine the two numbers by taking benefit divided by cost. The proper approach depends upon the constraints that are relevant to the decision problem. Ratios are applicable when there is a budget constraint and numerous levels of the same alternative can be undertaken up to the limit of the

---

*Gary S. Becker, "Investment in Human Capital: A Theoretical Analysis," *The Journal of Political Economy*, Vol. 70, No. 5, 1962; Burton A. Weisbrod, "Preventing High School Dropouts," in Robert Dorfman (ed,), *Measuring Benefits of Government Investments,* Brookings Institution, 1965, pp. 117-149; and Werner Hirsch and Morton J. Marcus, "Some Benefit-Cost Considerations of Universal Junior College Education," *National Tax Journal,* Vol. 19, March 1966.

The Analysis of Effectiveness

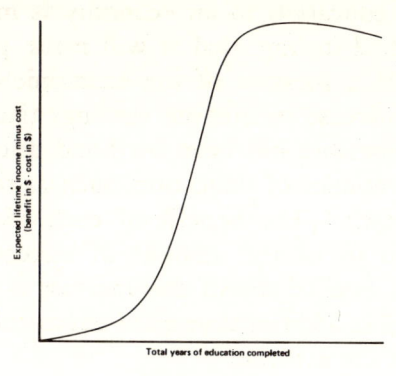

Figure 13

A Hypothetical Benefit-Cost Relationship

budget. The net-benefit approach is used when there is no budgetary constraint and when the programs are mutually exclusive, as would be the case with the present example. (One cannot obtain education only through high school and still complete a college course, nor can one obtain a high school education several times over.)

General Principles for Assessing Effectiveness

Because the benefit-minus-cost measure is highly aggregated, it provides a relatively uncluttered illustration of some guiding principles about assessing effectiveness. These principles are:

- The gauge of effectiveness is tied to the problem.
    - The output is a direct expression of the objective.
    - The means for generating the output is the problem of concern.
- Systems being compared that would affect output should be the same in all respects, except those being examined.
- The assessment should consider all of the major outputs.
- Correlation only suggests causality.

A discussion of the principles will conclude this chapter. First, the way in which benefit or effectiveness is gauged is closely tied to the question that is to be answered; that is to say, there are no universally useful ways to assess effectiveness. The assessment must be of an output that either expresses the objective directly or is so closely related to it that it can be substituted for it. In the example, the objective is to increase the total return to the economy. This is translated into the total lifetime income of individuals, which is presumably correlated with overall economic gain.

The problem must be concerned with the means by which the output is produced. In this example, the question was simply what number of years of schooling is of benefit to the economy? If the question had been "How can personal income be increased?" various means other than education would have to be included in the study.

The corollary to this line of argument is clear: a given set of measures of effectiveness of program elements will *not* answer *all* questions about decisions in education because, for one thing, in order to assess the effectiveness of solutions to many school district problems, it will be necessary to tailor measures to the problems *ad hoc*. Other reasons related to the need for value judgments and other issues will be discussed in Chapter Ten.

The second point the example illustrates (by default) is that the system being compared should be the same in all respects that are relevant to the problem, except in those aspects being tested. The students are one of the major components of a school system. As Weisbrod points out,* students who complete more years of schooling are different in their capabilities, on the average, than students who complete less; so their increased lifetime income might be due partly to these different capabilities as well as additional education. The only way to actually compare the several groups would be to select sets of students who had the same kind of capability and then compare the lifetime income of those who had completed more school with that of those who had

---

*Weisbrod, *op. cit.,* pp. 129-130.

completed less. Then if there were an increase in lifetime income, the point would have been proved. (A less satisfactory way to handle the problem is to perform a regression analysis. Unfortunately, in a number of cases, this may be the only tool available.) The failure to consider the students themselves and their capabilities as an integral part of the educational system often leads to faulty analysis.

In general, effectiveness is assessed so that different means of attaining a goal can be compared. Answers may be required to such questions as "Is the system doing well or poorly?" in which case the system would be compared with some stated or implicit goal. In another case the system may be compared with its own past performance; or with another essentially similar system, like another school; or with a different way of producing the same output. In any case, the purpose is to compare, and comparability between educational systems is especially difficult to achieve because of the multifaceted nature of nearly all educational activities.

The third principle is that any assessment of benefit should consider all major benefits that would be affected by the decision, even if some are not grossly quantifiable. In the example, nothing is said about the increased enjoyment and appreciation that an education can bring to everyday life, and yet this is a value with which educators are rightly concerned.

Finally, although correlations, such as lifetime income with years of schooling, suggest causal relationships, to feel dissatisfied with having to rely on them is justifiable. In the example, the additional income that goes with increased years of schooling may also be due to greater native talent, a higher social and economic position at the start, greater ambition, and so on. So, although it is extremely difficult to control all the explanatory variables well enough to make sure that results are dependent on only the variable of interest, this is still the ultimate goal and one worth working for. To achieve it will require a greatly increased body of rigorous research in education.

CHAPTER SEVEN

EVALUATING ALTERNATIVES IN SCHOOL DISTRICT PLANNING

Sue A. Haggart

Introduction

Evaluating alternatives in educational planning is both *the why* and *the how* of program budgeting for educational planning. The purpose of all the activities demanded by the program budgeting process is to investigate the consequences of alternative courses of action. The output of all these activities results in an organized information base for improved decisionmaking, and the analytical activities required in support of the program budgeting process provide a systematic way to make the best use of this information base.

As was stated earlier, program budgeting is a way of life—a way of thinking about where you are going, how to get there, at what cost, and with what benefit. Analysis is, of course, implicit in all the components of the program budgeting process and in all the activities that make a program budgeting system work. The name of the game, after all, is evaluating alternatives.

This section outlines the more basic techniques employed in the evaluation of alternatives, and discusses some of the considerations in using them in educational decisionmaking. This will not be an extensive discussion; there is a large body of literature about systems analysis and decisionmaking in general. Much of the treatment of the subject has been in the area of decisionmaking for defense, and, in recent years, in the area of program budgeting. For present purposes, the best discussions are found in Hitch and McKean, Fisher, and Quade.* These discussions are extensive, yet clear and concise. The ideas and techniques are almost directly transferable to the problems of educational decisionmaking.

It has been stressed that program budgeting is an approach to improved planning and that the process is more than budgeting and accounting by program. This idea—that the program budgeting process provides a better way of looking at decisionmaking problems—is the unifying thread of this book. Discussions about defining objectives, developing a program structure, and viewing the school district as a system in order to develop resource and effectiveness relationships provide the problem context. The chapters on the concepts of effectiveness and the assessment of program alternatives as well as the concepts of resource analysis and the determination of the cost of alternatives provide the analytical framework for seeking solutions. These all relate to the elements involved in the systematic selection of the preferred course of action that are briefly described below. For the most part, the descriptions are paraphrased from the more lengthy discussions by Hitch and McKean, Fisher, and Quade** and are outlined in this chapter for completeness of this discussion of program budgeting for improved school district planning.

Elements of the Analysis

1. *The Objective or Objectives.* What educational aims are to

---

*C.J. Hitch and R.N. McKean, *The Economics of Defense in the Nuclear Age,* Part II, Harvard University Press, Cambridge, Massachusetts, 1960; Gene Fisher, "The Role of Cost-Utility in Program Budgeting," in David Novick (ed.), *Program Budgeting: Program Analysis and the Federal Budget,* Harvard University Press, Cambridge, Massachusetts, 1965; and E.S. Quade, *Systems Analysis Techniques for Planning-Programming-Budgeting,* The Rand Corporation, P-3322, March 1966.

**Ibid.*

be achieved with the resources that the analysis is designed to compare? The choice of objectives is fundamental; if the wrong objective is chosen, the whole analysis may be addressed to the wrong question.

2. *Alternatives.* By what alternative combinations of resources may the objective be accomplished? The generation of new and sometimes better alternatives is often an important by-product of the analytical part of the program budgeting process; this is partly due to the interaction of the decisionmaker and the analyst but mainly due to the fact that additional analysis often results in a better understanding of the problems and the subsequent discovery of other alternatives.

3. *Costs or Resources Used.* Each alternative method of accomplishing the objective involves incurring certain costs or using certain resources. The resources (and costs) required for each alternative must be determined.

4. *A Model or Models.* Models are abstract representations of reality that help to perceive and clarify significant relations in the real world, to manipulate them, and thereby predict others. The model is needed to trace the relationship between inputs and outputs—resources and effectiveness—for each alternative to be compared.

5. *Criteria.* Criteria refer to the rules by which one alternative rather than another is chosen. They are the standards against which the contribution of a program toward meeting the program objective is measured.

The Process of Analysis

The elements of the analysis then become inputs to the process of the analysis (see Figure 14). The process begins, of course, with the alternatives to be evaluated. These are examined within the model that represents the input-output or the resource-effectiveness relationships of the system. It tells what can be expected from each alternative. Essentially, it shows the *cost* of the alternative and the *contribution* of the alternative in meeting an objective. A criterion is then used to weigh the cost against performance. The purpose is not to determine one ratio of

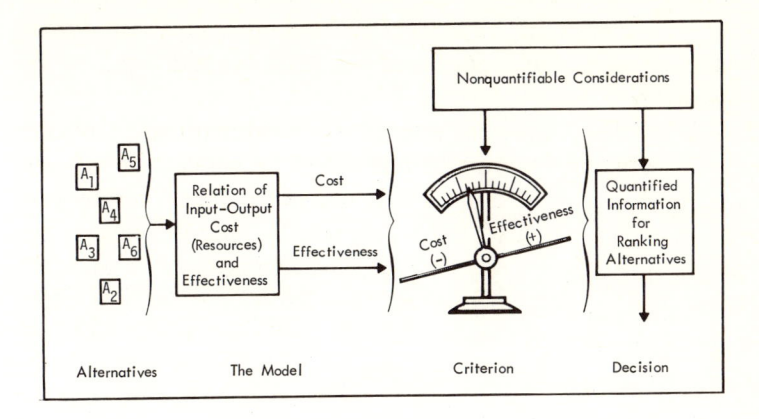

Figure 14

The Process of Analysis as Adapted from E.S. Quade

effectiveness to cost for an alternative but rather to rank alternatives to provide a part of the basis for selection among them. This is the quantified information for decisionmaking.

There is another important aspect of this process; it is the consideration of those dimensions of the problem that cannot be quantified—the qualitative or intangible factors that make it impossible to define a satisfactory criterion.

It might be a good idea at this time to interject a note of caution about the role of analysis in the program budgeting process. This was nicely stated by Fisher, who said:

> First of all we must be very clear about what the purpose of analysis really is—particularly in a long-range planning decision context. Contrary to what some of the more enthusiastic advocates of quantitative analysis may think, I tend to visualize analysis as playing a somewhat modest, though very significant, role in the overall decisionmaking process. In reality most major long-range planning decision problems must ultimately be resolved primarily on the basis of intuition and judgment. I suggest that the main role of analysis should be to try to *sharpen* this

intuition and judgment. In practically no case should it be assumed that the results of the analysis will "make" the decision. The really interesting problems are just too difficult, and there are too many intangible (e.g., political, psychological, and sociological) considerations that cannot be taken into account in the analytical process, especially in the quantitative sense. In sum, the analytical process should be directed toward assisting the decisionmaker in such a way that his intuition and judgment are better than they would be without the results of the analysis.*

This warning should be kept in mind when considering the ways to account for the nonquantifiable aspects of district problems and decisions. These ways are inextricably bound up in the totality of the analytical techniques. Before discussing some of the techniques of analysis and pointing out those especially useful in dealing with the qualitative factors that must be considered when a decision is made, it is appropriate to discuss the analysis itself.

Characteristics of a "Better" Analysis

It is not possible to say what makes a good analysis; it is possible to say what might help to make a better analysis. The fact that a set of procedures or exact rules still remains elusive is not sufficient reason for giving up the search for ways to make the best of what is available. The search continues—with the dialogue between opponents and proponents helping most to clarify both the problems and the solutions. Several actions may help in the quest for a better analysis.

First, be sure that the right problem is being addressed—that the analysis of the problem is seeking the answer to the right question. This includes not only developing alternative ways to do something, but also deciding what should be done. The right answer to the wrong question is, after all, rather useless. Considering the interactions of other activities as they have a bearing on the problem is important in deciding on the right problem. The complicating fact is that the really difficult problems are not isolated from their environment, and their

*Gene Fisher, *The World of Program Budgeting*, The Rand Corporation, P-3361, May 1966, p. 11.

solutions cannot be sought in isolation.

Assuming success in deciding the right problem to be studied and in designing the analysis to seek the answer to the right question, what is left? There is one important area over and above the analysis per se. It is the presentation of the results.

In the presentation of the analysis, the qualitative considerations should be identified. This includes both those taken into account in the analysis and those that could not be made an integral part of it. It is important to present the results of the formal quantitative analysis and to interpret the results with special attention to the assumptions and limitations of the analysis. In addition, the analyst should attempt to identify the important qualitative considerations that the decisionmaker should consider in weighing alternatives.

From the above discussion, there is no set of rules that can be followed in analysis for decisionmaking. Instead, there are guidelines that help in considering all facets of defining the problem and identifying solutions and that help in achieving the best possible use of the data available. It is a common-sense approach.

Some Techniques of Analysis

Cost-Effectiveness Analysis. The cost-effectiveness technique of comparing alternatives is the most widely-known and the most often misused technique. It is useful in comparing alternatives when either the *cost* (budget level) or the *effectiveness* (achievement) is held constant. Maximizing the ratio for the sake of the ratio alone can lead to some ridiculous extremes—like zero to infinite cost or zero to infinite effectiveness. But there is a way to make the technique meaningful. That is to specify the level of effectiveness and then to examine the *cost* of alternative means of achieving that effectiveness. Conversely, you can fix a single *budget level* and examine the levels of effectiveness that can be achieved through different alternatives. This is a particularly advantageous approach when examining higher-level problems with less well defined objectives. The ratio itself, however, can be a very simple guide to ranking alternatives when two conditions exist: (1) the scale of the activity is fixed and (2) the alternatives are not interdependent.

In sum, there are four purposes for which cost-effectiveness analysis can be used. The first is in the allocation of resources among major objectives. This is really a variation of the second and third purposes—the choice of alternative means to meet any given objective and the assessment of the merit of different objectives. The fourth purpose is to provide for the systematic generation of alternatives that were not initially identified.

The next three techniques all relate to the treatment of uncertainty. It is necessary to deal with uncertainty about the future itself, about the capability of new technical aids, about the effectiveness of new methods and operational procedures, and about the availability of resources. The techniques for doing this are sensitivity analysis, contingency analysis, and *a fortiori* analysis. Each of these will be mentioned very briefly and very simply.

Sensitivity Analysis. Sensitivity analysis is direct in both its purpose and its application. The key parameters of the alternative are varied to determine the sensitivity of the result—the ranking of the alternative—to changes in parameters. If you are uncertain about the cost of particular resources, a high, medium, or low cost is assumed for the analysis of the alternative. The same is true for uncertainty related to the effectiveness.

Contingency Analysis. In contingency analysis the purpose is to ascertain the effect on the ranking of the alternative of changes in the environment in which the alternative is to function or of changes in the criteria for evaluation. It might well be referred to as the "what-if" type of analysis, with the what-if's being external to the alternative. This is in contrast to a sensitivity analysis, where the parameters of the alternative are varied.

A Fortiori Analysis. The definition of *a fortiori*—"with greater reason or more convincing force, used in drawing a conclusion that is inferred to be even more certain than another"—provides the best explanation of the use of this technique. It is essentially stacking the cards against the alternative

Evaluating Alternatives in School District Planning 159

intuitively preferred by resolving all questions of uncertainty in favor of another alternative; if the initially preferred alternative still looks good, you have a stronger case. This same process could be used in reverse if you want to see how a new alternative compares to the initially preferred one. In this case, major uncertainties are resolved in favor of the preferred alternative.

There are many more ways to treat uncertainty, to perform system analyses in general, and to aid decisionmaking; this discussion has intentionally been limited to those ways that can be of immediate use to school district administrators in district planning activities and in the use of program budgeting.

One additional thought should be mentioned. Analysis does not necessarily mean number juggling. A great deal can be gained from just a systematic approach to defining the problem and seeking possible solutions. Numbers, of course, do help. Everyone knows that. Everyone also knows that some numbers are better than other numbers. The trick is to know as fully as possible the meaning of the numbers: What do they tell you? Where do they come from? On what are they based? The point that should be emphasized is that numbers alone do not make a better analysis; the important factor is the context in which they are used and how they are used. The process of trying to make explicit some of the qualitative considerations inherent in defining the problem and in seeking possible solutions probably contributes more to making a better analysis than amassing and manipulating data.

CHAPTER EIGHT

AN EXAMPLE OF THE ANALYSIS OF AN EDUCATIONAL PROGRAM

Margaret B. Carpenter and Sue A. Haggart

Introduction

This chapter will discuss the concepts, techniques, and problem areas involved in the *how* of analyzing an educational program. As a basis for discussion, the chapter will use the data from a developmental program, Project R-3, carried out in the San Jose Unified School District under California Senate Bill 28. The example will illustrate most of the aspects of analysis discussed in Chapters Six and Seven.

Description of Project R-3

There are 35,000 students in the San Jose Unified School District, in which Project R-3 is being conducted. San Jose, California, is in the center of an area characterized by a large Mexican-American population and by rapid industrialization. In some neighborhoods in downtown San Jose, the concentration of Mexican-American residents can run as high as 70 percent. But prejudice against Mexican-Americans is slight compared to what one might expect to find in some other areas of the United States, so that there are job opportunities for ambitious Mexican-Americans in the San Jose area.

Population growth in San Jose has been more rapid than in the state as a whole, which is itself characterized by rapid population growth. Population growth has had two effects. One is the loss of large areas of orchards and farmlands. In the past San Jose was known as a center for fruits and vegetables, but now many of the orchards are being cut down to make room for new homes. The other effect has been a large increase in nonagricultural employment, which more than tripled between 1950 and 1966. It is of particular interest that the electronics industry had become the largest single employer by 1966 in a town in which the canning industry had at one time been the largest employer.

Project R-3 was funded under California Senate Bill 28, which was passed shortly after the Watts riot. Part of that bill was aimed at improving the achievement of students in the seventh, eighth, and ninth grades who were at least one year below grade level in reading or math and who were judged to be capable of doing better. Such children are characterized as underachievers.

"R-3" stands, not as the reader might think, for the three R's—reading, writing, and arithmetic—but for readiness, relevance, and reinforcement. The concept behind the project is that the student is ready to learn when he is motivated; motivation is produced by showing the relevance of learning to the world of work; learning is made more lasting by reinforcement of acts which promote cognitive and affective development.

The objectives of the program were both short-term and long-term. The short-term objectives were to raise the students' achievement in reading and math beyond the normal for the target population, and to induce positive attitudes toward learning and education. The long-term objectives were to raise the educational and vocational aspirations of the students.

Three groups of students were chosen for the experiment. The program group which received the special treatment was chosen at random from a group of students in the eighth grade at Woodrow Wilson Junior High. These students were no more than two years nor less than one year below grade level in reading or math. (Actually, some of the students were above grade level in one or the other of these subjects.) The other criterion for student selection was chosen so that the project could be carried to successful completion. It was that the students would not be likely to move out of the district during the school year. Using these criteria, 17 boys and 17 girls were chosen for the program group.

The control group for comparison of academic achievement was chosen from another school in a similar socioeconomic area. This school had the same tracking program as Woodrow Wilson Junior High. All of the students were taken from the Y-track, comprised of students of average intelligence who were underachieving. No one in the district knew who the students in the control group were.

The third group was chosen for comparison on the basis of indicators of attitude toward school—primarily records of attendance and disciplinary problems. The comparison group consisted of all Woodrow Wilson eighth graders who qualified for the R-3 program but were not in it. The group was chosen from Woodrow Wilson students because the project personnel knew the backgrounds and environments of the students in this group, and also because these students would be treated with the same administrative policies for suspensions and expulsions as would the students in the program group.

The project had several components that could be grouped in a number of ways. In this chapter the project is divided into three parts: remedial reading and math, the study of occupational technology, and the involvement of parents and students in special activities. Each of these will be described briefly. The subject-matter content of the remedial reading and math was not changed from that of the standard eighth grade curriculum. Each was given during one of two periods to classes of 15 students each, approximately half of the size of a normal class. A diagnostic/prescriptive approach was used. Initial diagnosis of reading difficulties was made by means of the Durrell reading test, and of math from the profiles of the students' performance on subtests of the California Achievement Test in math.

Occupational technology was taught through a variety of means. In the classroom, gaming and simulation were used with groups of approximately 15 students each. This activity was geared to the reading and math curricula and took one period every day. The gaming/simulation activity, which is how this will be referred to below, was a highly structured representation of real-world situations. Students played the roles of actual people, such as a park director or a highway engineer. Each unit was supplemented by a study trip to a facility directly related to classroom work. There were about 19 study trips throughout the year. Students helped to make the arrangements for the study trips by use of a conference phone.

The third component was the involvement of parents and students in special activities. This will be referred to as *involvement* from here on. For involvement of the students, there were two study trips of four days each. One year a group went to Asilomar, a park on the Monterey peninsula; the other group went to Big Sur, a park on the coast further south that contains a grove of coast redwood. These study trips were again very highly structured. They were intended to break down the stereotyped roles of students and teachers in the classroom and to involve students in a prolonged and intensive learning experience. It was apparent that they accomplished both of these goals.

The parents of the students in R-3 were also involved in the program. Before school opened, they were asked to attend a preschool dinner, where they were told what the program was to be about and where their consent was sought for the students to participate in the program in general and in the intensive involvement trips in particular. Since this was a Mexican-American community, project personnel were afraid that a number of the parents would not approve of their girls going on the intensive involvement trips and thereby violating some of the traditions surrounding Mexican-American girls. However, this did not come to pass. In addition, the parents were invited to all of the study trips that accompanied the gaming/simulation activity, to the intensive involvement trips, and to several other dinner meetings throughout the year. At every one of these activities the parents participated along with the students and teachers. For example, they played some of the games during the dinner meetings; and, whereas the students were teaching the parents at the beginning, the parents were taking great pride in teaching their children toward the end of the sessions. Finally, the teachers made home visits to all of the parents during the course of the year to discuss some activity connected with their children's participation in the program. This assured that each visit had a clear purpose so that the parents were at their ease.

The results of the project can be expressed in terms of both its cost and effectiveness. The cost figures, however, are not completely relevant for planning purposes because the project was not originally designed with the objective of keeping cost down. Therefore, many of the costs are considerably higher than they probably need to be. For example, teachers in one of the other schools in the district became so interested in the intensive involvement trips that they decided to design their own. Many teachers donated their time to planning the trip, surplus foods were used, and instead of staying at the dormitories at Asilomar where the R-3 program was housed, the students went camping. The result was that this trip cost only a third as much as a trip for the R-3 program. Of course, because the students were camping, most of the time had to be spent in housekeeping chores so that the learning experience was not as concentrated as it was on the R-3 trips.

The effectiveness of the project can be expressed herein in two ways. The first, displayed in Figure 15, is academic achievement. In both reading and math, the program and control groups were fairly well matched at the beginning, but by the end of the year the program group had gained more in both reading and math than had the control. These gains were significant at the five percent level. The achievement testing was given under standardized conditions and under the supervision of a counselor.

There are only rough indicators for attitude change. These are given in terms of attendance and suspensions (see Figure 16).*

---

*Pre- and post-tests of attitudes toward school and career were also administered to the program group. Although these tests did indicate attitude changes in the desired directions, the reliability and validity of the measures are not known.

Average Reading Grade Placement
(from CAT)

	Boys		Girls	
	R-3	C-3[a]	R-3	C-3
Pre	6.7	6.6	6.9	6.4
Post	8.4	7.9	8.9	7.5
Gain	1.7	1.3	2.0	1.1

[a]C-3 denotes the control group.

Average Arithmetic Grade
Placement (from CAT)

	Boys		Girls	
	R-3	C-3	R-3	C-3
Pre	6.7	6.5	6.9	6.7
Post	7.9	7.0	8.3	7.5
Gain	1.2	0.5	1.4	0.8

Figure 15

Academic Gains

	Days Absent Per Pupil-Day	Days Suspended Per Pupil-Day
Fall Semester		
R-3	.084	.0008
C-3	.110	.0004
Spring Semester		
R-3	.098	.0020
C-3	.151	.0132

Figure 16

Attitude Indicators

These were expressed as a rate, that is, number of absences per student-day and number of suspensions per student-day, in order to take account of the different lengths of time and the different numbers of students in the fall and spring semester and in the R-3 and the comparison groups. There is no way to measure the significance of these differences. Both the program and comparison groups had more absences and suspensions in the spring semester than they had in the fall.

Other results are of interest. One of these had to do with parent attendance at the program functions. This averaged 85 percent for all program functions, compared with about 16 percent for PTA meetings and other school functions. Of great importance to the school and the community was the improvement in the school image in the community. School personnel knew that professional agitators were trying to stir up trouble against the school, but in recent years the agitators have been unsuccessful. The school principal attributes their lack of success primarily to the influence of the R-3 program. Finally, the school has gained a reputation for innovation within the district and among other California school districts, evidenced by many visits to the school by people interested in the program.

The program has been given in toto up to this point, and there is no way, therefore, to know which of the *components* discussed is primarily responsible for the achievement gains and for the attitude change. Project personnel would very much like to experiment in order to isolate the effects of the various components. Then a school district wanting to institute a program of this kind could choose those components which were most effective, if any of them are without the others. This experiment, however, was not funded. Nevertheless, the project personnel are going to continue to follow the students who have been in the program. Information will be gathered on their academic progress, including the courses chosen in high school as well as their grades and scores on standardized tests; and on student attitude, primarily as evidenced by suspensions, expulsions, attendance, dropouts, police contacts, and clubs joined. If possible, patterns of college entrance and vocational choice will be noted, for of course these are what the program primarily was aimed to change.

Generation of Equal-Cost Alternatives

In using Project R-3 as a basis for illustrating the analysis of educational programs, every effort has been made to convey the intent of the demonstration program. However, great liberties have been taken with the cost of the program. Because of this a word of caution is necessary at the very beginning: The cost of the alternatives, of their components, or of the specific items of equipment used in this illustration does not reflect the cost of the program in the San Jose Unified School District. The purpose is to show how cost analysis may be done so that the results are useful in the evaluation of alternative programs. The emphasis will be on *analysis for planning* rather than on *accounting for budgetary or financial control.*

This distinction is an important one. It demands an approach quite different from the traditional cost accounting procedures. The most basic difference concerns *what* is included in the cost estimate of the program. This means we are really interested in resource analysis as contrasted to cost analysis; we want to know what the dollars are buying. Having a cost-per-student measure of alternative programs is not sufficient. For decisionmaking purposes we want to know the requirements for special teachers, new equipment, additional facilities, and so on. We can then translate these requirements into an estimate of cost.

In analysis for planning, one might use techniques for translating requirements into cost estimates that would be unsatisfactory from a cost accounting point of view. In developing an estimate we would be happy using, say, $12,000 per year for a teacher—without breaking the $12,000 down by the amounts for each regular budget appropriation category such as instruction, retirement fund, or fringe benefits. This kind of breakdown is, of course, required in cost accounting for budgetary control or accountability. But our main concern is to provide information about the resource demands of the alternative programs and to use a monetary measure of these demands as a convenient way to compare alternative configurations of the R-3 Project.

The Project R-3 of the illustration may be described in terms of three basic components: the remedial reading-and-mathematics component; the intensive involvement of the students, with parental involvement; and the gaming/simulation component. Various mixes of these components have been identified as *options*. These, along with the cost for units of 30 students, are shown in Table 23.

The following assumptions are used in the calculation of the estimated cost of each option and in the generation of the equal-cost alternatives. For each component requiring classroom instruction, a regular class of 30 students is separated into two classes of 15 students each. Each classroom is remodeled, in a sense. The floors are carpeted, walls are painted, and new furnishings are added. This is in addition to the special furniture (trapezoidal tables, for example) and equipment of each component. The classrooms can be used for six periods per day; utilization rates above this level require the preparation and outfitting of an additional classroom. The estimate for this is $3,000 for the classrooms and $2,000 for the furniture.

An Example of the Analysis of an Educational Program

Table 23

Cost of Options
(for units of 30 students)

Components of Project R-3

#1 Remedial Reading and Mathematics
#2 Intensive Involvement and Parental Involvement
#3 Gaming/Simulation

Options

A Components #1, #2, and #3 .... $27,130
B Components #2 and #3 18,990
C Component #1 only 13,140
D Component #2 only 8,675
E Component #3 only 10,315
F Components # 1 and #3 18,455

Instruction estimates are based on one incremental period for every two classes of 15 students. That is, one class of 15 is taught by the teacher of the regular 30 students and the other class of 15 is taught by the additional teacher. No special training is required for the teacher. And there is no special qualification needed to teach the classes of any component. It is assumed that the cost of instruction is $11,715 per year, based on a five-period instructional day. This figure includes the salary of the teacher and all fringe benefits. The estimate for instruction is, on this basis, $2,345 a class period. These supporting cost details are given in Table 24. The cost of equipment and materials is also given in Table 24.

The cost related to the classroom is separated from the cost related to the number of students that use the classroom (perhaps six different classes of 15 students each). The cost related to the classroom (shown in Table 25) varies from $5,610 for Option E, *Gaming/Simulation Only,* to $8,660 for Option A, *All Components.* The cost related to the number of students receiving classroom instruction (Table 26) varies from $4,705 for Option E

Table 24

Supporting Cost Details

Item	Unit Cost ($)	Cost/30 Students ($)
Remodeling Classrooms	3,000	–
Furniture	2,000	–
Classroom Materials		
Reading & mathematics	350	–
Gaming/simulation	50	–
Classroom Equipment		
Reading & mathematics	2,200	–
Gaming/simulation	560	–
Equipment for Involvement	500	–
Materials for Student Use		
Reading	~ 16	475
Mathematics	~ 14	425
Gaming/simulation	~ 12	360
Intensive Involvements	–	6,775
Parental Involvements	–	1,400
Gaming/Simulation Trips	–	2,000
Instruction (per period)	2,345	–

Table 25

Classroom-Related Cost[a]

Item	Option A ($)	Option B ($)	Option C ($)	Option D ($)	Option E ($)	Option F ($)
Remodel Classrooms	3,000	3,000	3,000	--	3,000	3,000
Furniture	2,000	2,000	2,000	--	2,000	2,000
Classroom Materials						
Reading & mathematics	350	--	350	--	--	350
Gaming/simulation	50	50	--	--	50	50
Classroom Equipment						
Reading & mathematics	2,200	--	2,200	--	--	2,200
Gaming/simulation	560	560	--	--	560	560
Involvements[b]	500	500	--	500	--	--
Classroom-Related Cost	8,660	6,110	7,550	500	5,610	8,160

[a]This is the cost to provide the space, equipment, and materials for two classes of 15 students each. The cost of the alternative is based on being able to use the classrooms for six periods a day.
[b]This is the cost of equipment for both games of the intensive involvement—the Land Grant Game and the Oceanography Game.

Table 26

Student-Related Cost[a]

Item	Option A ($)	Option B ($)	Option C ($)	Option D ($)	Option E ($)	Option F ($)
Remedial Reading						
Materials	475	--	475	--	--	475
Instruction	2,345	--	2,345	--	--	2,345
Remedial Mathematics						
Materials	425	--	425	--	--	425
Instruction	2,345	--	2,345	--	--	2,345
Gaming/Simulation						
Materials	360	360	--	--	360	360
Instruction	2,345	2,345	--	--	2,345	2,345
Trip expense[b]	2,000	2,000	--	--	2,000	2,000
Involvements						
Intensive	6,775	6,775	--	6,775	--	--
Parental[c]	1,400	1,400	--	1,400	--	--
Student-Related Cost	18,470	12,880	5,590	8,175	4,705	10,295

[a]Based on 30 students.
[b]Based on approximately 20 trips per year with an average cost of $100 per trip.
[c]Based on experience data with 30 students. This includes the cost of 3 dinner meetings with the parents.

to $18,470 for Option A. The cost of the involvements (for groups of 30 students) is also shown in Table 26.

There is now enough information to look for some equal-cost alternatives. In evaluating the effectiveness of the alternatives, Option A has been chosen as the basic alternative for comparison. This is the option that includes all the components of Project R-3: the remedial reading and mathematics, the intensive involvement of the students, the parental involvement, and the gaining/simulation component. The following alternatives are selected:

Alternative	I:	Option C for 90 students	$24,320
	II:	Option D for 90 students	25,025
	III:	Option E for 150 students	29,135
	IV:	Option F for 60 students	28,750

The cost of each of these alternatives is shown in Table 27 and is within ten percent of the cost of Option A. This is simply an arbitrary rule chosen for this illustration. Notice that it eliminates Option B, at a cost of approximately $32,000, from consideration as an equal-cost alternative. Option C for 90 students makes use of the classrooms for the six periods of the day; additional students would require the remodeling and outfitting of additional classrooms and would make the cost of Option C more than ten percent over the cost of Option A. This would result in the elimination of Option C for more than 90 students as an equal-cost alternative.

From what might be called the decision matrix of Table 27 we have selected the set of equal-cost alternatives used in the following discussion on comparing the effectiveness of alternative programs. A different set for a budget level of about $45,000 could have been selected just as easily.

In an effort to keep this discussion brief, just the flavor has been given of the ideas involved in making the results of cost analysis useful in the evaluation of alternative courses of action. The important consideration is that of providing the decision-maker with information about the resources needed for each alternative as well as the cost of the alternative. In an actual

Table 27

Generation of Equal-Cost Alternatives

Item	Option A ($)	Option B ($)	Option C ($)	Option D ($)	Option E ($)	Option F ($)
Classroom-Related Cost	8,660	6,110	7,550	500	5,610	8,160
Student-Related Cost	18,470	12,880	5,590	8,175	4,705	10,295
Cost for 30 Students	27,130	18,990	13,140	8,675	10,315	18,455
Cost for 60 Students	45,600	31,870	18,730	16,850	15,020	28,750
Cost for 90 Students	72,700[a]	44,750	24,320	25,025	19,725	47,205[a]
Cost for 120 Students	91,200	57,630	37,460[a]	33,200	24,430	57,500
Cost for 150 Students	118,330[a]	70,510	43,050	41,375	29,135[a]	75,955[a]

Note: Option A—Remedial Reading & Mathematics, Involvement, Gaming/Simulation.
Option B—Involvements, Gaming/Simulation.
Option C—Remedial Reading & Mathematics, only.
Option D—Involvements, only.
Option E—Gaming/Simulation, only.
Option F—Remedial Reading & Mathematics, Gaming/Simulation.

[a] Additional classrooms required if over 60 students in Option A or C and if over 90 students in Option F.

An Example of the Analysis of an Educational Program 175

evaluation one would need much more detailed information than has been given in this illustration. One would need a good picture of existing resources, how they are used and with what effectiveness. This is necessary not only to determine the incremental cost of the specific alternative but also to compare the effectiveness of the alternative with the effectiveness of current programs. Information of this nature is readily available within an operational program budgeting system. In fact, organizing the informational data base to permit the systematic evaluation of alternatives is the primary objective of a program budgeting system.

Comparing the Effectiveness of Equal-Cost Alternatives

First, the primary objectives of each of the components of the R-3 program will be discussed. Originally, the program was designed so that all of the components would support one another in attaining the two objectives: improved achievement in reading and math, and an improved attitude toward education. But when we consider each component separately, it does seem that we can identify one or the other of these two objectives as being the primary objective of a given component. For example, the primary objective of the reading and math program was clearly to improve the students' academic achievement in reading and math. Some change in the students' attitude toward school might have been induced because of improved achievement, but the *primary* objective was improved achievement.

On the other hand, the involvement appeared to be oriented to improving the attitudes of both the students and their parents toward school. (Actually, the involvement also changed the teachers' attitudes toward their students and toward the students' parents as well.) Many of the project personnel believe that the most essential part of the whole R-3 program was the parental involvement because it opened lines of communication that had not existed before. The parental involvement was required for a variety of reasons. Of course, the parents' consent was required for the students' participation in the program, but there were also effects on the way the parents looked at the role of education in their children's lives. Before Project R-3, the parents had lacked a realistic appreciation of modern requirements for entry skills into the job market. Many of them had grown up making a living on the farm or in the canneries, and they did not understand that these jobs were becoming far less important for their children than some of the more highly technical jobs that were developing in San Jose. This lack of appreciation, coupled with strong family ties, resulted in parental urging that the students quit school so that they could contribute to the family income. Many families had large numbers of children and needed this extra money.

Although it would seem that the involvement was primarily aimed at attitude change, some of the project personnel thought that the intensive involvement trips were really the most influential component for improvement in academic achievement, as well as for attitude change. They believed that this was because the trips provided a dramatic break with traditional instruction, and that they got the students away from the negative triggers that they have learned in their prior school experience. These people pointed out that even the limited intensive involvement trip that was conducted at the other school actually resulted in improvement in academic achievement. (We can think of a number of reasons for this; for instance, much of the school was involved in planning this intensive involvement trip, and therefore the teachers' attitudes toward their students were changed, as well as the other way around.) Whether the involvement really was principal in improving academic achievement will have to be resolved by further experimentation. Lacking this experimentation, all that can be done for the present is to point out the effects of the two different assumptions on the choices that one would make among the components. The one assumption is that the improvement in academic achievement primarily came from the reading and math program, and the other assumption is that it was caused by the involvement.

The third component, gaming/simulation, showed how the program in reading and math was related to the world of work. Thus, it reinforced the reading and math and it also effected attitude change. Therefore, it is assumed that gaming/simulation

An Example of the Analysis of an Educational Program 177

had both objectives.

Figure 17 shows which of the components is assumed to have which primary objectives. Academic achievement is primarily attained through the reading and math program, supported by gaming/simulation. A positive attitude toward school is induced by the involvement, and also supported by gaming/simulation. And there is a question as to whether the involvement was important for improving academic achievement.

Let us now consider various aspects of measures of effectiveness. One aspect has to do with the effects of the program over a longer period of time than has been discussed up to now. Figure 18 displays the rate of growth in achievement in reading by grade. Normal growth, which is represented by the dashed line, would be indicated if a student was achieving at the fifth grade level in the fifth grade, at the sixth grade level in the sixth grade, and so forth. The rate of growth for Mexican-American students is shown by the solid line. Because the Coleman report (Coleman, *et al.*, 1966)

	READING & MATH	INTENSIVE INVOLVEMENT & PARENTAL INVOLVEMENT	GAMING/ SIMULATION
ACADEMIC ACHIEVEMENT	X	?	X
POSITIVE ATTITUDE TOWARD SCHOOL		X	X

Figure 17

Primary Objectives of R-3 Components

gave reading achievement levels only for the sixth, ninth and twelfth grades, the growth rate by grade can be inferred only very roughly, as indicated.

A program like R-3 is intended to raise the growth rate at least to normal and, ideally, to provide sufficient initial growth that the student makes up for prior years of underachievement. Figure 19 shows some of the possibilities. The R-3 program succeeded in the eighth grade in raising the students' growth rate to 1.8 months per month, as represented by the sharp peak, while in the ninth grade the growth rate was 1.1 months per month. In the future the students may drop back to their original achievement or to normal growth, or they may even continue to grow at a somewhat greater rate than normal.

Another aspect of effectiveness is the effect of changes in one achievement measure on other measures not affected by the program directly. Logically, one might think that if a student's performance in reading has been improved, his performance in other subjects would also improve, particularly those such as science that require reading skills. Therefore, perhaps Project R-3 has also raised the students' achievement in science above normal growth, as suggested by the upper dash-dot line in Figure 20. But it is also quite possible that the science program has suffered by comparison with the R-3 activities. In that case, the students' performance in science may even drop below the normally low achievement for this population. Thus, we must measure the students' achievement in *all* areas of interest so that we will know what the indirect effects are, if any.

Other measures also are needed, especially if the program involves more than, say, 100 students. In that case, background data will be needed of the type that is being collected for the evaluation of all of San Jose's compensatory programs (Rapp, *et al.,* 1969). These data are required so that the effects of varying backgrounds on student achievement can be isolated from the effects of the programs. The San Jose survey will assess background in five areas: the parent's view of the child, the parent's view of the school, family history, language patterns (important for Mexican-American populations), and economic status. Follow-

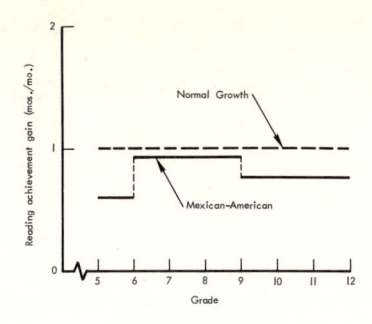

Figure 18

Long-Term Growth in Reading Achievement

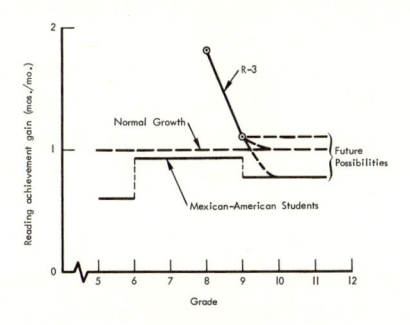

Figure 19

Long-Term Growth in Reading Achievement for R-3 Program

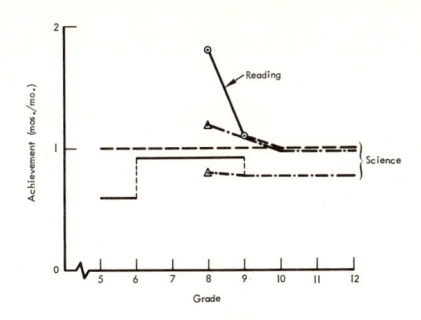

Figure 20

Effects of Reading Achievement Gains on Achievement in Science

up information of the type that will be gathered on those who participated in R-3 is also needed because, of course, planners are primarily concerned with longer-term effects. Recall that among the data to be gathered are dropout rate, police contacts, patterns of college entrance, and patterns of vocational choice.

Now, let us compare the hypothetical effectiveness of the equal-cost alternatives that have been described previously, and that were chosen so that the decisionmaker might concentrate his deliberations on effectiveness. These comparisons will be made using two different assumptions. The first assumption is that the reading and math programs were primarily responsible for gains in academic achievement. Figure 21, based on this assumption, shows growth in reading achievement versus the number of students involved in the alternative programs. The first point on the figure, labeled "all," represents the 1.8 months per month gain attained by the 30 students in the R-3 program. (At present, of course, "all" is the safest alternative to choose because there are no data on the effectiveness of the others.)

If the components are recombined into the equal-cost alternatives, there will probably be changes in achievement growth and there will also be changes in the numbers of students involved. For example, although the gaming/simulation activity might not induce as much achievement gain as would the total program, it could be provided to five times as many students. It might, however, be too close to the dashed line—indicating one month per month, or normal growth. The dashed line is critical because the State of California considers any achievement growth less than this to be unacceptable. This would mean that, although the involvement could be given to 90 children for an equal cost, it would not be acceptable if the achievement it induced fell below the critical minimum, as suggested. If the district is not required to meet a minimum standard in achievement gain, it will be possible to trade off achievement gain on the one hand and the number of students reached on the other. This might be an important consideration if the schools need visibility. In that case the gaming/simulation would always be the best choice, because it is the least expensive per student.

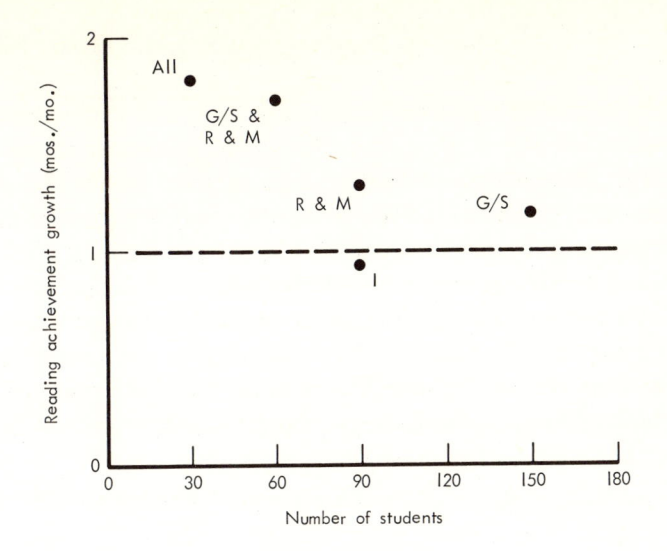

Figure 21

Effectiveness of Alternatives—First Assumption

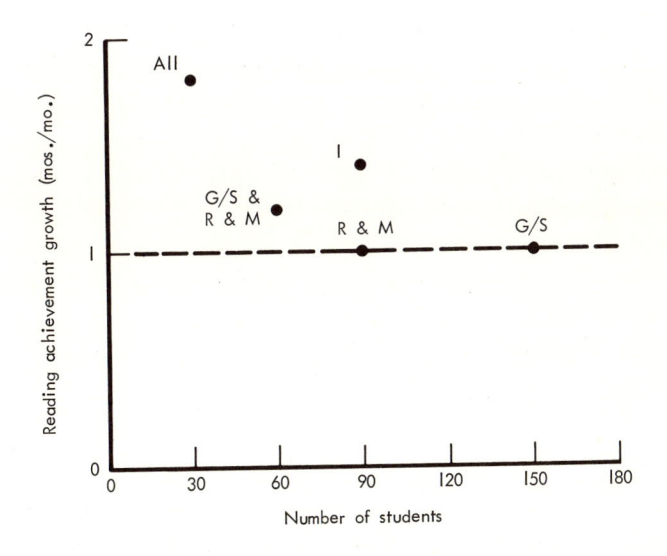

Figure 22

Effectiveness of Alternatives—Second Assumption

The other two alternatives shown may more than meet the minimum requirement, so that the choice between them would depend on whether one felt it more important to provide a higher rate of achievement to fewer students or a lower rate of achievement to more students. Because the reading and math program is not particularly innovative, one might be more interested in the gaming/simulation plus reading and math, even though it can be given to only 60 students.

Suppose it is assumed that the involvement was primarily responsible for the achievement gain rather than the reading and math. Figure 22 is based on this assumption. Again, all components working together account for a 1.8 months per month growth in reading achievement for 30 students, but reading and math and gaming/simulation have dropped because they have been assumed to contribute relatively less to reading achievement. In fact, either of these alternatives might not be acceptable because they appear to fall on the critical line. The involvement has moved above the line, and since the involvement applied to 90 students, it looks like a very attractive alternative. In fact, it would appear that the involvement might be superior to the combination of gaming/simulation with reading and math, both in terms of achievement and number of students reached. On the other hand, in some districts it may not be possible to maintain discipline among the students for the extended period that they must be away from the school and home on the intensive involvement trips. If this is a significant problem for the district, the involvement would be an unsafe choice, and it would be better to select the gaming/simulation and reading and math.

Let us now include another measure of effectiveness in our analysis. Two measures of effectiveness—one, growth rate in reading, and the other, an index of attitude change for each program—are shown in Figure 23. This index was derived by assuming that each alternative would induce a change in attitude relative to the change induced by the R-3 program. Thus, the index of attitude change for the R-3 program is unity, and the

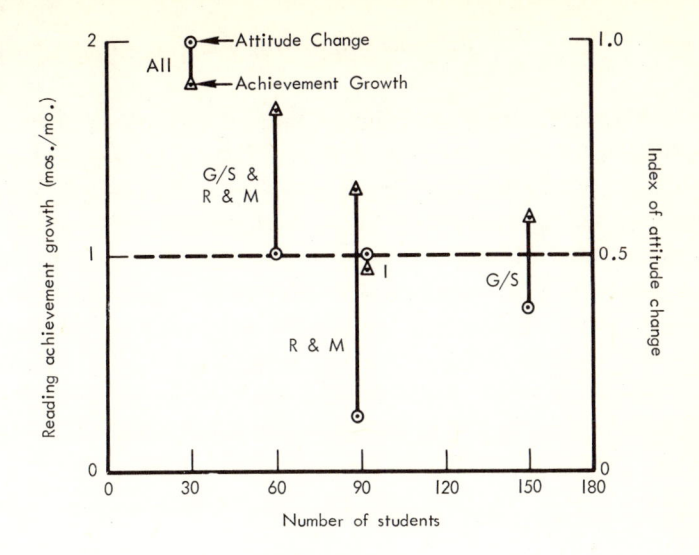

Figure 23

Two Measures of Alternatives—First Assumption

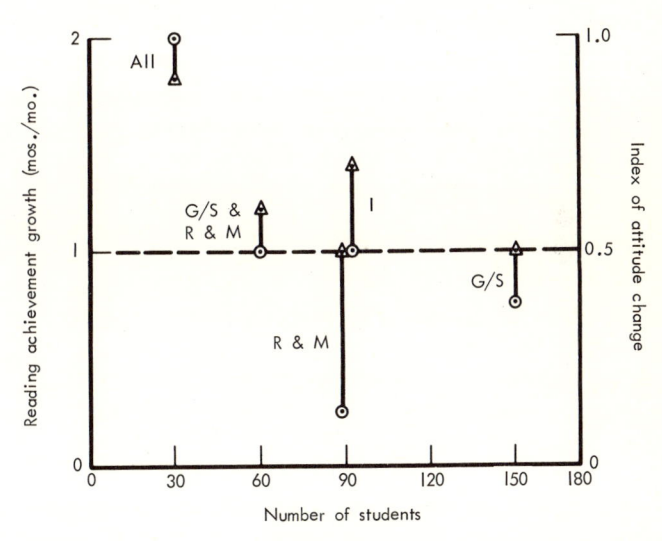

Figure 24

Two Measures of Effectiveness—Second Assumption

other alternatives have indices less than this.* As before, gaming/simulation alone looks risky because it is not being reinforced with backup programs. In addition, it may induce relatively little attitude change; reading and math look even poorer in this regard, while the involvement is too low on achievement gains. Note how the addition of the second measure supports the superiority of the combination of reading and math with gaming/simulation over reading and math alone (refer to Figure 21). Thus, we may want to accept smaller numbers of students and have reinforcing programs, as in the gaming/simulation and reading and math, where we buy achievement gain and attitude change for 60 students, or we may prefer to buy less of each for 150 students with the gaming/simulation alone. Which one a decisionmaker chooses will depend upon whether he considers gains per student or numbers of students reached more valuable.

Supposing it is believed that the greatest contributor to achievement gain was the involvement. Then there would be a situation something like that depicted in Figure 24. Now the choice is even more clearly in favor of the involvement over the gaming/simulation. The gaming/simulation and reading and math cannot compete with it on any measure and only gaming/simulation alone is superior—in terms of numbers of students only.

This chapter has gone through this kind of analysis to demonstrate how it can assist decisionmakers in choosing among alternative programs by considering effectiveness alone. It also demonstrates the value of being able to attach measures of effectiveness to alternatives. (Recall that we could only hypothesize what the effectiveness would be.) But even though the analysis had to be made in the absence of solid data, at the least it has made subjective judgments explicit and related them to one another in an orderly way.

*A slight digression at this point will help to explain the rationale behind this figure. Analysts have a tendency to lump all measurables in single indices for the sake of simplicity of manipulation and presentation. For example, the number of students in each alternative program might have been included in the indices. Although this would have made for a very pretty picture, it would have been almost impossible to interpret because too many variables would be combined in a single point. As far as possible, it is better to keep measures that are significant in their own right separate.

CHAPTER NINE

EVALUATING INNOVATIVE EDUCATIONAL PROGRAMS

Marjorie L. Rapp and Gerald C. Sumner

Introduction

As more and more school districts implement a program budgeting system, there will be an increased demand for meaningful evaluation of current programs and of alternative programs. In addition, because of the Congressional mandate that Title I programs for disadvantaged children be evaluated, educational evaluation has assumed a more important role than ever before. In the wake of this mandate has come an accelerated need for "the design and specification of accurate, reliable and sensitive systems of observation, measurement, testing and, in the final analysis, judgment."*

And yet Doxey Wilkerson says that "currently available research in this field typically reports ambiguous outcomes of unknown or amorphous educational variables. This unhappy 'state of the art' is likely to encourage contradictory but equally

---

*"Testing and Evaluation/Two Views," *The Urban Review*, Vol. 2, No. 3, December 1967, p. 5.

premature tendencies in educational decisionmaking."*

Against this background of need, and of dissatisfaction with techniques for meeting it, this chapter considers some ways of planning evaluations so that the decisionmaker will be provided with the information he needs: clear-cut evidence about innovative programs that can be meaningfully compared with current school practice.

The developmental aspect of these innovative programs is in itself forcing a change in the role of evaluation. Of necessity the shift is from the concept of the traditional short-term highly structured experiment wherein all the variables are tightly controlled, to a concept of long-term, developmental evaluation in an atmosphere where variables are not controlled, but rather accounted for. The role of the evaluator is being changed, although his task remains unchanged—to collect all the evidence he can, so that judgments can be made about the effectiveness of an innovative program in achieving its objectives. But rather than being looked upon as an experimenter manipulating variables, he is considered an integral part of the staff of a developmental program.

Three Functions of Evaluation

The parameters of the evaluation design are determined by the use to which the evaluation is to be put, the ultimate user of the results, and the capabilities of the school information system. There are three basic functions served by evaluation: to support decisionmaking in program adoption, to support decisionmaking in program improvement, and to support research for a better understanding of the educative process.

Evaluation results that specify what achievement gain is being produced by what resource mix for which segment of the population can be combined with a cost analysis of the program resources to provide the essential ingredients for a cost-effectiveness analysis.** This information can then be used to aid the

---

*"Programs and Practices in Compensatory Education for Disadvantaged Children," *Review of Educational Research*, Vol. 35, No. 5, December 1965.

**Margaret B. Carpenter and Sue A. Haggart, "Cost-Effectiveness Analysis for Educational Planning," *Educational Technology*, October 1970, pp. 26-30. (See Appendix D.)

decisionmaker in choosing among alternative programs.

Evaluation for program improvement is concerned with the details of each program, and the results are used within the program on a short-term basis to improve the operation of the program in meeting its stated goals. In this role the evaluator becomes the focal point in a feedback loop, gathering information about the effectiveness of the program that can then be used to improve program design.*

In addition to these action-oriented uses for evaluation results, the researcher can use them in conjunction with other results to improve his understanding of the educational process. Then, over a longer time span, the research results can be fed back to decisionmakers to aid decisionmaking in initial program selection and continuing program improvement.

A precondition for evaluation is the specification of the program to be evaluated, the relevant effectiveness measures for the program, and the types of students for whom the program is designed. The evaluator translates the above specification into an evaluation model that may vary from the simple to the complex. The complexity of the model depends, of course, on the number and kinds of programs, students, and effectiveness measures that are to be considered. The evaluator's model describes the manner in which the inputs are assumed to effect the outputs (e.g., achievement).

The type of model adopted depends somewhat on how the evaluation results are to be used. For example, if they are to be used for program improvement, then the model should reflect the details of the program, so that the effect of each can be determined and program changes made when necessary. On the other hand, a detailed model *may* not be required if to support program adoption one simply wants to know which of two programs is more effective for a designated mix of students. Unfortunately, the payoff from using a simple model that does not place much emphasis on understanding the educational process is correspondingly small. The use of simple models has dominated evaluation and research efforts for many years and has

*See Appendix B.

failed to produce much knowledge that could be used to improve the educational process.

The more emphasis that is placed on evaluation for understanding the educational process, the larger is the requirement for a more varied mix of inputs, for more detailed measurements, and for a more complex analysis, and thus, for a better designed school information system. Also, if the evaluation results are to be used for program improvement, then the information system must be able to make faster responses to information requests.

Because the school information system will largely be shaped by the requirements for evaluation and resource analysis, it should be designed to meet these needs. Information systems designed in a vacuum—generally from readily available data—rarely, if ever, support the data requirements of the decisionmaker.

Planning for Evaluating

Planning the evaluation should be one of the phases of designing an innovative program. The assumption that no final decision will be made at the end of the first try-out period needs to be made explicit; therefore, a report couched in terms of the strengths and weaknesses of the innovation, with a view toward capitalizing on the former and remedying the latter, is a help to the decisionmaker. It is necessary, above all, to guard against making premature decisions about the worth of innovation.

No matter how well educational innovations may be planned, until the programs are actually in the classroom, it is not possible to know how all the components are going to interact. It seems only fair to everyone concerned to plan for a try-out period during which the main role of the evaluator is that of observation and information gathering. At the same time, the assessment techniques for measuring change should be administered. The analysis of the data, plus observation, will more than likely yield the cures that will lead to improvement. As this process is repeated, the outcome of the innovative program will become apparent. It will either respond and improve, thus establishing its worth; or, if repeated trials incorporating attempts at improvement do not succeed, there will be solid ground on which to base a decision about not incorporating this innovation into the educational program structure.

Several factors need to be taken into account in planning the evaluation, so that the decisionmaker will have the kinds of information needed to assess the value of an innovation in relation to the other standard, or current, programs. The first task is to specify the objectives in such a way that they accurately reflect the goals of the innovative program, and then to state these objectives in ways that are observable and measurable. While it may be meaningful in a general sense to say that one of the objectives is to improve students' ability to express inner creative impulses, this is not an acceptable objective as stated because it is not observable or measurable. If this objective is rewritten "to improve students' ability to express themselves creatively," the spirit of the objective is not violated, but it is possible to define its components. By eliminating the words "inner" and "impulses," the objective has been stated in such a way that it is now amenable to some form of measurement. It is still necessary to further define what is meant by "express themselves" and "creatively" before being able to specify the means of assessment. In writing objectives, care must be taken to ensure that any word used can be defined operationally, if one is to attempt an evaluation.

Another task in planning evaluation is to make provisions for measuring progress toward meeting the stated objectives. In order to do this, subjective as well as objective judgments will have to be used. It is on the areas of attitude change that attention needs to be focused. If there are no suitable commercial tests available, tests may have to be constructed. If the concern is measuring change, and the same instrument is administered before and after the implementation of an innovation, it is not necessary to worry about the reliability and validity of the instrument to the same degree as it would be if the instrument were to be used for predictive purposes. It is necessary to make sure, however, that it is the changes in progress toward meeting the objectives as stated that are being measured.

Measuring devices need not always be sophisticated; sometimes, something as simple as a count of events is more reliable than the self-reports of young children. For example, if one of the objectives is to improve participation in group activities in a kindergarten setting, the most direct measure of improvement may be to have adult supervisors keep a tally of participation at stated intervals throughout the term.

Evaluating innovative programs is currently a pioneering effort, and, as such, affords a unique opportunity to develop simple assessment measures that are directly related to objectives.

In planning an innovation, the rationale is always to effect some kind of change. This could be either a change in the quality of output or a change in the utilization of resources. In the school setting, these changes are often stated in terms of improvement of some kind. In order to be able to make a clear-cut decision, a definition of what is considered a sufficient improvement to warrant adopting a new program is required at the outset. Although "improvement" is not specific enough as a statement of objective to yield to evaluative techniques, there are actually ways of defining it usefully. It is possible, for example, to specify that if a youngster that is not participating in group activities at the beginning of the year is observed to join in later, *this* is improvement.

Once the objectives have been stated, the measuring instruments chosen, and the success criteria specified, it is necessary to make certain that it is indeed the stated objectives that are being evaluated.

Considerations in the Experimental Design

Experimental design is essentially a problem of organizing the observation of various alternatives and of specifying criteria and instruments of measurement. There are times when evaluators must face the problem of compromising tenets of "good" experimental design to accommodate the realities of implementation (political, economic, and social realities).

The experimental design should be so structured as to accommodate all the data requirements for the evaluations. Often, one bit of information will serve several evaluation purposes. For instance, reading-achievement gain may be the criterion for several programs. For any *one* program, it is a measure of the effectiveness of a specific set of educational inputs in achieving an objective. It can also be used to compare the amount of gain to be expected from several different mixes of inputs. Finally, if it is also related to student and teacher characteristics, it serves to further an understanding of the variables that contribute to the achievement of sub-sets of the student population.

Throughout the life of the research effort, objectivity requires adherence to the experimental design. However, decision rules should be incorporated that allow midstream course changes; rigid implementation of impotent programs (as well as frequent program changes) may do injustice to the cost-effectiveness of overall research, not to mention the students taking part in the program.

Experimental Control

To the extent that the variables to be measured are affected by inputs other than the program alternatives, the design should provide control on those inputs. Control accomplishes two purposes: (1) it increases the representativeness of the experiment with respect to those inputs, in turn enhancing generalizability of experimental results to the target population; (2) it allows the analyst to test for interaction between program inputs and non-program inputs (e.g., a program input may be effective for children of certain backgrounds, but not for others). Where there is no interaction, the problem of generalizing from innovative programs to all schools will require far less heroism because representation over the non-interactive controls is that much less important. In addition, the presence or absence of interaction is useful information about the educative process.

The fixed-level budget for any experimental program requires that a selection be made with regard to the number of possible combinations of inputs and levels of inputs. It is possible that economic expediency will preclude controlling an experiment by some of the important non-program variables. In this case, one may at least want to set up control *groups* for the program alternatives. The control group is a handy expedient when there are insufficient resources to formally incorporate non-program effects into the design, or when there is uncertainty as to which non-program effects are important. Setting up a control group involves designating a class or school that embodies all characteristics (student, teacher, curriculum, etc.) of the experimental class or school, except that the purposes of the experimental program are met therein by "conventional" means. A control group provides an experiment with only very limited generalizability, answering little more than whether the particular students in the experiment might have done better or worse without the special program.*

To some extent, the benefits of control groups, or of controlling on individual variables, are tentative. Educational experiments lack the relative homogeneity of experimental conditions encountered in the biological and physical sciences; it is in fact difficult to even approximate the ideal of setting up independent experimental trials where some inputs are held constant and other inputs are varied in a known manner. Careful planning is necessary to minimize some of the more obvious sources of this experimental "looseness."

One such source, for example, arises from the fragmented nature of many innovative programs. Children often participate in a "standard" district program for part of a day and in an innovative program for another part. Even assuming no duplication of material from one program to the other, interactive effects will need to be taken into account. If teachers in a standard program try to capitalize on the learning experiences of the innovative program, can all achievement gain be attributed to the innovation? Are children likely to have negative reactions to the standard part of the program in contrast to the innovative part? Ways must be found to take account of these possibilities so that neither too little nor too much gain is attributed to the innovative program per se.

*Even if controlling by individual variables is possible, control groups may be desirable in order to "standardize" achievement—measuring methods used in experimental programs (especially if those methods bear little commonality with conventional tests).

Selection of Students and Teachers

In the selection of teachers and students to participate in programs, there are a number of considerations. There is often a tendency (because of practical considerations) to fill programs with volunteers—both students and teachers. The motivation of these people may not reflect that which is typical in the larger setting, and thus the program results may not be applicable in the large. For this reason, random selection is preferred. If a program appeals to most of its target population, then something close to random selection can be obtained. In selecting experimental programs, one criterion should be their ability to obtain a representative sample from their target populations.

In a transient population there is always a serious problem of program dropouts. For evaluation results to be valid reflectors of long-term effects, a sufficient number of participants must be observed over a fairly long period of time. One alternative is to consider dropouts when determining initial sample sizes, but this is uncertain and costly. Another alternative is to select non-transient participants, but this may bias the sample. There is no easy solution, but dangers should be recognized.

Measuring Achievement

The specification of inputs and their organization into some sort of experimental design provides the framework for collecting observations on the alternatives being evaluated, observations that provide indicators of the relative effectiveness of those alternatives. It might be worthwhile to reflect on the question of what the observations can hope to show.

In the first place, the achievement-related variables that are measured will probably not be the real criteria on which one would wish to base his preferences; it is more likely that they will be surrogates that in some sense embody those criteria, but have the virtue of measurability.

Second, given the vagaries of attaching objective meaning to the utility concept in the context of education, evaluation can only go as far as making ordinal distinctions among alternatives. It is not clear, for example, that a program which produces a gain of

.8 grade equivalents is worth twice as much as one which produces a gain of .4 grade equivalents, just as progress from the first to second grades probably does not have the same utility to society as progress between the third and fourth grades.

Accuracy

These observations notwithstanding, the usefulness of evaluative observations depends on their being accurate; this implies watchfulness in the selection of achievement-related variables, in the selection of instruments, and in the interpretation of test results. The objective is to provide basic data for a preference ordering with respect to effectiveness among competing program alternatives. Accordingly, the observations must have sufficient accuracy to enable the evaluator to discriminate consistently among those alternatives (i.e., if the experiment were replicated a number of times, the variance of the observations should be small enough so that comparisons among alternatives almost always lead to the same ordering of alternatives).

Achievement-Related Variables

The achievement-related variables obviously should reflect the educational goals of the research effort. They should also be measurable and relatively convenient to observe. However, it is also necessary to avoid the trap of measuring only that which is readily quantifiable. There is always a tendency to evaluate a program solely in terms of achievement because post-test measures are available in the form of standardized achievement tests. If there are other program goals, they must be evaluated, even if measures need to be constructed for a specific purpose. If another program goal, for example, is to increase the ability of students to work together in the solution of a problem, this must be evaluated along with achievement gain.

Instruments of Measurement

The measuring instruments should reflect the instructional content of the programs being evaluated. If a given instrument provides observation on more than one achievement-related variable, and if the variables are eventually combined to compare against some composite criterion, then the testing instrument should reflect a balance consistent with the weights that are implicit in that criterion. The instruments must also be sensitive to differences in emphasis and timing of components of instruction. This is a critical factor when the instruction interval is short, and is in fact an argument against interim testing; after all, aside from social and political considerations, long-run educational objectives are more important than the short-run aspects of getting there. On the other hand, time is a luxury, and the interests of an efficient research effort encourage relatively frequent monitoring of the programs to keep them moving in profitable directions (such a pity that educational research lacks the speedy experimental vehicle that genetics found in the fruit fly). To suggest that instruments of measurement be sensitive to program differences is not to recommend that they be completely tailored to the differences; the objectivity of evaluation requires that measures be comparable despite program differences.

Scoring Modes

Finally, in interpreting measurements the evaluator must discern which scoring mode is appropriate for which purpose. Raw scores and grade equivalents are essentially *absolute* scores; percentiles and standard scores reflect achievement levels *relative* to those of all test participants. Because the distribution of absolute scores is wider for the higher grades, it is possible that over a period of years, a poor student may advance in terms of relative score (e.g., from the 20th to 25th percentile) while he is losing ground in terms of grade equivalents gained; the question is whether the instructional program for that student is doing a more or less effective job than the instructional program of the average student who remains at the 50th percentile, while picking up a full grade equivalent each year.

Need for New Approaches to Measurement

It may be advisable to allocate a portion of research effort toward the study of relatively new measurement methods or the development of tools that are currently in the experimental stages. Sole reliance on traditional measures may reveal only part of what a program has to offer; it should not be surprising that innovative instructional programs may require innovative evaluation techniques.

Planning for Future Implementation

Concurrent with the planning for innovative programs should be the planning for future implementation. Since reproducibility of a program is always an implicit and often an explicit goal of an innovation, it should be one of the criteria used in the selection of programs. Many things can be done on a small scale that do not lend themselves to replication on a large scale. Class size can serve as an example. If a program is based upon the theory that in the primary grades achievement is best facilitated by instruction in very small groups, then a series of questions needs to be asked. Can the school district considering the innovative program afford the salaries for a sufficient number of teachers to implement it? Can the school district attract a sufficient number of teachers to carry on such a program? Does the school district have sufficient facilities to house such a program, or would it need to build additional facilities; and, if so, what is the likelihood that the funds to do so would be available? If all the answers are in the affirmative, then an innovative program based on the theory of small-group instruction would be a good idea. If, on the other hand, the answers are in the negative, alternative ways of meeting the objective might be explored. Could one teacher and two aides carry on the program as well as could three teachers? If so, it might become feasible for most districts, in terms of personnel and facilities, and should be tried. If, on the other hand, the program can only be carried out by three teachers, each in a separate classroom, and could not be implemented by most districts, it probably should not be undertaken.

A host of problems relating to facilities, personnel, equipment, and logistics needs to be considered in the light of the desirability that innovative programs be reproducible. In the long run, it is better to grapple with them at the same time that decisions are made about introducing innovative programs than to be faced with the problem of trying to adapt a successful program to fit within a new set of constraints. This is closely tied to the necessity to identify the resource requirements of both the innovation and the operational program so that the cost may be determined.

Long-Term and Short-Term Program Assessment

Another concern is with the question of timing: Are the changes to be effected by an innovative program to be long-term, or short-term, or both? Consider, for example, a program at the ninth grade level in which the stated objective is to raise the reading achievement level by raising vocational aspirations. Here the need is to provide for both short-term and long-term evaluation. In an innovative program that cuts across many objectives and two time spans, it is advisable to return again and again to the stated objectives to instill confidence in the evaluation plans.

Even if spectacular reading gains are realized, for example, the stated objective of raising vocational aspiration should not be neglected. In the long run this is really the objective, and in its assessment lies the true measure of the effectiveness of the innovative program.

In this example, what is really being discussed is effecting attitudinal changes in the students. The hypothesis is that an improvement in the attitude of the youngsters toward school can help them achieve at a level closer to their potential.

Raising a youngster's vocational aspirations can be translated into motivating him to seek a higher order of occupation than would generally be expected of him. While it is not possible to measure motivation directly, it is possible to measure behavior traits that are postulated to be highly correlated with motivation. In this case, baseline data are needed about the kinds of occupations the program population normally enters. From the records of students with the characteristics of the current sample, some sort of schedule that allows them to indicate the employment they would like to have can be constructed. Both the kinds of occupations they normally enter and the kinds of occupations to which it is hoped to make them aspire can be included. This schedule can be administered at the beginning and at the end of the special program and can measure short-term expressed changes. But the real assessment of the success of the program will come after graduation from high school. At that time a series of questions can be asked. In the answer to those questions lies the long-term success or failure of the program. In the long-term sense:

- Did more students finish high school than is usually expected from this population?
- Did more students go on to college than usual?
- Did more students enter employment fields of a more skilled nature than is usual for this population?

If the answers to these questions are affirmative, the motivational aspect of the program can be considered successful, as reflected in raised vocational aspirations.

The ongoing evaluation of a demonstration project has been discussed and some of the more important variables that need to be considered have been delineated: the kinds of changes to be effected, the timing of the assessments, and the criteria to be established.

Developmental Aspects of Evaluation

It was stated at the outset that the evaluation was to be ongoing, and that the nature of the innovative program is developmental. Therefore, it is necessary to think about some of the special problems this poses as contrasted with an educational experiment that is designed to be completed and evaluated within a term of a year.

If the precepts have been followed, the first year of operation will produce the data specified at the outset and a host of observations and hunches. Because the success of any school undertaking depends to some extent not only on the materials used and the methods of instruction, but also on the attitudes and feelings of the teachers and other adults involved, it will be desirable to get their reactions. Here, the evaluation will be subjective, and largely oriented toward making suggestions for improvement. Opinions will be sought about how the youngsters reacted to various aspects of the innovation. If new materials were written, for instance, information will be needed about any difficulties teachers may have encountered in using them. A series of questions specifically tailored to the components will be devised to elicit their reactions. Students' opinions also serve as a guide to improvement. Students can be asked what phases they enjoyed, and what they found difficult or exciting.

As these pieces of information are put together, the immediate strengths and weaknesses of the innovative program will become apparent and will become a basis for changes that need to be made.

Here is where the ongoing developmental nature of this kind of evaluation becomes important. This philosophy of assessment is oriented from the outset toward program improvement rather than toward making a judgment at an early stage. The concentration of purpose is on objectives, not on a prescribed methodology. Therefore, the program designers and evaluators are free from the constraints of exact replication, and can use the experience gained. If, for example, it becomes apparent that some of the material being tried out fails to interest the students, it can be changed. If several teaching techniques are being used at the same time and one or two seem to be more successful than others, those that are unsatisfactory can be dropped, and those that are producing results can be emphasized. At the same time, it is important not to lose sight of the fact that it will be necessary not only to compare the innovation with a standard program, but also to satisfy basic experimental design.

An example can best illustrate the importance of experimental design; it is an important point because it is closely related to the problem of obtaining unequivocal results.

In the first phase of a specific demonstration program, a population within the school was tested, from which both the participants and controls were to be chosen. A list was made of all eligible students—some were assigned to the treatment group, the rest were controls. One of the short-term objectives was to raise achievement level. At the end of the term, the treatment group had made more than satisfactory gains—but so had the controls. A little sleuthing turned up several facts that had not been taken into account in the original plans. As students were taken out of classes to participate in the innovation, their places were not filled. Therefore, the control classes, which should have been larger to be more in keeping with the usual class size, were about the same size as the program classes, and the effect of reduced class size was lost. The controls had also been given the same measures of attitude as the treatment group, and they may have reacted to this attention. Also, the controls were in the same classes as the treatment group in the afternoon, and they may have reacted to the general excitement of their friends.

On the basis of these data, the recommendation was made for the following year to have the controls in another school whose population was similar, and to administer nothing to them but the pre- and post-achievement tests. The identities of the control students were unknown to the staff of their school. At the end of the year, under these conditions, the achievement gains of the treatment group were greater (statistically significant) than gains made by the control group.

In addition to being germane to the problem of trying to get unequivocal data about a demonstration program, the question of the effects in a school on youngsters not participating in special programs needs to be considered.

The example illustrates that if youngsters are removed from regular classes to participate in a special program, it is necessary to assess the effect on the regular classes. The parameters of the standard program that are changed by the introduction of an innovative program must be made explicit and their assessment provided for. If, for example, computer assisted instruction is being used, and several children at a time leave the classroom, temporarily reducing class size, there is a need to assess the effects of this opportunity for the teacher to work with a smaller group. We must guard against attributing any and all achievement gains in this kind of situation to the computer.

Finally, what effect is it going to have on the decisionmaker when the proponents of an innovation that he has agreed to have developed tell him that the results will not really be known until four or five years later? We need to remember that in the example two objectives were specified—a long-term objective couched in motivational terms and a short-term objective of raising achievement level. If, during the developmental phase, the predicted gains in achievement are attained, they will represent an improvement over the current program. From that point of view, it is reasonable to continue with the program development.

However, when the long-term motivational aspects are assessed, the decisionmaker will be faced with another decision. If at that time academic achievement has been improved and the other objectives have been met, the decisionmaker can be rather confident that for the described population he has a better program than he did before. He now has a better basis for allocating scarce resources with which to expand the program.

But suppose, on the other hand, that although academic achievement was improved, the other objectives were not met. Now he must make a different decision. Now he must determine whether or not this kind of innovation is the best program he has for raising achievement level, or whether there is, perhaps, a better way of meeting that objective. It is at this point that the evaluation data enter the program budgeting process. In addition to the information he will have about an innovation, such as objectives and expected changes, the decisionmaker will need detailed information about all aspects of this innovation. This includes information about such items as personnel requirements, special equipment, new materials, field trips—all the details that need to be considered on the cost side of the cost-effectiveness picture. The decisionmaker now has the informational basis for assessing the new program in the light of his total ongoing program resource requirements and their effectiveness in meeting his objectives.

He may then be confident that he is implementing not only

those programs that will be of maximum benefit to the students under his jurisdiction, but also those that make the best use of his limited resources.

CHAPTER TEN

THE USE OF PROGRAM BUDGETING IN DECISIONMAKING

Margaret B. Carpenter

Introduction

Throughout the preceding chapters, program budgeting has been proposed as an aid to decisionmaking and as a medium of communication. This chapter will illustrate some of the many ways in which such assistance and mediation may be provided. Examples will be drawn from current issues and problems* in education in order to provide concreteness. Two disadvantages to this approach need to be recognized: the timely nature of the issues means that their impact will diminish as time passes; but while they are at issue, their controversial nature may elicit an emotional involvement that can obscure the major point of the chapter—that program budgeting can assist decisionmakers and the public at large in a variety of ways by providing insight into problems in education.

The use of program budgeting to provide a framework for

_____
*We may think of an issue as being a problem whose solution is a matter of public debate.

collecting, organizing, and analyzing information about the school district's activities has been treated in previous chapters. However, its use is not restricted to the resolution of problems only within the jurisdiction of the school district. It can also help to clarify issues in education that lie within the authority of other leaders in the educational community or that require action by other civic groups. In discussing examples of these kinds of contributions, this chapter will treat five major points: First, because of the multi-faceted nature of public education, any categorization of school district activities, such as a program structure, cannot deal explicitly with every issue. Second, by providing information about program cost and effectiveness, program budgeting by a school district can contribute directly to the solution of the bulk of the problems within the jurisdiction of the school district. Third, problems whose solution requires joint action by the district and other formal or informal groups can be clarified, at least in part, by information provided within the program budgeting system. Fourth, sometimes such information can be used to argue for a school district's point of view, even when the district cannot take direct action. Finally, the data required to support program budgeting may provide more accurate measures for comparisons among districts.

Educators must struggle with many problems, some of which have to do primarily with the internal operations of the public schools. Others are posed by concerns arising in the community at large. In almost all cases, the solution the educators choose will ultimately affect either the cost or the success of the schools' activities, although many of the effects can be very indirect or relatively small. Problems may involve *any* aspect of education, from the design of classrooms to the use of the schools as instruments of social change. Some may be problems that have recurred ever since the public schools (or any schools, for that matter) were first set up. The teaching of controversial ideas is an example. Others may be relatively transient, like changes in requirements for certification of teachers or whether a particular teacher should be retained. Because problems can focus on any aspect of the operation of the public schools, including their relations with other educational institutions and with the community at large, there is no reason to expect that any single, or even multiple, categorization of educational activities, such as a program structure, will deal directly with every issue. Any manageable categorization that is specific enough to actually describe a given district's activities must slight many problems.

But since decisions typically concern problems, and the program structure can deal explicitly with only a few of them, how can we assert that program budgeting is an aid to decisionmaking? Critics of program budgeting* have stressed this apparent inconsistency. Our answer to them is twofold. First, a program budgeting system (as opposed to an accounting scheme) should ensure that problems are put in the proper perspective vis-a-vis the school district, by demonstrating their impact on the cost and effectiveness of the district's primary programs. Second, the program-oriented data that program budgeting requires are more likely to be useful for problem-solving than are data gathered to support the traditional budget.

Categorization of Problems in Public Education

Problems in public education are so diverse that it is difficult to categorize them. A three-way division seemed, finally, the most appropriate—first, by whether or not solutions to the problem would affect programs; second, by the scope of action that the solution to the problem would require; and, finally, by program orientation.

Issues whose effects on the cost or the effectiveness of the programs cannot be assessed, such as the prohibition of schoolwide ceremonies specific to particular religions, cannot be illuminated by program budgeting. Issues of this kind will not be considered.

The number and influence of formal organizational entities or informal groups that must take action in order to resolve the

*Aaron Wildavsky, "The Political Economy of Efficiency: Cost-Benefit Analysis, Systems Analysis, and Program Budgeting," *Public Administration Review*, Vol. 26, No. 4, December 1966, pp. 292-310.

problem to any degree can be referred to as the *scope of action* of the problem. Two examples will clarify this concept. An individual school district, or even an individual school for that matter, can improve the teaching of science in the district by using more up-to-date curricula and materials. In contrast, a nation-wide network may be set up to ensure that the results and implications of educational research and development are readily available to *all* schools in consistent, understandable form. In this case, many schools must work together and with one or more organizations that have the communication of research results as one of their main objectives. Thus, the scope of action in the former case is the individual district; but, in the latter case, joint action by many districts and perhaps other organizations is required. The desire to improve the teaching of science may well have been instigated by nation-wide concern about the need for young scientists, and the improved materials may have been developed by a committee composed of scientists and teachers from all over the country. Still, the solution to the problem lies in the independent actions of individual districts. The "scope of action" of a problem is one determinant of the manner in which program budgeting by a school district can contribute to the resolution of the problem.

A brief list of categories by scope of action is shown in Table 28. Because of the relative autonomy of American school districts (and even of some individual schools), most problems in American public education focus on actions to be taken by the districts acting essentially independently. This does not mean that problems with a larger scope of action do not exist, but that they are often not thought of, or not at issue, because of the primacy of the school districts. So it is not surprising that the bulk of the issues used as examples will have a relatively small scope of action.

The third way to categorize problems in education (reading across the table) is by their program orientation; that is, whether they concern one or a few programs directly, whether they cut across several programs, or whether they concern the district as a whole. Obviously, problems that affect intradistrict concerns and that have the same orientation as one or more of the primary programs in the program structure are most readily dealt with by

Table 28

Some Contributions of a School District Program Budgeting System to the Solution of Various Categories of Educational Problems

Categorization of Problems by Scope of Action	Contribution of Program Budgeting by a School District to Problem Solution
School district Program orientation:	May demonstrate effect on cost or effectiveness (or both) of one or several programs by:
One or several programs	Showing direct effect on each program involved.
Aspects common to several programs	Showing direct effect on each program involved.
District as a whole	Demonstrating effects on size or composition of program budget and possibly on individual programs.
School district and community	May contribute in any of the ways listed above. May show the effects of the introduction of additional constraints by the community or of increased community support.
More than one district	Program-oriented data furnished by each district may improve comparability of districts.
School district (or districts) and other educational institutions	Program-oriented data furnished by each district may improve comparability of districts. May demonstrate the effects of decisions made outside the district on the cost or effectiveness of district programs.
Institutions other than school districts	No contribution.

program budgeting. For example, issues involving curriculum or student populations with special characteristics will fit neatly into the program structure. An auxiliary categorization by school would facilitate the consideration of program-oriented problems as they apply to individual schools or even to classes within them. Some issues will cut across several programs because they concern an aspect of operation common to each. An example is class size. There is a small group of problems that concern the district as a whole—its size, the length of the school year, and so on. Solutions to these problems may affect the program structure and the program budget as a whole or may lead to the addition of new programs to, or the subtraction of old ones from, the program structure.

Halfway down the table is the class of problems that has to do with joint actions by the school district administration and by groups within the community of which the district is a part. Again, program budgeting information may be able to demonstrate the effects of such issues on the programs involved. Nevertheless, even though it may be quite clear that a particular solution to an issue will have *some* effects on the operation of the school district, the exact nature of those effects may be unforeseeable. Often the resolution of such issues further complicates the task of the district administrators by introducing additional constraints on the courses of action they may pursue. On the other hand, community involvement may encourage greater community support for the schools, with a resulting expansion of available resources.

So far, we have been concerned with problems that require action only by independent school districts—either by the school system itself or by the schools and the surrounding community. Many problems in public education require the joint action of several school districts or groups of districts (as, for example, the districts within a given state). These problems can have the same orientations, vis-a-vis a district's programs, as the intradistrict problems, but additional considerations may often be introduced.

The Use of Program Budgeting in Decisionmaking 209

For example, such problems may often involve explicit or implicit comparisons of one or more aspects of the districts being considered. At present, the descriptors of these aspects are often so aggregated or simplified that they are only superficially related to the characteristic they are supposed to represent and are not readily comparable from one district to the next. Hopefully, because it requires careful definition of program-oriented data, program budgeting will either improve the chances that districts will be compared only on the basis of legitimately comparable aspects or will make incomparability more evident than it is now.

Program budgeting by the school districts can make another type of contribution to the resolution of problems requiring action by one or more districts and other educational institutions; namely, it can be used to demonstrate the effects of decisions made *outside* the district on the cost and effectiveness of district programs. District administrators can use such demonstrations to support their positions in general debate or to argue for (or against) such decisions.

Examples of the Use of Program Budgeting in Dealing with Issues

Some specific examples will clarify these points. To see how each example could be dealt with by a program budgeting system, refer to the partial version of the program structure shown below, which combines the categorizations by "what is to be learned" and then by type of student. It retains the numbering scheme but omits several programs, which is why some numbers and letters are missing. Alongside the program structure, the information describing the resources and effectiveness of each program that would complete the program description in a standard program document would be indicated. This information would almost always comprise quantitative and qualitative descriptions of the several aspects of program input and output (as opposed to a single number). The program document format would appear somewhat as follows:

	Program	Resources	Effectiveness
1.	Learning fundamental intellectual skills		
	A. Language and communication skills		
	1. Regular program	$R_1, R_2, \ldots R_n$	$E_1, E_2, \ldots E_m$
	2. Programs for the educationally disadvantaged	$R_1, R_2, \ldots R_n$	$E_1, E_2, \ldots E_m$
	3. Programs for exceptional students	.	.
	B. Mathematical and reasoning skills		
	1. Regular program	.	.
	2. Programs for the educationally disadvantaged	.	.
	3. Programs for exceptional students	.	.
2.	Learning about the world	.	.
4.	Preparation for employment or occupational training	.	.
5.	Preparation for higher education	.	.
9.	Auxiliary services to students		
	A. Transportation	etc.	etc.

Intradistrict Problems

This discussion follows the categorization of problems in public education discussed previously, beginning with issues that require action on a single program within the school district and progressing to those that require action by several school districts and other educational institutions.

An example of a program-oriented issue is the introduction of the so-called new math into the public schools. Such basic math would be an element in the first program (Program 1B). The change in this element has probably affected its cost only slightly by requiring new texts and some teacher retraining. The more significant effect has been on the success with which the schools that use the new math are now teaching basic mathematical concepts and arithmetic skills (to students and their complaining parents). What has happened, in essence, is that the objectives of Program 1B have been redefined. Now students at the elementary level are expected to develop an understanding of the fundamentals of mathematics, rather than concentrating almost solely on the development of skills of arithmetic manipulation. An alternative to this approach could have been to add the new conceptual material to much of the drill and practice work in the traditional curriculum, thereby retaining the former emphasis on manipulative skills. This would have increased the resources devoted to Program 1B and its cost.

The public debate concerning the teaching of reading provides a similar example (Program 1A). Where a change in subject matter is the basic issue, the cost of the program may be little affected, but if additional resources are to be devoted to the program (such as special teachers, additional teaching time, additional teachers and so on), the cost of the program will clearly change. Ideally, program budgeting should be just as useful in either event—whether cost or effectiveness is being changed. But for practical purposes, program budgeting is most useful for resolving problems that hinge on the allocation of resources, because the techniques and facts needed for the analysis of cost are far better developed than are those for the analysis of effectiveness.

There are at least two reasons for this. First, in the past and at present, the budget rather than performance has largely dictated decisions in the public sector. Hence, tools for analyzing the budgetary effects of decisions have been relatively well developed. Second, the availability of a universal measure, the dollar, makes it seem easy to determine the cost of a program—although the real cost in basic resources or in opportunities foregone may be hidden.

Returning to the examples of issues, one of intense current interest is the problem of improving the achievement of educationally disadvantaged children. One way to attack this problem is to provide instructional programs especially tailored to such children. These are often termed *compensatory education* (Programs 1A2 and 1B2). Compensatory programs are similar to other programs that treat a particular group of children needing educational services that are different from those provided for the general student population. Programs for special categories of students have been part of the responsibilities of the public schools for years. Programs for the physically handicapped and for the mentally retarded are examples.

The per-student cost of compensatory programs is generally high and could severely burden a district that has a high percentage of educationally disadvantaged students, if all the eligible students were to participate. But up to now, federal funds have provided almost all the additional support of such programs, so that their additional expense is not borne by the district. A number of compensatory programs have resulted in improvements in student achievement. The current question is not *whether* student achievement can be markedly increased but *how* it can be most efficiently increased.

To return to our immediate concern, such programs should have direct impact on the primary programs in terms of *both* cost and effectiveness; hence, their relevance to primary objectives can clearly be shown. Unfortunately, most recommendations for compensatory programs, such as those in the Passow report,* have included no estimates of cost or effectiveness to guide a choice among them.

Many compensatory programs include the participation of parents and other concerned citizens in activities such as summer workshops, serving as teachers' aides, assisting in preschool programs, and so on. These are examples of programs requiring the action of both the school district and the surrounding community. The cost of such activities to the school district, in view of the number of people contributing, may be very low, yet they may appreciably increase the effectiveness of the major school programs in a number of ways. It may be quite impossible to estimate what, or how significant, these changes will be until the programs have been in operation for several years.

*A. Henry Passow, *Toward Better Schools, A Summary of the Findings and Recommendations of a Study of the Schools of Washington, D.C.,* Teachers College, Columbia University, New York, September 1967.

A varied group of important problems affect the activities that cannot be allocated to primary programs. Program budgeting, for example, is concerned with problems of educational planning and has to do with the way administrative tasks are carried out. The implementation of the methods of system analysis can improve educational planning, but at the least the larger districts may need the full-time services of a system analyst. This cost should eventually be more than offset by savings accruing from more efficient planning, or from improvements in the effectiveness of program elements, or from both.

Many problems have to do with what might be considered the "mechanics" of teaching—class size, team teaching, tracking, and so on. Changes in each of these aspects of the instructional process may alter the cost or effectiveness of instruction. Some, such as tracking, may not alter monetary cost appreciably, if each tracked grade has enough total students to form a full class per track. Often such changes are thought of as being made across-the-board rather than in one or a few programs. The program structure encourages the consideration of the appropriateness of each change for each program in turn.

The way the school district is organized and operated as a whole is currently at issue. Very large districts, such as those in the big cities, are thought to be too unwieldy to be responsive to community desires, while very small districts are presumed to be unable to provide the variety of services they should. The decision on the appropriate size for a school district is usually made on the basis of desired quality or political considerations—not primarily because enlarging or reducing the district will change costs. The resolution of the problem cannot be assisted by analysis *within* a program budget, but the effect on the program budgets and the program structures of the districts involved can be major. Comparisons of existing program budgets with those that would result from changing the size of the district can be used to estimate the magnitude of these effects. The effects on the *effectiveness* of specific programs may also be large. If the effectiveness of a district is construed to include diversity as one of its desirable attributes, combining small districts may increase effectiveness. The combined districts may be able to afford more special teachers, such as for foreign languages or fine arts. On the other hand, if there are different types of programs in the smaller districts because of local control, the overall diversity may also be quite large, even though each district may have a very limited program. If greater responsiveness to community desires results in greater parental support of school activities, splitting up large districts also may increase effectiveness.

Another problem affecting the district as a whole is the question of the most desirable length for the school year. Year-round schooling, for example, would cost more than the traditional nine-month school year, but because school facilities would be used more fully, the costs would not rise in proportion to the increase in time. At the same time, in principle, students could complete basic requirements in something like three-quarters of the time currently needed. A question of this kind has implications for the cost and effectiveness of every activity in the school district and thus affects the program budget as a whole.

School integration has continued to be a salient issue in education for a number of years, despite its slow pace. Generally, it cannot be accomplished to any degree without considerable additional cost. Bussing often is an expensive or token solution unless it accompanies changes in the way the district is organized. The Berkeley School District, for example, has split its elementary schools into grades K-3 and 4-6, and uses bussing to achieve a better racial mixture at the elementary level. San Francisco has considered building educational parks, among other things, as more effective than bussing and changing district boundaries. The cost of these strategies, which primarily involve the organization and logistic aspects of the district, is felt almost entirely in support-type or nonallocated programs.

At the present time, considerable work is going on to determine how the racial mix in the school relates to the students' achievement in scholastic terms.* It appears that the achievement

---

*James S. Coleman, *et al., Equality of Educational Opportunity,* U.S. Office of Education, Washington, D.C., 1966; Robert E. Jenkins, *Educational Equality/Quality. Report No. 1. Program Alternatives,* San Francisco Unified School District, December 1967.

of students in a minority group improves as more and more of them are introduced into a school which originally contained few of them, until a plateau is reached. Thereafter, introduction of more minority children appears to cause their scholastic achievement to fall off. The possibility that such a relationship exists casts doubt on the use of a different measure of "effectiveness" of integration programs. This measure is simply the comparison of the degree with which the population in each school mirrors the racial mix in the community as a whole and has been used as a criterion of effectiveness of integration programs.* Such a criterion may conflict with primary objectives in individual schools if the "minority" group is close to being a majority in the community, because then the students may be beyond the plateau in achievement and be approaching the declining side. If such is the case, major revisions of the district's boundaries or massive compensatory programs may be preferable to school integration alone.

It is not the purpose of this book to take a stand on such questions as integration *versus* compensatory education, and the like. Both are needed, with genuine integration the eventual goal. But at this point the discussion is more narrowly oriented. The intent is to illustrate how program budgeting helps to shed light on the relationship of such a complex problem to the primary objectives of the public schools. As far as *cost* is concerned, most integration programs affect the cost of support-type activities and cannot be allocated to primary programs. As far as effectiveness is concerned, it is apparent that student achievement and racial mix *are* related in a complicated way, but this relationship casts doubt on the criterion of success that has been used in the past—that is, the racial mix in each school. If the relationship between racial mix and student achievement could be more clearly defined, programs for school integration could be judged on the basis of their contribution to the success with which the schools can attain their educational goals, rather than on the basis of the racial mix

*Carroll F. Johnson, *White Plains Racial Balance Plan*, White Plains Public Schools, White Plains, New York, July 7, 1967.

of the community. Educators and the community would then be in a better position to choose among various plans for integration.

The other reason for bringing up school integration is to point out that it is an issue that cannot be resolved by actions taken by the school district alone. Not only must the community refrain from hindering the schools' efforts to integrate, but if the problem is to be solved in any real sense, the community must actively support its own integration. School integration alone may eventuate in social integration, but many communities—Negro, Spanish-surname, and white minority groups alike—are too segregated already for school integration to be applicable without major changes in the school districts and communities.

Problems Involving More Than One District

Frequently, neighboring districts cooperate so that they can provide special programs that they could not afford separately, such as vocational and adult education programs. In cases such as these, program budgeting can show what individual programs would cost in comparison with the consolidated program, in order to estimate the anticipated gains to be had from the arrangement. Such arrangements further complicate the program structure even as they increase the contributions of the district to the community.

Problems Involving Other Educational Institutions

There are many institutions other than the school districts that have both direct and indirect effects on district operations. State departments of education and the Office of Education are examples. Frequently, the resolution of issues requires action by these institutions, and often that action is guided by comparisons among school districts—comparisons of both their cost and effectiveness. So the use of measures like assessment tests for comparative purposes becomes an issue in itself. Educators are well aware that such simple measures are abused. As suggested earlier, it is hoped that eventually program budgeting can help to provide legitimate, comparable measures of cost and effectiveness so that questions about the relative success or failure among a group of school districts can be more fairly answered.

The issue of assessment tests is, of course, part of the broad and complex problem of educational effectiveness—the issue of the relations between district programs and the success of students both in and outside of school. These relations may be unclear even for the traditional achievement tests, as the controversy surrounding the Coleman report demonstrates.* They are even more debatable as general measures of the community's social and educational health, such as the dropout rate, the unemployment rate, the rate of entrance into vocational schools or higher education, and so on. Such measures *are* related to the general effectiveness of the district's public schools, but other variables (such as the economic status of the community) must be taken into account before the relationships can be stated in a meaningful way. Far more research is needed to establish these relationships. It is to be hoped that the system-analytical aspects of program budgeting will help encourage such research.

Scope of Action Entirely Outside the District

There are many issues in education that can have marked effects on the cost or effectiveness of the operation of a school district and that are out of the control of the district entirely. A prime example was the 1967 strike of teachers in Florida—essentially a confrontation between the teachers and the governor, with the legislature acting as a third party. The school districts were damaged both during and after the strike and paid for it in higher salaries and disheartened teachers (some of whom left the state), according to the *Saturday Review*.** In cases decided primarily on political grounds, program budgeting at the school district level may do little more than show what the long-run effects may be; although, this can be an important contribution. Put another way, analysis may help clarify what the real costs (benefits lost) of a political decision might be. In this event the districts might be able to argue their side more effectively if they were armed with the

*Coleman, *op. cit.*
**James Cass, "Politics and Education in the Sunshine State," *Saturday Review*, April 20, 1968, pp. 63-65, 76-79.

planning information available from the program budgeting process.

A similar issue is that of the means to be used to support the schools—what should be the apportionment of the cost of school operation among local, state, and federal funds? As in the preceding problem, the program budget can only record the results in terms of the total funds within which the district must operate. Program budgeting at the state and federal levels, however, would be very useful as a tool for determining more effective allocation of funds among programs, states, and districts.

Summary

The preceding discussion can be summarized by displaying a distribution of the issues just touched on among the categories discussed at the outset of this chapter—some problems have been added for further illustration—as shown in Table 29. Some of the issues will affect primarily the effectiveness of the district programs (new math), others will affect primarily their cost, and some will affect both (compensatory education). Issues can be relevant to a single program (reading achievement) or can cut

Table 29

Some Examples of Issues Categorized by "Scope of Action" and Program Orientation

Categorization of Problems by Scope of Action	Examples of Issues
School district	
Program orientation:	
One or several programs	"New math," reading achievement, compensatory education, program budgeting.
Aspects common to several programs	Class size, team teaching, tracking, technological aids, pay raises.
District as a whole	Size of district, length of school year.
School district and community	Compensatory education, integration.
More than one district	Inter-district programs.
School district (or districts) and other educational institutions	Assessment tests, amount of state support of special programs, dissemination of research results.
Institutions other than school districts	Florida teachers' strike.

across several programs (tracking). They can be oriented to primary programs (reading achievement) in the curriculum or they can affect programs that are not allocable to primary programs, such as central administration (program budgeting). They can have to do with the district as a whole (district size) or can require joint action by both the district and the community (integration). Although most issues seem to require action at the district level, the resolution of some may hinge on joint action among districts (joint programs) or among districts and other educational institutions (assessment tests). And finally, some issues may have profound effects on the operation of a district, but be essentially out of its range of action (teachers' strike).

CHAPTER ELEVEN

CONSIDERATIONS IN DEVELOPING A PROGRAM BUDGETING SYSTEM

Sue A. Haggart

Introduction

The development of a program budgeting system for school district planning demands the active participation of almost all district personnel. This means participation by all levels within all functional areas—educational research, curriculum development, testing, evaluation, instruction, counseling, personnel selection, and teacher training; not just administration, finance, and budget. If the individuals in these areas are to participate in the design and development of a successful program budgeting system, they must be provided with information about the nature and purpose of the program budgeting system itself.

In this participation, emphasis must be placed on the role program budgeting is to play in the decisionmaking process of the district as well as on the requirements the program budgeting system will levy on the individuals in the district organization. If, in the design phase, there is an excessive amount of emphasis on the development of the program structure and the development of a program cost accounting nomenclature, a very real possibility exists that the result of the attempted program budgeting effort will be just another accounting system.

The purpose of this chapter is to outline some steps that might be taken to lessen this possibility. These steps will be discussed in terms of their relationship to the development of a program budgeting system. The discussion will provide some general guidelines for the development of the system; no step-by-step outline for developing it will be, or should be, provided. The reason for this will, it is hoped, be apparent as the discussion unfolds. A necessary beginning for the discussion must concern the meaning of program budgeting as used in this report.

In the imbroglio over the threat of program budgeting and the need to rescue functions, agencies, and personalities from its clutches, characteristics, or features, of program budgeting have been buried. This is partly due to the fact that program budgeting means quite different things to different people. The list of features shown below provides a means of picturing these different ideas; the features of program budgeting are rather loosely ranked from the more simple to the more complex, as follows:

- Output-related arrangement of items of expenditure by program.
- Capital budget items included by program.
- Extended time horizon for planning.
- Resource/cost model developed.*
- Criteria and measures of effectiveness developed.*
- Up-to-date financial plan.
- Mechanisms for control of funds by program.
- Organizational alignment by program.

To some people, program budgeting must include all of these features or it is not program budgeting. To others, program budgeting development stops after you have rearranged the expense budget by program, after you have extended the time horizon of the budget, or after you include capital budget items in

*These features are, of course, the basic tools needed for the systematic analysis of alternative courses of action.

the display of the expense items.

To many, program budgeting, as a tool for long-range planning, has merit even without the budgetary control aspect, if, and this is an important *if,* the system-analytical aspect has been developed. This is the point of view from which this chapter is written. The analytical capability need not be sophisticated; it can be as simple and as direct as described throughout this book. Computers and automated management information systems are useful aids, but are not prerequisite to achieving a workable system-analytical capability. A great deal can be accomplished with quantified common sense, especially when it is tempered with a conscious effort to account for the nonquantifiable facets of both the problem and potential solutions.

Program budgeting, by providing a framework for organizing the educational and operational data of school districts and by providing consistent guidelines for the analysis of the data, offers the means to make the most of the effort expended on educational planning. A program budgeting system encompassing the first six features of the above list can be designed, and effectively used, to achieve this improvement in school district planning.

Problem Areas in Developing a Program Budgeting System

As a discussion device, the features of program budgeting and the impact they collectively have on the design, implementation, and operation of a program budgeting system have been sketched in Figure 25. The effects of these impacts are grouped into four broad areas: (1) the area of data-related problems, (2) the area of people-related problems, (3) the area of system effectiveness, and (4) the area of the cost of the system. These areas are not contrived, but rather are natural focal points of concern in developing a program budgeting system.

In most cases, additional features cause an increase in all of the problem areas. An exception might be, for example, the successful development of a resource/cost model. In the near-term activity in the development of the program budgeting system, this feature would generate significant data-related and people-related

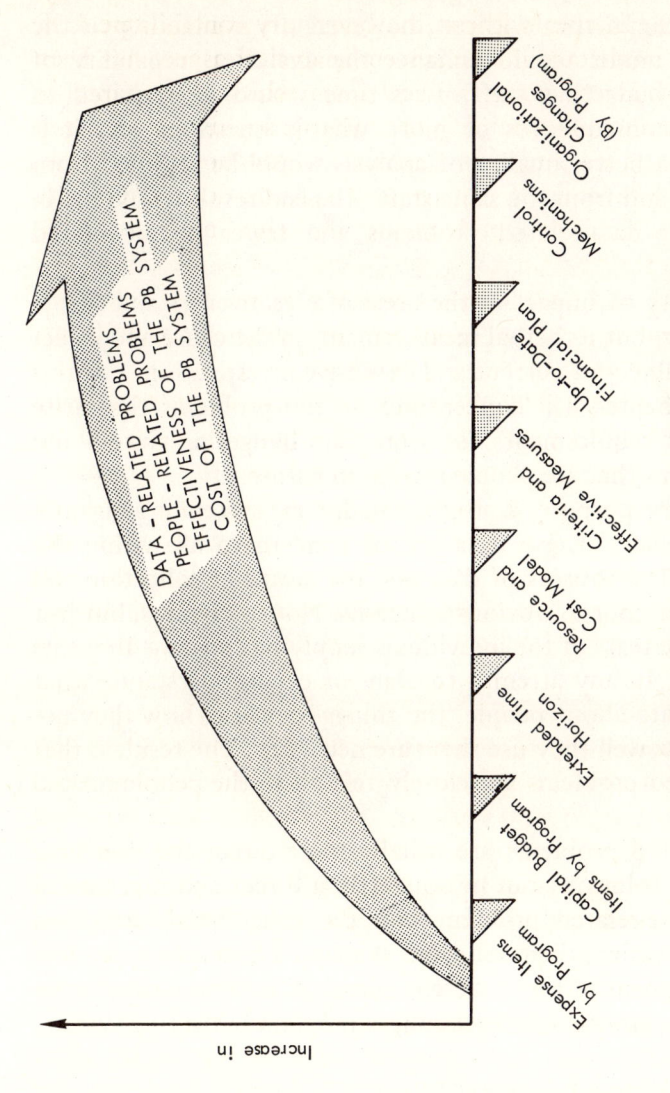

Figure 25

The Impact of Features of a Program Budgeting System on Its Design, Implementation, and Operation

problems; constructing the model demands an extensive data collection effort and, more importantly, model builders are a scarce resource. In the long run, however, the availability of the resource/cost model would enhance the analytical capability of the program budgeting staff. Less time would be required to examine the consequences of more what-if questions and it is possible that a better quality of analysis would be attained from the same data and from the same staff. The end result would be, in essence, fewer data-related problems and fewer people-related problems.

The reality of impact in the areas of effectiveness and cost is relatively clear, but its actual measurement, in the cause and effect sense, is the subject of current and extensive investigation. For this reason, this chapter will concentrate on the problems that arise from the data requirements for a program budgeting system and on the problems that are people-related in nature.

By its very purpose, a program budgeting system is a gigantic consumer of data. These data are of concern to all within the organization. The sources of data and the means of collection and analysis are, of course, obvious concerns. Not so obvious, but just as real, are the fears of the individuals supplying the data about its intended uses. In any attempt to plan—or even understand—what is going on, data about people, the things they use, how they use them, and how well they use them are necessary. The result is that the data-related problems are closely related to the people-related problems.

Data-related problems are usually more direct and mechanical, and their solutions can be sought in a direct and mechanical manner. People-related problems, on the other hand, are often subtle and pervasive; their solutions demand a different approach. A basic component of this different approach is "knowledge"—the catalyst in the process of developing a program budgeting system.

Program Budgeting Educational Effort

As mentioned earlier, almost all personnel of the district should participate in the development of the program budgeting system. This means that all personnel should know what is happening; they should know what their role is in the development of the system; they should know what demands the system might make on their operations; and they should be encouraged to have a voice in the development of the system. Knowledge of this nature demands an educational effort that parallels the development of the system. This is true whether or not the development of the system is being done by persons within or outside the institution.

The extent of the educational effort should be broad enough to include all levels of the district's organization; it should not be limited to the top administrative staff. For example, the district personnel concerned with the development of criteria for the evaluation of educational innovation, compensatory education programs, or other educational changes have a vital part in the development of the program budgeting system; they contribute to the system-analytical aspect of program budgeting that makes the system more than just another accounting system. The effectiveness of their contribution can be increased if the educational effort includes information about their interface with the design and operation of the program budgeting system.

Coordination of Development Activities

Another facet of the educational effort that parallels the development of the program budgeting system deals with coordinating the activities of development. It is necessary to spell out who does what and with what authority. For the most part, this is a people-related problem area. And again knowledge serves as the catalyst in the process; the more the members of the organization know about what is expected of them, and why, the less are they inclined to jealously guard their bailiwick of information or to wait for the finished product and then react. They all become participants in the development of the system and, through this participation, increase the likelihood that they will be users of the operational system.

In this coordinated effort, it is logical to identify the main and supporting cast of characters. It is suggested that, once the group has been designated, every attempt be made to quite frankly publicize its existence, to define its authority and to support its task. The group should be clearly visible within the organization and its members should cut across organizational lines. In addition, the group should be recognized as having some operational life after the design and implementation phases of the program budgeting system; a temporary committee has rather obvious shortcomings. One of the main functions of the group would be to organize the educational effort described earlier.

Another function of the group (and also part of the educational effort) is the development of the techniques that enable the district administrators to use the program budgeting system output. This means a definition of the role of program budgeting in the decisionmaking process as discussed in Chapter One.

Developing an Analytical Capability

There is another problem area that is partly data-related, but for the most part people-related. That is the development and maintenance of an analytical capability. In most current efforts to develop a program budgeting system, the lack of an analytical capability has been identified as a major problem. The best way to solve the problem is still largely a matter of conjecture. One possible approach might be the most direct—just begin, going from the more simple to the more complex techniques and, in the process, learn. Concurrent with this approach, two activities would be carried on. One activity would be the initiation of a training program. The other activity would be an attempt to separate those analytical techniques required for the routine operation of the program budgeting system from those required for the development of supporting models (student flow model, for example) and of estimating relationships. Those techniques required for the routine operation of the program budgeting system would be the first area of study in the training program. This effort should be reinforced with the development of the more complex techniques by a central analytical staff. There are, of course, many trade-offs within the different approaches to developing and maintaining an analytical capability. The point is that solutions to the problem are well within the state-of-the-art.

We have discussed the steps that can be taken to ease the development of a program budgeting system. In review, these are:

1. The initiation of an educational effort concerned with what program budgeting is, what effect it will have on the individuals of the district, and how individuals of the district can help in its development.
2. The setting up of a coordination group with a delineation of its authority and an identification of its role in the development and operation of the program budgeting system.
3. The development of strategies for attaining an analytical capability.

Activity Areas in Developing the System

For discussion purposes, a distinction has been made between data-related problems and people-related problems; this distinction remains a useful guide in seeking solutions to the overall problems of developing a program budgeting system. It should be obvious that solving the people-related problems as a first order of business would have a direct effect on the magnitude of the data-related problems.

In the schematic of activity areas in the development of a program budgeting system shown in Figure 26, it is rather easy to trace the origin and flow of data requirements. Less clear, however, is the "who does what" requirement so necessary to the effective development of a program budgeting system. In some respects, the people who possess the data can be identified as the starting point for the "who does what" requirement; the important idea is to bring these individuals into the development of the system at an early time.

For example, there should be lines of communication set up between the individuals concerned with the development of curricular changes, individuals concerned with evaluation of educational programs, and individuals with knowledge of the resources needed to achieve a particular activity or program

INVENTORY OF EDUCATIONAL SYSTEM

- Describe student population
- Describe resource base

  Personnel
  Staff support
  Facilities
  Equipment
  Supplies
  Other

- Describe community profile

  Socio-economic
  Demographic

- Define management structure

  Administration hierarchy
  Decision process
  Information system

- Determine data availability

DEVELOPMENT OF STRUCTURAL ASPECT

- Define broad goals
- Define operational objectives
- Identify activities
- Define programs
- Define program elements
- Develop program structure

  (Group activities)

DEVELOPMENT OF ANALYTICAL ASPECT

- Determine resource requirements
- Determine cost of activities
- Develop program cost estimates
- Develop estimating relationships
- Determine criteria of effectiveness
- Determine measures of effectiveness
- Identify alternatives
- Evaluate alternatives

RESOURCE AND COST MODEL DEVELOPMENT

DEVELOPMENT OF DATA BASE

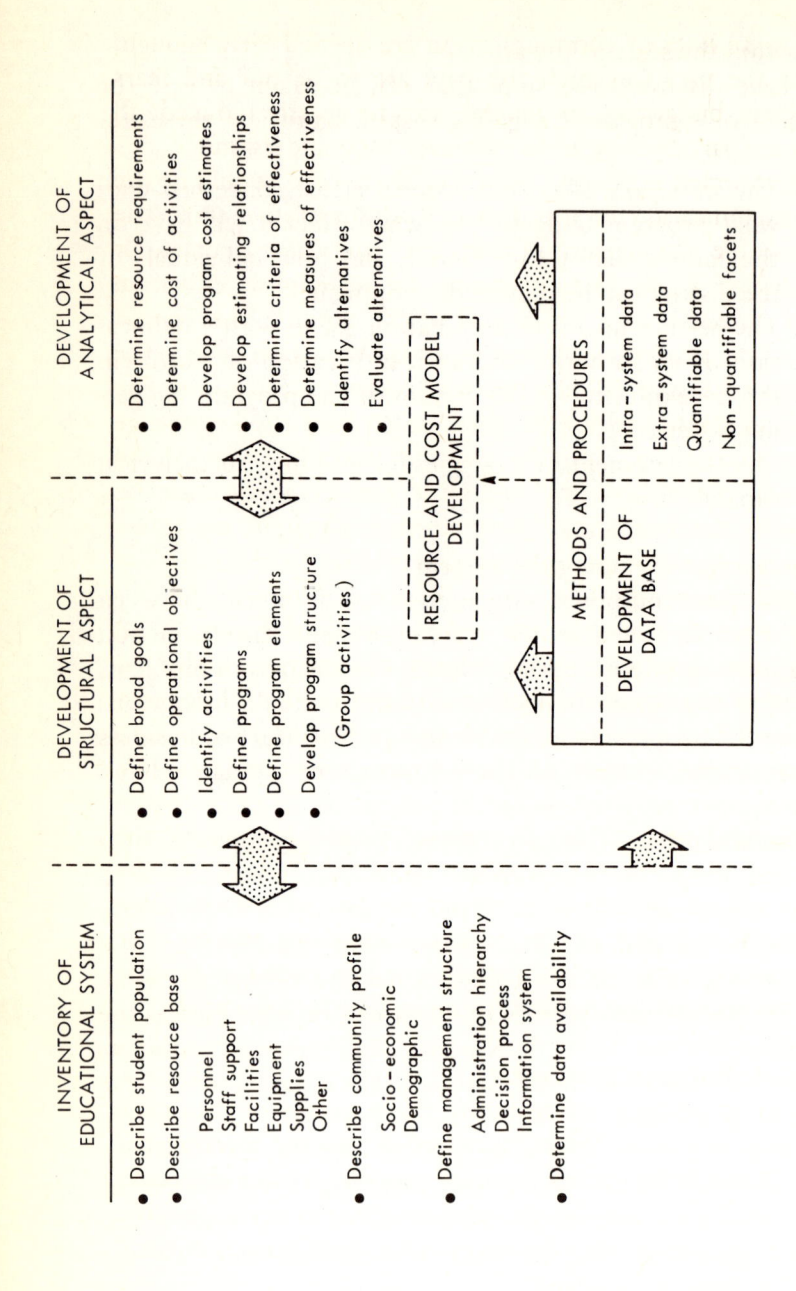

METHODS AND PROCEDURES

Intra-system data
Extra-system data
Quantifiable data
Non-quantifiable facets

Figure 26

Schematic of Activity Areas in the Development of a Program Budgeting System

change. If these lines of communication are opened early enough, fears about the uses to which the data are to be put and fears about program budgeting, in general, can be greatly reduced; all individuals are participating in an endeavor they understand.

Not mentioned explicitly, but certainly needed, would be the line of communication to the district's administrative staff—the level responsible for ensuring that the particular activity or program change is, in fact, a means to accomplish either an operational objective or a broad goal of the district. This line of communication, as well as all lines of communication among the activity areas of Figure 26, is a two-way communication line. The lower levels of district administration, which have the knowledge to generate alternatives, must be aware of the objectives of the district; and, conversely, the top-level district staff must be provided with the output of the analytical effort of the lower levels. It is through this process that the evaluation and selection of alternatives is accomplished.

If we were to rearrange the activity areas of Figure 26 to reflect the "who does what" requirement, the activities under the development of the structural area would be primarily the concern of the top-level decisionmakers and planners; efforts by individuals in the other activity areas would flow to this structural area. In a sense, all the other activities would be supportive to the activities in the structural area. This, of course, would be during the developmental phase of the program budgeting system. In the operational system all activities would be part of the decision-making process and part of the program budgeting process. The purpose is, as has been stressed throughout this book, to provide the organized information needed for more informed decisions.

Developing the Program Structure

Program structuring—categorizing the activities of education into programs based on their contribution toward meeting the objectives of education—is an iterative process. As the objectives are initially identified and the program structure is developed, the process serves to clarify the objectives. This clarification, in turn, facilitates the program structuring.

The process is continued, with the goal being to achieve a workable program structure. The program structure then provides a format for the program budget. The program budget, itself, is a display of the expenditure consequences, over time, of activities resulting from current policies and decisions. Combining this with the program plan that includes output measures results in an organized information base—an informational framework—that is useful in assessing current programs and in evaluating the alternatives in terms of their impact on the cost and effectiveness of all the programs. This is in keeping with the overall concept of PPB as a management tool in educational planning—the purpose of the planning being not only to achieve better educational results but also more effective use of resources.

The activities of program structuring and their relationship to other activities in implementing PPB are shown in Figure 26. The central location of these activities involved in developing the program structure is not accidental. The structure is based on the needs, the goals, the objectives, and the activities of the district.

The program structure, through programs, relates activities (and their resources) to objectives. The meaning of the word "objective" as used in this discussion of the program structuring process should be made clear. The term "objective" is used as a broad, but still measurable, goal or purpose rather than a performance objective or behavioral objective. Schematically, the nature of the program structure might look like that in Figure 27. The program structure organizes information about cost and effectiveness of programs, subprograms, and program elements. This organization reflects the goals and purpose of the educational system.

Both the nature and the role of the program structure have changed since PPB was first introduced. The change can be traced through the directives of the former Bureau of the Budget issued since 1965. In Directive 66-3 of October 12, 1965, the program structure was "a series of output-oriented categories which, together, cover the total work of the agency." In Directive 68-2 of July 18, 1967, this statement was made: "The program structure groups the activities of an agency into a set of program categories

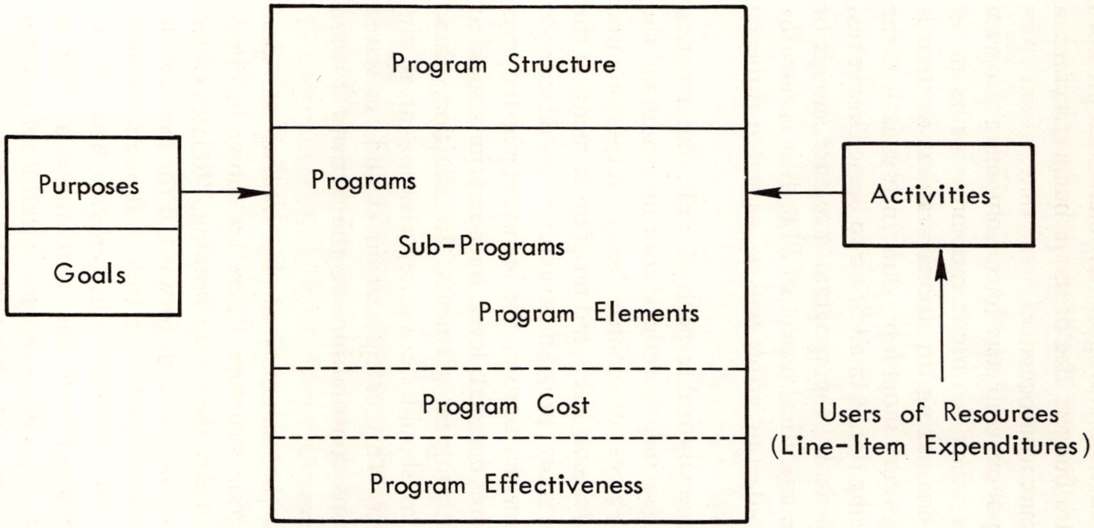

```
┌─────────────┐
│  Activities │
│             │
└──────┬──────┘
       │
Users of Resources
(Line-Item Expenditures)
       ▼
┌──────────────────────────────────┐
│ Program  │         │      │      │
│ Structure│         │      │      │
│          │Sub-Programs    │      │
│          │         │Program     │
│          │         │Elements    │
│          │         │      │Program
│          │         │      │Cost  │
│  Programs│         │      │      │
│          │         │      │Program
│          │         │      │Effectiveness
└──────────────────────────────────┘
       ▲
       │
┌──────┴──────┐
│Purposes│Goals│
└─────────────┘
```

Figure 27

Nature of the Program Structure

that facilitates analytic comparisons of the costs and effectiveness of alternative programs." Analysis is explicitly mentioned. In April of 1968, Directive 68-9 added the idea of the program structure in support of the decisionmaking process.

Thus, today there is an emphasis on developing a program structure that is *closely tied to the decisions to be made* at different levels of decisionmaking. In decisions about matters of purpose and direction, what should be done? How is it being done? How well is it being done? In addition to being closely tied to the decisions to be made, the program structure should be designed to support the analytical aspect of PPB. If it is not, the result of the program budgeting effort will be, as stated earlier, a new accounting system.

In supporting the analytical aspect of PPB, the program structure should be organized to reflect information about the main areas of choice—areas of choice being output-oriented programs at the higher decision levels and program elements at the lower decision levels. In short, program structures should provide informational support for decisions at the highly aggregated level and at the lower, more detailed level of operation, such as particular instructional program elements. In addition, these output-oriented programs should be a categorization of all the activities of the district. This categorization should, as stated earlier, be based on the contribution of the activity toward meeting specific objectives.

These points can be summarized by looking at some characteristics of a program structure. These are shown in Figure 28. The characteristics under the broad heading, "Relates Objectives and Activities," are fairly straightforward, if the usage of the word "objective" is recalled. The fourth item, "allows for growth of flexibility," will be discussed later. In general, these are the characteristics of a program structure that make a program structure, and the resulting program budget, a useful information display. Information is provided about what is being done and how the resources are allocated.

The characteristics listed under "Supports Decisionmaking" require more explanation. An explanation is most easily provided

Relates Objectives and Activities

    o Identifies objectives
    o Provides measurable objectives
    o Includes all activities
    o Allows for growth (flexibility)

Supports Decisionmaking

    o Illuminates priorities
    o Highlights trade-off areas
    o Promotes realistic analysis
    o Provides for imaginative change
    o Is manageable

Figure 28

*Characteristics of a
Program Structure*

by asking questions about a few currently used or illustrative program structures. The discussion of these program structures will then be followed by the presentation of a proposed program structure for education.

The HEW program budget is shown, in part, in Figure 29 and an "Illustrative Program Structure for a State Department of Education" is shown in Figure 30. Notice not only the broadness of the programs but also the fact that the programs reflect the areas of choice within the jurisdiction of the different levels—the federal and the state levels. Each of the few broad programs of these two program structures covers many program elements whose activities contribute toward meeting the purpose of the broad program. Notice the relatively small number of programs that encompass all the activities. Six programs in the "E" of HEW cover an expenditure of approximately $4 billion. In the illustrative state-level program structure, there is only a slight increase in the number of programs. But again, these programs are the areas of choice within the jurisdiction of a state department of education.

PROGRAM DISTRIBUTION OF BUDGET AUTHORITY

(In $ millions)

Program Category and Subcategory	1968 Actual	1969 Estimate	1970 Estimate
Education			
Development of basic skills	2,380.0	2,289.3	2,179.0
Development of vocational and occupational skills	269.3	268.3	304.1
Development of academic and professional skills	1,330.9	966.2	1,020.7
Library and community development	87.9	86.8	96.0
General research (nonallocable research)	25.7	25.6	31.1
General support	35.5	41.3	45.3
Total	4,138.3	3,677.5	3,676.2
Health			
Development of health resources	2,315.0	2,185.7	2,395.6
Prevention and control of health problems	457.1	480.8	480.5
Provision of health services	7,345.7	9,980.3	10,739.0
General support	48.5	54.9	64.4
Total	10,166.5	12,701.8	13,679.4

Figure 29

Partial Program Budget for the Department of Health, Education, and Welfare

o Provide general support of school districts
      Support for current operations
      Support for facilities acquisition
o Equalize educational capability of school districts
o Support special programs
      Designated categories of students
      Designated programs
o Provide central educational services
o Provide central administrative services
o Support educational research and development
o Coordinate Federal programs
o Administration

Figure 30

Illustrative Program Structure for a State Department of Education

Considerations in Developing a Program Budgeting System   235

The number of programs has been mentioned. Why is this important? Remember that the program budget is, in part, a display device geared to organize information in support of the decisionmaker. The decisionmaker is a human being with a limit in his ability to comprehend and act on the information in a massive display of detailed data about every facet of numerous activities. This logical and necessary limitation on the number of programs in a program structure translates into one of the characteristics of a good or workable program structure—a manageable number of programs.

The Pearl River program structure is shown in Figure 31. Imagine a five-year projection of cost out to the right of the program structure itself—the program budget. What does this reveal about the priorities within the district? Is the planner really interested in knowing how much is spent on Basic Instructional Services as opposed to Supporting Educational Services and Other Supporting Services? Is there a reasonable basis for trade-off analysis? Is there an interest in making trade-offs among these three programs? It is, of course, possible to do cost-effectiveness

Program Code	Program Description
	Basic Instructional Services
60	Language arts, including English and reading
61	Science and health
62	Mathematics
63	Social studies
64	Physical education, intramural, and interscholastic athletics
65	Business
66	Foreign language
67	Unified arts, including industrial arts, homemaking, driver education, and mechanical drawing
68	Art
69	Music
70	Special and vocational education
	Supporting Educational Services
71	Library services
72	Guidance and psychological services
73	Medical services
74	Adult education and summer school
	Other Supporting Services
80	Pupil transportation
81	Operation and maintenance of plant
82	District management
83	Debt service
84	School lunch

Figure 31

Pearl River Program Structure

analysis *within* the programs listed under each of the broad categories. For example, how effectively is mathematics taught using the current level of resources and instructional methods? What alternative methods might be developed and evaluated? And so on. This goes back to the statement that the program structure should be designed to provide informational support for all levels of decisionmaking.

Analysis at this program element level is necessary. In fact, most of the "analysis" is done at this level. But, the structuring of the program elements into subprograms and then into programs that are goal-oriented increases the information needed to make broad decisions *from a more informed position.* Careful selection of the programs will immediately result in a pay-off by showing where the resources are being spent.

Another question can be asked: Does the Pearl River program structure provide for imaginative change or is the status quo locked in because the program structure reflects subjects that are being taught today and reflects the organization of the school district? The program structure should allow for growth by showing the impact of adding new "subjects" at the program element levels. The total program impact in terms of cost and effectiveness should be visible without having to revamp the basic program structure. If all the educational, or more precisely the instructional, programs are grouped together, very little additional information about the educational impact of particular changes is provided to the decisionmaker. In order to provide this information, a goal-oriented program structure is needed for the instructional activities of the district. This structure should enable the decisionmaker or curriculum developer to focus attention on more narrowly defined educational problem areas.

But there is still another question: Does this program structure and the resulting program budget convey sufficient information about how resources are being spent to achieve the *educational* goals of the district? Or about how well the resources are being spent? What program structure helps provide support of this nature to the educational decisionmaker? If the structure is "arranged" by level, then the assumption might well be: The goal

Considerations in Developing a Program Budgeting System 237

is to advance students from one level to another. If this is the goal of education, then these program structures make some sense.

If, however, more reasonable goals can be translated into program objectives, then the activities of the educational system can be categorized into programs based on their contribution toward meeting the objectives of education.

There has to be some middle course between looking at the total instructional program cost as one lump sum and looking at the instructional program cost fragmented into a multitude of costs by individual subject. This means the effort should concentrate on developing a program structure for the instructional program, per se.

In Chapter Two, Development of a Program Structure, an attempt was made to do just that. As shown in Figure 32, the instructional program is grouped into five major programs based on what the student is learning. The other programs concerned with the management and support of the educational process are also categorized by a commonality of purpose. In some cases, these non-instructional or non-learning based programs have

```
Learning Fundamental Intellectual Skills Program
    Language and Communication Skills (subprogram)
    Quantitative and Reasoning Skills (subprogram)
    Study Skills (subprogram)
Learning About the World
    Learning about U.S. and Other Societies
    Learning about the Physical World and Living Things
    Learning about Literature and the Arts
    Learning Knowledge and Skills for Everyday Application
Development of the Individual Physically, Socially, and Emotionally
    Physical Development
    Development of Means of Self-expression
    Development of Interpersonal Relationships
Learning Knowledge and Skills in Preparation for Future Employment
    or Occupational Training
    (classified by occupation)
Learning Academic Subjects to Prepare for Higher Education
    (classified by academic subject)
Assessment, Guidance, and Counseling Services
Program Development and Evaluation
Instructional Resources and Media Services
Auxiliary Services to Students
    Health Services
    Transportation
    Food Service
Community Services
```

Figure 32

Programs Organized by What Is to Be Learned and by Other Student-Oriented Objectives (Traditional subjects are program elements.)

objectives of their own. In other cases, workload-type measures are used as measures of program effectiveness.

To repeat a few facts from Chapter Three, The Program Budget and the Traditional Budget: The program structure used as the format of the program budget, as shown in Figure 33, provides information about the instructional and non-instructional activities of the district. On the other hand, the traditional budget, as shown in Figure 34, provides information about the size of the total budget and about the line items of expenditure. It provides almost no information about what is happening in the educational component of the district's expenditure. A better picture of the difference in information content is shown in Figure 35—"A Crosswalk Example." The traditional budget information is given in the first three columns. Notice that the Account No. 200, "Instruction," is a lump sum of $15.9 million. In a program budget, the dollars shown as the total instruction line item would be shown according to the specific instructional programs of the program structure.

In Figure 28, shown earlier, several characteristics of a program structure were listed. These characteristics were the guidelines for designing the program structure shown in Figure 32. In general, most of the characteristics of a good program structure are present in the program structure. The program structure allows for growth by providing stable, goal-oriented programs that are sufficiently broad to encompass a wide variety of program elements (subjects, for example) in the future and are still adequately definitive to provide a basis for measuring how well program objectives are being met.

In order to use the program structure as a basis for analysis at the *program* level, it must be possible to specify objective-oriented programs and measures of effectiveness, either single or multiple. It can be argued, rather strongly and rightly, that precise specification of either the objective-oriented, broad programs or their measures of effectiveness is a long way off. Specification adequate for appropriate analysis at the program element level is possible. In the analytic middle, so to speak, is the subprogram level. Because of these difficulties at the program level, analysis at

Program Number	Program Description	Year 1	2	3	4	5
		($ thousands)				
1	Learning Intellectual Skills	4,655	4,905	5,265	5,630	6,025
2	Learning About the World	4,445	4,785	5,130	5,484	5,875
3	Developing the Individual	2,700	2,920	3,135	3,350	3,590
4	Preparation for Employment	805	865	930	995	1,070
5	Preparation for Higher Education	665	720	765	820	880
	Direct Instruction Total	13,270	14,195	15,225	16,280	17,440
6	Assessment, Guidance & Counseling	990	1,035	1,105	1,185	1,275
7	Development & Evaluation	425	455	490	525	560
8	Instructional Resource & Media Services	250	240	260	275	295
	Instructional Support Total	1,665	1,730	1,855	1,985	2,130
9	Auxiliary Services	1,085	1,185	1,310	1,445	1,595
10	Community Services	700	110	110	115	120
11	Operations & Maintenance	2,840	3,050	3,190	3,480	3,750
12	Capital Outlay	450	725	1,325	1,695	2,195
13	Administration	2,560	2,805	3,010	3,215	3,445
	Total	22,570	23,800	26,025	28,215	30,675

Physical Data		(Numbers)				
Students						
	Elementary	20,000	20,510	21,510	22,180	23,070
	Junior High	7,500	7,780	8,090	8,415	8,750
	Senior High	6,500	7,070	7,355	7,650	8,155
	Total	34,000	35,360	36,775	38,245	39,775
Teachers		1,260	1,310	1,365	1,416	1,473
Total personnel		1,900	1,975	2,055	2,135	2,220
Schools		45	46	47	49	51
Square feet, in thousands		3,250	3,285	3,320	3,450	3,570

Figure 33

Program Budget Example

Account Number	Description	Cost ($ thousands)	Percent of Total Current Expense
100	Administration	580	2.6
200	Instruction	15,945	72.2
300	Health	290	1.4
500	Transportation	280	1.3
600	Operations	1,760	8.0
700	Maintenance	915	4.1
800	Fixed Charges	1,100	5.0
	Subtotal	20,870	94.6
900	Food Service	500	3.2
1100	Community Service	700	2.2
1200	Subtotal, Current Expense	22,070	100.0
1200	Capital Outlay	500	
	Subtotal, Current Expense and Capital Outlay	22,570	
1400	Transfers	250	
	Subtotal, Expenditures	22,820	
	Reserves	3,000	
	Total, Expenditures and Reserves	25,820	

Figure 34

Summary of Traditional Expenditures and Reserves Budget

Account Number	Account	Total	Instructional Programs[a]						Noninstructional Programs						
			1	2	3	4	5	Assessment, Guidance, and Counseling 6	Development and Evaluation 7	Instructional Resources and Media 8	Auxiliary Services 9	Community Service 10	Operation and Maintenance 11	Capital Outlay 12	Administration 13
100	Administration	580	--	--	--	--	--	--	50	--	--	--	--	--	530
200	Instruction	15,945	4,410	4,210	2,560	760	630	915	355	215	--	--	--	--	1,890
300	Health	290	--	--	--	--	--	--	--	--	290	--	--	--
500	Transportation	280	--	--	--	--	--	--	--	--	280	--	--	--	--
600	Operation	1,760	--	--	--	--	--	--	--	--	--	--	1,760	--	--
700	Maintenance	915	--	--	--	--	--	--	--	--	--	--	915	--	--
800	Fixed Charges	1,100	245	235	140	45	35	50	20	10	15	--	165	--	140
	Subtotal	20,870													
900	Food Service	500	--	--	--	--	--	--	--	--	500	--	--	--	--
1100	Community Service	700	--	--	--	--	--	--	--	--	--	700	--	--	--
	Total Current Expense	22,070	4,655	4,455	2,700	805	665	965	425	225	1,085	700	2,840	--	2,560
1200	Capital Outlay[b]	500	--	--	--	--	--	25	--	25	--	--	--	450	--
	Total Current Expense and Capital Outlay	22,570	4,655	4,455	2,700	805	665	990	425	250	1,085	700	2,840	450	2,560
	Percentage of Current Expense[c]	100.0	21.1	20.1	12.2	3.6	3.0	4.5	1.9	1.1	4.9	3.1	12.9		11.6

[a]Instructional Programs: 1. Learning Fundamental Intellectual Skills
2. Learning About the World
3. Development of the Individual Physically, Socially, and Emotionally
4. Learning Knowledge and Skills in Preparation for Future Employment or Occupational Training
5. Learning Academic Subjects to Prepare for Higher Education

[b]Provision of physical plant and equipment.

[c]These are percentages of "Current Expense" excluding "Capital Outlay." This conforms to current practice.

Figure 35

Crosswalk Example
(In $ thousands)

the subprogram level offers a more productive path to getting the most out of a program budgeting effort.

Objectives at the subprogram level are easier to specify, measures of effectiveness are easier to determine, and both are easier to agree on. Analysis at this level should serve as a means to achieving a better definition of the goals of education and should aid the search for measures of effectiveness. This will be realized if analysis is jarred out of the comfortable area of program elements or subjects, especially out of the reading-mathematics rut.

The program structure should be designed to support analysis for educational planning. In turn, the needs of analysis should be considered in developing a program structure for education. The goal of the program structuring aspect of program budgeting for education is to develop a workable program structure that provides the information necessary for all levels of planning. This goal can be realized if the program structuring effort is done concurrently with the analysis of educational alternatives and with the development of an analytical capability.

APPENDIX A

ALLOCATION OF STUDENTS AMONG GROUPS*

Gerald C. Sumner

The allocation of students described in this appendix was performed as part of Rand's study of the San Jose Unified School District's Project R-3, a demonstration program conducted under the auspices of the California State Department of Compensatory Education as provided for in Assembly Bill 938. The technique provided the means for establishing classroom heterogeneity among the students in the project. Although the description is specific to Project R-3, the method generalizes to a rather flexible range of allocation requirements; this flexibility is also discussed.

Before the semester was underway, it was necessary to divide the seventh graders into class-size groups. The groups were to be internally heterogeneous with respect to sex and scholastic abilities, but between-group differences were to be small; thus, there would be no semblance of tracking and each group could be regarded, to some extent, as a separate replication of the same

---

*This paper was presented to the Association of California Administrators in Compensatory Education held at the Oakland Hilton Hotel, March 8, 1971, and published by the Rand Corporation as P-4584, March 1971.

Allocation of Students Among Groups

experiment. The guiding strategy was to establish an objectively reproducible selection procedure, a method free of intentional or unintentional bias.

There were to be 12 groups of equal size; each group would have proportional representation by sex and each would represent a full range of reading and arithmetic abilities as manifested in raw scores achieved on the CAT, which was administered in January.

At the start of the semester (February 2) 253 students were enrolled (136 boys and 117 girls). Five students had not taken all of the CAT tests, but were assigned proxy scores.* The mean and median raw scores and the raw score distributions were as follows:

	Mean	Median
Total reading	57.52	53
Total arithmetic	47.26	44

The raw score distributions are displayed below:

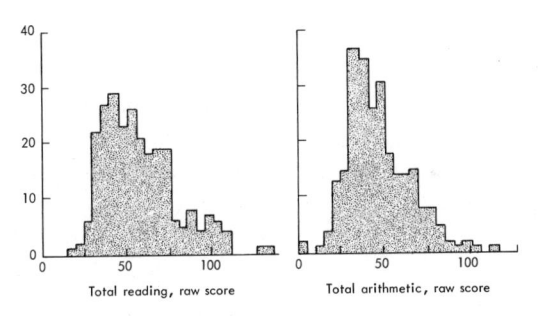

*Proxies for three students were extrapolated from relative placements in the Title I testing administered the previous October as follows:

$$_i\tilde{X}_J = \bar{X}_J + S_J \left(\frac{_iX_o - \bar{X}_o}{S_o} \right)$$

where $_i\tilde{X}_J$ = proxy for the *i*th student

$\bar{X}_J$ = mean score of the January testing

S_J = standard deviation of the January testing

We now describe the scheme used to allocate 252 students into 12 groups of 21, such that each group contains 3 students from each of 7 reading-ability rankings (reading septiles) and from each of 7 arithmetic-ability rankings (arithmetic septiles).* The remaining student was to be arbitrarily assigned to one of the groups.

The students were first ordered according to the reading raw scores. The top 36 students were assigned to the first septile, the next 36 students were assigned to the second septile, and so on down to the last (seventh) septile. Each student was assigned a number corresponding to his reading septile. Next, the students were similarly divided into arithmetic septiles, and assigned

---

$\overline{X}_o$ = mean score of the October testing

S_o = standard deviation of the October testing

$_iX_o$ = score received by the *ith* student on the October test.

Since the previous test included only Title I students, who presumably would score lower on the average, the respective assignments probably are positively biased.

Because the other two students were not included in the October testing, the January test data corresponding to the nonmissing score were substituted. For example, if the reading score was missing for the *ith* student:

$$_i\widetilde{X}_{read} = \overline{X}_{read} + S_{read} \left(\frac{_iX_{math} - \overline{X}_{math}}{S_{math}} \right)$$

*The choice of 7 ability rankings (rather than, say, 5 or 10 rankings) was primarily a matter of convenience. For the problem at hand, the number of rankings could have been as small as 2 or as large as 21. Smaller numbers would provide less heterogeneity and larger numbers would allow less freedom for allocating the sexes. The "sensible range" for this case would therefore lie between 5 and 12. Since the allocation procedure is more straightforward when the number of rankings is an exact divisor of the group size, the likely candidate for this case is 7 rankings.

Allocation of Students Among Groups 245

corresponding identifiers. Using the two-digit identifier thus assigned, the joint distribution of students across the two ability measures was charted on a 7 by 7 matrix:

Arithmetic Septiles

	1	2	3	4	5	6	7	
1	21	8	4	2	0	1	0	36
2	7	11	11	3	2	1	1	36
3	5	9	4	7	4	5	2	36
4	2	5	5	12	3	6	3	36
5	1	1	8	8	3	6	9	36
6	0	2	1	3	16	9	5	36
7	0	0	3	1	8	8	16	36
	36	36	36	36	36	36	36	252

(Reading Septiles)

The numbers in the cells indicate how many students were in the respective categories; numbers on the margins provide row (reading septile) and column (arithmetic septile) totals.

A distribution pattern for each of the 12 groups was designated (in sequence) by choosing 3 non-zero cells from each row and from each column of the matrix.

After each pattern was designated, the cell numbers were decremented by the number of selections from the respective cells and the marginal totals were adjusted to reflect the new sums. When designating any particular pattern, it was permissible to select the same cell more than once; the selection rules were:

1. If the cell number was zero, the cell could not be chosen;
2. If the cell number was non-zero but less than one-third the margin total, it could be chosen once;
3. If the number was one-third the margin total, the cell had to be chosen;
4. If the number was between one-third and two-thirds of

the margin total, the cell had to be chosen once but could also be chosen twice;

5. If the number was two-thirds the margin total, the cell had to be chosen twice.

These rules guaranteed that pattern designation would proceed in such a manner that the 12 patterns could be exactly accommodated by the 252 students. Furthermore, the rules precluded the necessity to select a cell three times and minimized the need for double selections. Within these restrictions, care was taken to distribute each pattern fairly evenly over the matrix. The selection of the first two and last two patterns is indicated by the asterisks in the illustration below:

Pattern 1

21*	8*	4	2	0	1	0	36
7*	11	11*	3	2	1	1	36
5	9	4	7*	4	5*	2	36
2	5	5*	12*	3*	6	3	36
1	1	8*	8*	3	6	9*	36
0	2	1	3	16*	9*	5*	36
0	0	3	1	8*	8*	16*	36
36	36	36	36	36	36	36	252

Pattern 2

19*	7*	4*	2	0	1	0	33
6*	10*	10*	3	2	1	1	33
5*	8*	4	6*	4	4	2	33
2	5	4	11*	2*	6*	3	33
1	1	7*	7*	3	6	8*	33
0	2	1	3	15*	8*	4*	33
0	0	3	1	7*	7*	15*	33
33	33	33	33	33	33	33	231

Pattern 11

4*	1	1*	0	0	0	0	6
1*	1	1*	1	0	1*	1	6
0	1*	1	2*	1	1*	0	6
1	1*	1	2*	0	1*	0	6
0	1	1	1*	1*	1	1*	6
0	1*	0	0	4*	1	0	6
0	0	1*	0	0	1	4*	6
6	6	6	6	6	6	6	42

Pattern 12

2*	1*	0	0	0	0	0	3
0	1*	0	1*	0	0	1*	3
0	0	1*	1*	1*	0	0	3
1*	0	1*	1*	0	0	0	3
0	1*	1*	0	0	1*	0	3
0	0	0	0	2*	1*	0	3
0	0	0	0	1*	2*	3
3	3	3	3	3	3	3	21

Allocation of Students Among Groups

The next task was to match students to the patterns designated. The patterns were taken one at a time and students with identifiers matching the chosen cells were selected. This selection was arbitrary (unsystematic) except that the ratio of boys to girls was either 11 to 10 or 12 to 9 and both sexes were distributed fairly evenly over the pattern. The extra student (number 253) was arbitrarily assigned to the ninth group; his test scores would have placed him in cell 6.6.

Finally, the 12 groups were shuffled and assigned the labels used in the R-3 program (A: 1, 2, 3, 4. B: 1, 2, 3, 4. C: 1, 2, 3, 4). The 12 groups are illustrated, along with the R-3 labels, in Figure 36 in the order of designation. Boys are indicated by B's, girls by G's.

It may be of interest to examine how well this procedure performed its task of allocating students into groups that uniformly mirror the central tendency and variability of the overall student population. Table 30 provides comparisons with respect to reading and arithmetic scores. The groups are identified by their R-3 codes. Means and standard deviations are given for each of the 12 groups, for each of the 3 lettered groupings (A, B and C), and for the overall population.

It is also interesting to compare the variability of the group means with that which might have occurred had the students been allocated by simple random methods. The standard deviation of the means of the groups is computed as

$$\sqrt{\frac{\sum_{g=1}^{12} (\bar{X}_g - \bar{X}_o)^2}{12}} \begin{matrix} = 1.6 \text{ (reading)} \\ = 1.6 \text{ (arithmetic)} \end{matrix}$$

where $\bar{X}_o$ is the mean for all 253 students. Had groups been allocated at random, one could have expected the standard deviations to be in the neighborhood of

$$\frac{S_o}{\sqrt{12}} \begin{cases} = 4.6 \text{ (reading)} \\ = 3.9 \text{ (arithmetic)} \end{cases}$$

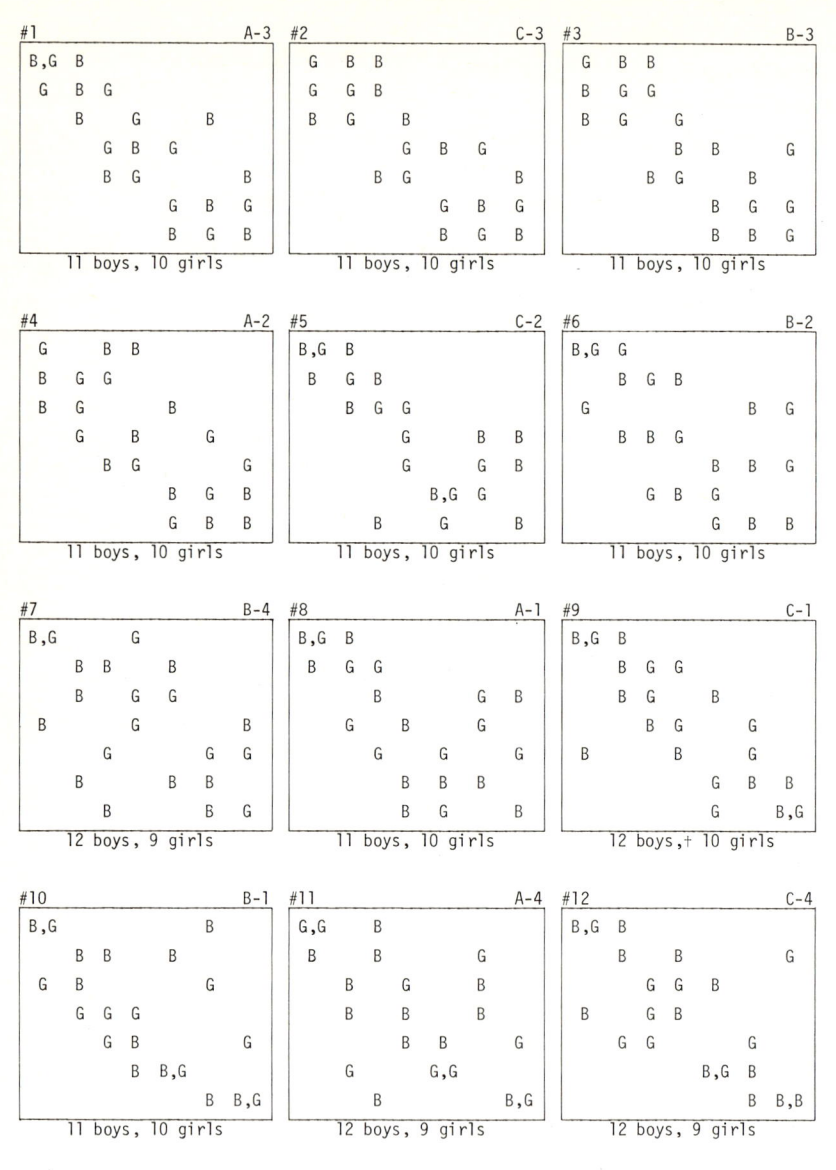

```
#1                    A-3    #2                    C-3    #3                    B-3
B,G  B                       G    B  B                    G    B  B
  G  B  G                    G    G  B                    B    G  G
     B     G     B           B    G     B                 B    G     G
        G  B  G                      G  B  G                    B  B        G
        B  G           B             B  G           B           B  G     B
              G  B  G                      G  B  G                    B  G  G
              B  G  B                      B  G  B                    B  B  G
      11 boys, 10 girls             11 boys, 10 girls             11 boys, 10 girls

#4                    A-2    #5                    C-2    #6                    B-2
  G     B  B                 B,G  B                       B,G  G
B    G  G                    B    G  B                       B  G  B
B    G           B              B  G  G                   G              B  G
     G  B        G                    G        B  B          B  B  G
        B  G           G                 G        G  B                 B  B  G
              B  G  B                      B,G  G                    G  B  G
              G  B  B                      B    G     B                 G  B  B
      11 boys, 10 girls             11 boys, 10 girls             11 boys, 10 girls

#7                    B-4    #8                    A-1    #9                    C-1
B,G        G                 B,G  B                       B,G  B
     B  B     B              B    G  G                    B    G  G
        B     G  G              B           G  B          B    G     B
B           G        B             G  B        G                 B  G        G
        G        G  G                G     G     G        B           B     G
     B     B  B                      B  B  B                       G  B  B
     B           B  G                B     G     B                 G     B,G
      12 boys, 9 girls             11 boys, 10 girls             12 boys,+ 10 girls

#10                   B-1    #11                   A-4    #12                   C-4
B,G              B           G,G     B                    B,G  B
     B  B     B              B     B           G             B     B           G
G    B              G           B     G     B                G  G  B
     G  G  G                    B     B           B       B    G  B
        G  B           G              B     B           G       G  G           G
           B  B,G                  G       G,G                       B,G  B
                 B  B,G            B                 B,G                B  B,B
      11 boys, 10 girls             12 boys, 9 girls             12 boys, 9 girls
```

†Includes the extra student.

Figure 36

Allocation of Students by Septile and Sex Among Groups

Table 30

Group Means and Standard Deviations

	Reading		Arithmetic		
Group	Mean	Std. Dev.	Mean	Std. Dev.	n
A-1	55.52	18.77	46.95	20.12	21
A-2	56.71	19.63	47.76	16.95	21
A-3	61.38	24.99	48.86	18.50	21
A-4	55.62	16.74	46.33	16.49	21
A total	57.31	20.41	47.48	18.10	84
B-1	56.29	21.66	47.29	17.79	21
B-2	57.43	22.80	47.29	15.87	21
B-3	58.86	21.64	47.19	15.74	21
B-4	56.71	19.85	47.81	18.01	21
B total	57.32	21.54	47.39	16.89	84
C-1	56.27	19.78	44.32	18.29	22
C-2	59.29	24.42	50.86	24.20	21
C-3	59.76	20.64	46.29	16.41	21
C-4	56.48	18.79	46.33	13.91	21
C total	57.93	21.06	46.92	18.79	85
Overall	57.52	21.01	47.26	17.93	253

where S_o is the standard deviation of the overall.

The sex ratio in the larger group was 136 boys to 117 girls, or 11.33/9.75. Eight of the smaller groups were assigned 11/10 ratios, three had 12/9, and one had 12/10. Short of partitioning some youngsters, there is no allocation with ratios more uniformly near that of the overall ratio (136/117).

The preceding pages describe an objective method for allocating students into groups so that each group includes the same representation of two quantitative measures of scholastic achievement. The method can easily accommodate a more flexible set of initial conditions:

1. With more effort, a third controlling variable (i.e., ranking criterion) could have been formally incorporated into the procedure. For example, students could have been ranked according to their scores on the language section of the pre-test. The two-dimensional matrix would then become a three-dimensional matrix characterized as having seven rows (reading septiles), seven columns (arithmetic septiles), and seven files (language septiles). Then, the allocation to each of the twelve groups would be such that three students are included from each file as well as from each row and column. Even more controls may be added, but with increasing difficulty.
2. The control variables need not be quantitative; the method would be equally useful for insuring representation across socioeconomic or cultural variables. For example, in some compensatory education programs it might be desirable to allocate students along a three-way ranking scheme using reading pre-test scores for one ranking criterion, racial or ethnic characteristics for the second, and a subjective assessment of English-speaking ability for the third.
3. Although it is administratively convenient for the control variables to split the student population into rankings of equal size, this is not necessary if the

Allocation of Students Among Groups

number of students selected from each ranking is proportional. Thus, in the example above, student allocation to groups should be dictated by the relative sizes of the racial-ethnic rankings (thereby obtaining proportionality, with the racial-ethnic mix of the population being considered).

APPENDIX B

EVALUATION AS FEEDBACK IN THE PROGRAM DEVELOPMENT CYCLE*

Marjorie L. Rapp

The dictionary defines "evaluation" as "fixing the value of; estimating the force of; appraising." Words such as "fixing" and "value" have discrete and unchanging connotations. They have shaped the role of evaluation for many years, certainly in the field of education.

If we accept this definition, we view evaluation as a function—one of the functions to be performed in an experiment, a demonstration program, or in the classroom.

As function, evaluation is static, rigid, and has a critical purpose. It is essentially a grade-giving device. The classic

---

*Parts of this material were presented at a meeting of the Association of California Administrators in Compensatory Education held at the International Hotel, Los Angeles, March 23-26, 1969, and at the Conference of Miller Mathematics Specialists held in San Diego, California, March 23-25, 1969. The ideas presented herein are an outgrowth of work with the San Jose Unified School District on evaluating compensatory education programs, and were published by The Rand Corporation as P-4066, April 1969.

Evaluation as Feedback in the Program Development Cycle 253

experimental design in education is an example of this type of evaluation. It is generally used for the purpose of determining the superiority of some form of education, be it method or material, over another. It is often used (misused) to seek evidence with which to support a bias on the part of the experimenter, rather than as a means of free inquiry.

Evaluation may be viewed statically as *function*; but it may also be viewed dynamically as *process*. As such it becomes flexible and inquiring with program improvement as its purpose. Used in this way it provides for adaptability.

Evaluation now becomes part of a cycle of planning, implementing, observing, and correcting. To each of these phases of a continuous sequence it provides feedback which can be used for program development. It becomes a tool useful to the decisionmaker.

In each of the phases of this cycle we are essentially asking a series of questions. If they are carefully worded, the evaluative process will be able to provide at least tentative answers.

The question underlying the *planning* stage is *Where do we want to be at a given time in the future?* This, after all, is the primary purpose of undertaking a new program—to change the direction in which we are going. This question must be translated into an expression of the formalized objectives of the program—objectives so written that they clearly spell out what the future goal is, and so written that progress toward that goal may be measured. It is in the planning stage that provisions for evaluation must be made, and measuring instruments so chosen that there will be no doubt that the data they provide relate accurately to the stated goals.

In *implementation* we stimulate answers to the question *How do we get to where we want to be?* We translate these answers into the execution of program plans. Decisions about the characteristics of personnel especially suited to the nature of the program and about instructional content and strategy are made in this phase of the cycle. These means of arriving at the goal must also be evaluated so that we will have a measure of how well suited to achieving our objectives are the ways in which we have chosen to arrive there.

Observation will continue throughout the program with a view toward ultimately answering the question *What progress are we making toward our goal?* In its intermediate phases it will provide a measure of the adequacy of planning and implementation. If the measuring instruments have been carefully chosen to reflect the objectives of the program, and the means of attaining them, the answer will be suggested.

Correction is the use of the data collected in the observation phase to answer the question *How can we improve our planning, implementation, and observation?* Here we address a host of questions related to all the phases of the program development cycle. We should have information about which aspects of our program are most successful, which are least successful, and how well suited to achieving our goals are the personnel, the curriculum materials, and the instructional strategies.

If our evaluation has been well planned and executed, it will provide feedback to every phase of the developmental cycle.

It will enable us to assess the adequacy of our planning. In the light of our data we will know better whether we wrote our objectives to truly reflect our aims, and whether our measuring instruments accurately specify them. If not, we can restate our objectives, or seek better measurements. Our experience may lead us to change our objectives; perhaps our direction should shift. We may find that we have multiple objectives, some of which are not being assessed; we can make provision for this.

The evaluation will indicate whether improvements need to be made in our implementation. It should provide an indication of the efficiency with which we are moving in the direction of our goals. If it is unsatisfactory, we should have alternative strategies which can be implemented, or our mix of strategies might need to be changed.

Our observations will be improved by our evaluation. The adequacy of the measuring instruments will be assessed, and we will learn whether they are really relevant to our objectives. Our subjective observations will enter the cycle also, and will suggest directions for program improvement which will need to enter the

Evaluation as Feedback in the Program Development Cycle 255

planning and implementation cycles of the evaluation process.

Finally, correction is the heart and soul of evaluation as process. With relevant data, we are now in a position to make changes as the program develops; changes which are planned for in an orderly fashion and which, because they are based on observation, have a good chance of advancing the program in the specified direction.

The process as described here in terms of program development is equally applicable to any teacher. It provides a framework for self-evaluation with a view toward self-improvement. This kind of improvement would have as its larger goal, of course, the goal of all development in education—providing the best we can give to our children.

The very act of undertaking a new program implies the awareness of a need for improvement, of a dissatisfaction with the status quo, and of a desire to change direction. By its very definition a developmental program is a striving for a new path, perhaps by new means. The direction it takes may be dictated by hunch, or previous experience, or observation. The original plans for a new program should be considered tentative. They should certainly be based on the soundest grounds available at the time of their inception. But we should be aware from the outset that we are doing something new, possibly untried in the past, or that we are putting together a set of plans which seem plausible, but which have not been put to the test. We should approach the development of a new program with an open-mindedness, a willingness to change as data from the evaluation process become available to us. Every aspect of the program should constantly be scrutinized with a view toward correcting and improving it. We must always be careful not to fall into the trap of becoming inflexible when we have at hand the means of implementing improvements as we progress in a new direction.

The process of evaluation is analogous to that of navigation. When you are concerned with getting a ship from one port to another, you cannot be certain that it will be expedient to maintain your original course until the end of the trip. At the outset, you plot the best course you can, taking account of whatever data are available about tides, currents, winds, possible storm tracks, etc. But even as you plot the course you know that to pursue it doggedly might be fatal, and you are aware of the necessity to constantly check your progress and be ready to change course if it seems advisable. If you run into adverse currents you do not buck them, but alter your direction to make the best possible progress toward your destination under those circumstances. You never lose sight of the fact that your purpose is not to stay on a given course, but to arrive at a stated destination.

Evaluation used as a navigational aid can keep a program headed for its destination at the same time that it corrects for the necessary deviations from the projected course, not all of which could have been anticipated during the planning stages. By freeing us from over-commitment to our original idea which, after all, can be no more than an attempt to reach a destination by a specified route, process-oriented evaluation wisely used can ensure that we correct as we proceed and help us to arrive at our goals.

APPENDIX C

PROJECTIONS OF ENROLLMENT

Margaret B. Carpenter

The use of enrollment projections in program budgeting requires a somewhat different approach from that generally used in education because program budgeting shifts the planning horizon further into the future. This different orientation may require the development of new techniques for enrollment projection.

Enrollment determines the long-run requirements for school buildings—a function that educators are all familiar with; it also determines the long-run requirements for equipment, teachers, transportation, and other basic resources. Beyond this, the specific characteristics of the expected student population, such as racial and ethnic composition, composition by age groups, and so on, determine the needs for special programs such as programs for the gifted or for the mentally retarded. In conjunction with descriptions of school programs, including class size, textbooks, and the like, enrollment projections result in estimates of resource requirements throughout the period of projection.

Projections of enrollment can play another role in educational planning. If they are sufficiently detailed to predict the anticipated characteristics of the student body, particularly ability, they can also provide estimates of future changes in program effectiveness. Foreseeable changes in effectiveness may presage the need for special programs.

Current Techniques for Projecting Enrollments

The Office of Education has developed several models for projecting enrollment in the United States. One of these is a grade-progression model, called DYNAMOD, in which enrollment in each grade is computed as a certain percentage of the enrollment in the preceding grade (with other elaboration). This has been a standard technique for projecting enrollment for many years. It suffers from a serious shortcoming, because it cannot take account of shifting school populations, both within and without the district. As is well known, migration often confounds efforts to predict population in small areas.

Another technique used by the Office of Education is essentially a population model based on predicted birth rates and death rates, with enrollment rates projected for the various age groups. In this model, changes in enrollment rates are assumed to be linear.

At the other end of the scale, there are the predictions of enrollment for the coming year made by individual school principals. Different methods are used to arrive at these figures—interviews of home owners, information on the characteristics of new housing developments (such as price range, number of bedrooms, and so on), the loss of residential housing to freeway developments, and the like. All of these items of information contribute usefully to estimates of forthcoming enrollment.

All the models used by the Office of Education are so highly aggregated that they are essentially useless at the school district level, where the particularities of the district largely determine the specifics of enrollment within it. For precise school-by-school projections of enrollment for the coming year, predictions made for individual schools probably offer the best approach. But we need other tools because these methods are inadequate for projections much beyond one year into the future. A new housing development, for instance, could very easily be built and fully occupied within a year.

Curve Fitting

What is needed, then, are techniques that fall somewhere between the highly aggregated models used at the national and state levels and the very specific but necessarily short-range techniques used by individual schools. At present, there are two possibilities open: curve fitting and projection by planning departments. Simple curve fitting, which uses a curve fitted to past data to estimate future enrollment, is the less satisfactory. A straight line or a growth curve may be used. The latter is analogous to the compound interest curve in banking; the former estimates each year's enrollment as a constant factor times the enrollment of the preceding year. There are other kinds of curves that can be made to fit the data more exactly; but, in general, they tend to go out of control when they are used for extrapolation—that is, they have unfortunate tendencies to wobble or to become extremely steep or extremely flat. (As an aside, the growth curve is not an exact representation of the behavior of populations because populations change at a changing, not a constant, rate. However, if we try to use a changing rate, we run into the difficulties of uncontrollability just mentioned.)

Accuracy. Figure 37 gives an idea of how well curve fitting can project enrollment. The solid line shows actual enrollments in a California school district. A straight line was fitted to data on the left-hand half of the figure and then projected into the next five years. Enrollment data covering a ten-year span showed how well the straight line would fit what actually happened. At first glance, the projection seems surprisingly good, being less than two percent above the actual enrollments five years later. However, two percent would be over 500 students in this district—the size of an elementary school. For this particular district, the growth curve provides a poorer fit for the data, as shown in Figure 38. It is nearly eight percent above the five-year prediction.

In order to see how curve fitting works for districts of various sizes, information from several districts was examined. These

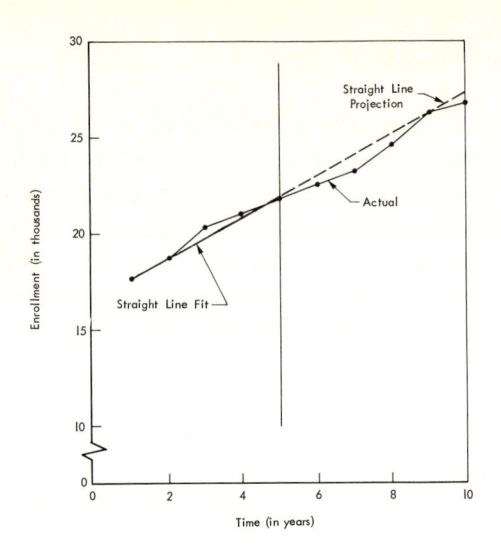

Figure 37

*Use of Curve Fitting to Project Enrollment:
A Straight Line*

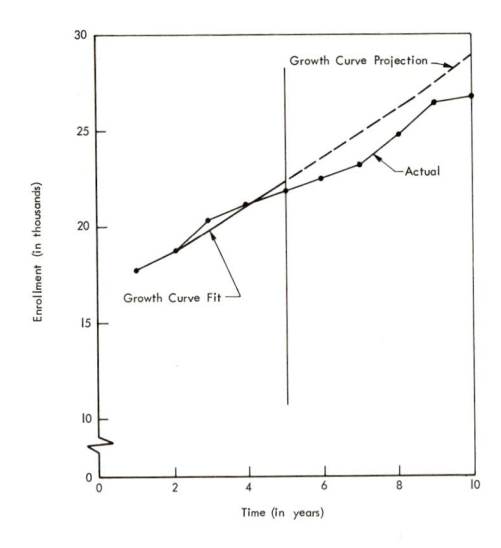

Figure 38

*Use of Curve Fitting to Project Enrollment:
A Growth Curve*

Projections of Enrollment

districts varied in enrollment size from a few hundred to over 20,000. Curve fitting was used to extrapolate from five years of data to two years in the future. That extrapolation was then checked with the enrollment that actually occurred. The results are summarized in Figure 39. We see that the curve fitting technique provides a better projection for the larger districts, being, on the average, only a few percent in error on the two-year projection, but for the smaller districts the average error in just two years is an embarrassing 15 percent.

One reason why using fitted curves to project enrollment seems to be better for large districts may be that social inertia inhibits very large fluctuations in total enrollment over a period of a few years. This may not hold, however, for a district of less than a thousand students, when such a small community can be radically changed by the introduction of new industry or new housing within a period of a year or so.

Subareas. For many school districts, it will be useful to break the district into a number of homogeneous subareas—homogeneous in terms of the socioeconomic type of population that may be found there. This will be helpful not only in projecting enrollment but in establishing criteria for student achievement. One particular district in California—a fairly large one that is probably typical of many—seemed to partition into three demographically homogeneous zones. One was an inner city zone that was slowly declining in population, which contained a fairly large concentration of a minority group and whose land was essentially filled with housing, business, and industry. In contrast, the suburban zone contained much desirable open land that was rapidly being developed with tracts of relatively expensive housing on the hillsides. This was a typical mushrooming suburban zone, with enrollment growing at a rate of about 25 percent a year. If this zone were examined only in conjunction with the inner city, that kind of trend would be masked to some extent by the slowly declining enrollment in the older zone. Between these two zones was a transition zone containing a mixture of older and newer housing. It was relatively stable.

The analysis of each of these zones separately provides far

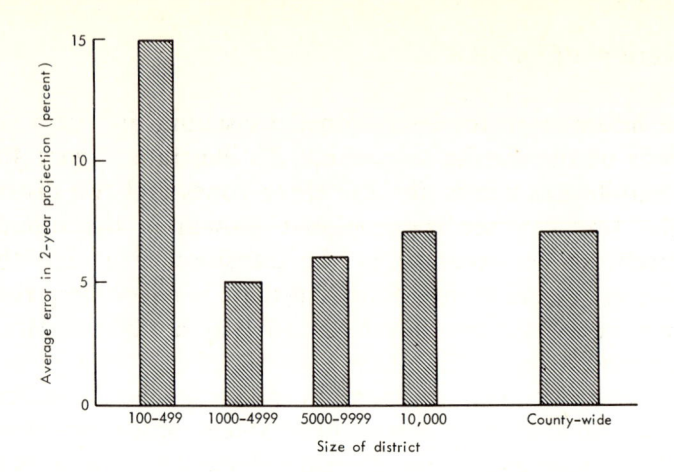

Figure 39

*Error in Projection Related to District Size
(Fitted curve projections)*

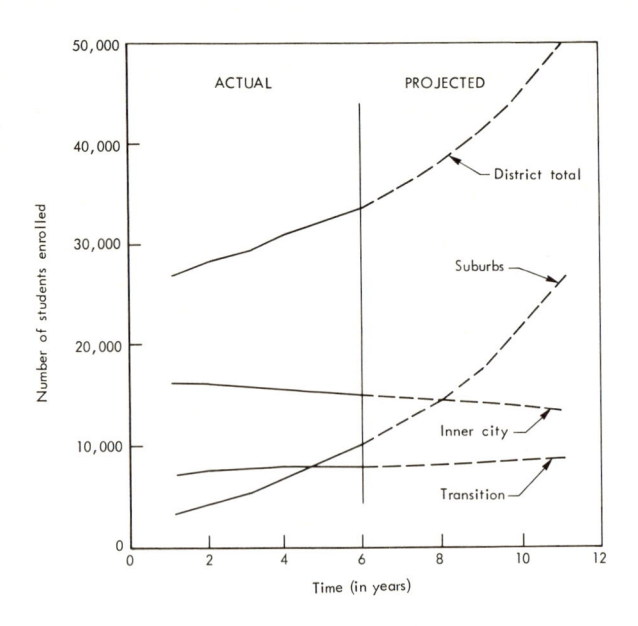

Figure 40

Enrollment Trends by Zone

Projections of Enrollment

more information for educational decisionmaking than does the analysis of the district as a whole. To illustrate, Figure 40 shows the enrollment trends for the three zones and the district as a whole. One can see the explosive growth in the suburbs, the relatively stable situation in the transition area, and the slow decline in the inner city. Note that there is a very steep rise to the right projected for the suburbs, which may not be accurate, as will be discussed later.

One of the major problems in analyzing school enrollments in subareas of districts is determining which enrollments draw from which demographic areas. Because elementary, junior high, and high school districts do not have coincident boundaries, this becomes a little complicated. Figure 41 shows a hypothetical school district with the demographic zones—the inner city, the transition, and the suburb—shown by different shading. Superimposed on this are hypothetical boundaries for junior high schools and high schools. Note, for example, that although one of the high schools is located in the transition zone, it appears to draw a considerable portion of its students from the other zones. Similarly, the junior highs that are located in the suburbs appear to draw many of their students from the transition zone. Because housing, industry, and other land uses tend to occur in clusters, it will probably be necessary to use data on student residence to determine to what extent the school populations actually represent each zone. Although not based on student residence, Figure 41 does not account for the geographic overlap of zones by school district boundaries. The mixing of students from different demographic zones is desirable from an educational point of view, but it means that some care is needed in analyzing enrollments by zone.

Grade Progressions. A similar problem exists in trying to use curves fitted to grade progression as a way of projecting enrollment. In order to do this, one must know which schools students go to when they pass, say, from elementary school to junior high school. That means, again, that detailed data on student residence are needed. One would surmise that using grade progression data for extrapolating enrollment would provide

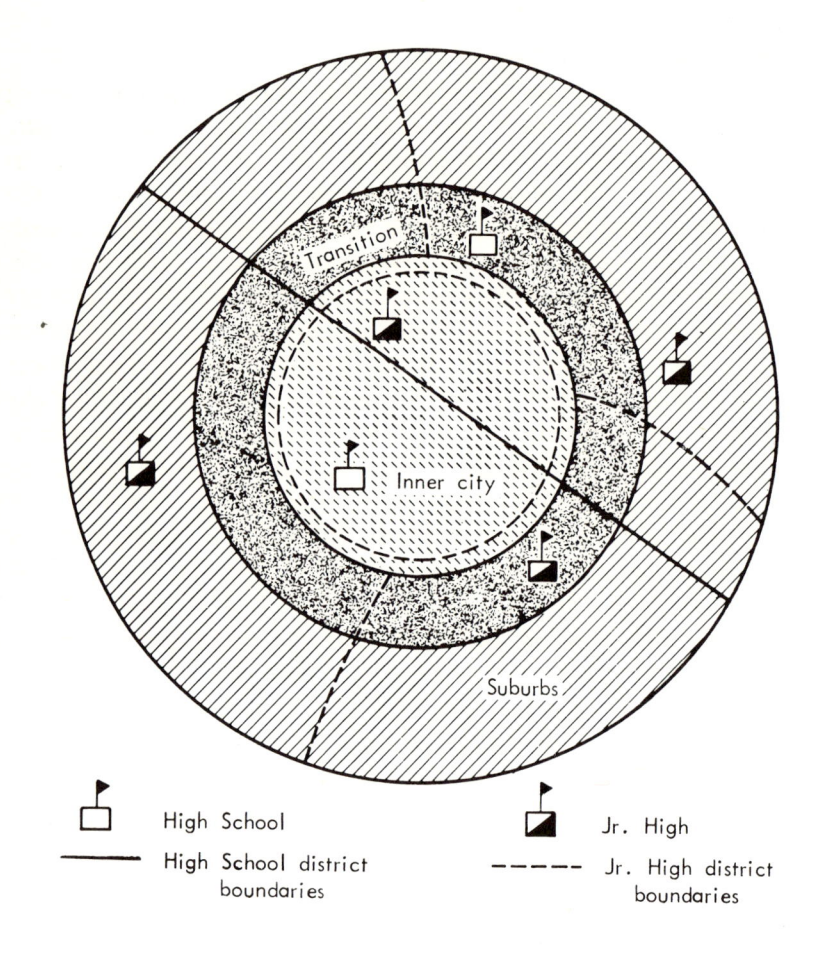

Figure 41

School District Boundaries and Demographic Areas

added accuracy, because one would be using the additional knowledge that the students of the year before were entering the next higher grade, and would assume the student population to be relatively stable. This surmise was not verified because we did not have enrollment data by grade for a sufficient number of years.

Planning Department Projections

Other methods are an improvement on blind extrapolation of past trends. At present, some county planning offices make longer-range forecasts of population for relatively small areas within a county. Planners use the projections of population for the county that have been supplied by the state, in conjunction with their own detailed knowledge of the development patterns within the county. They also take account of the total available land for habitation within the small areas, called the *holding capacity.* Taking these aspects of development into account, and using some informed guesses, planners project population in detail within the county. From projections such as these, projections of enrollment can be derived from enrollment ratios for the different age groups that have obtained in these areas in the past.

Figure 42 presents the error in two-year projections of enrollment by a county planning office. Data from the same county that were used to test the accuracy of projections using fitted curves (shown in Figure 39) are shown as dotted lines in Figure 42. Notice how much better the planning office projections are for the small districts than for those that simply extrapolate past trends. In fact, these projections are somewhat more accurate for districts of all sizes, being a few percent less in error except for the districts ranging between 1000 and 5000 in enrollment.

Techniques Under Development

The fact that planning office projections are better than extrapolation supports the hope that systematic combinations of information on land use, population trends, industrial development, land availability, transportation networks, and cultural preferences can eventually yield significantly improved projections of enrollment. It should be clear, however, that the interactions

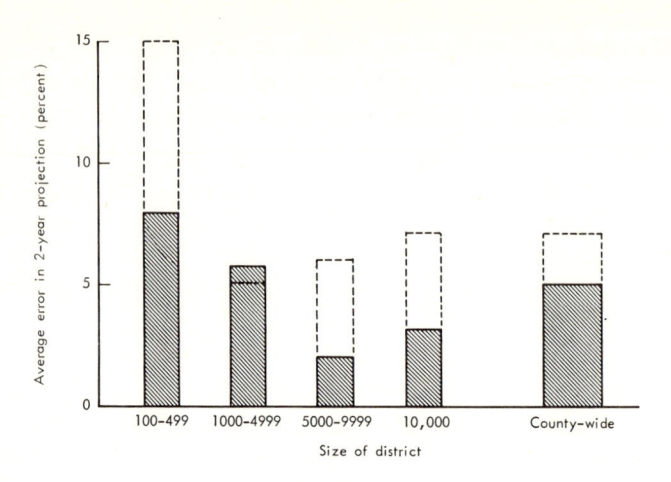

Figure 42

*Error in Projection Related to District Size
(Planning department projections)*

among these agencies of society are complex. More extensive and more detailed data, and possibly the use of automated data-handling equipment, are required to study them adequately. The development of models and games for analyzing urban growth and its interaction with the political process is now under way at several research institutions. Most of these models have not yet been applied to real data, so that it is not known how successfully they can predict. All are still under development and can make no claim to being effective substitutes for the informed judgments of experienced planners. Nevertheless, it would seem likely that further refinement of these models cannot help but provide better means for estimating enrollments in the future. To help evaluate the potential usefulness of these models, the following sections describe them, within the limits of the presently available documentation.*

*Much of what follows is condensed from J.P. Crecine, *Computer Simulation in Urban Research,* The Rand Corporation, P-3734, November 1967.

Most of the models of urban development are computer simulations that deal with various combinations of activities and land uses on the one hand and geographic units or land sites on the other. *Activities* are defined to comprise retail and commercial business, basic employment (as opposed to commercial employment), education and other civic activities, housing, and transportation.

Transportation Models
A number of major metropolitan transportation studies, such as those for Chicago and Pittsburgh, have used essentially the same model of urban spatial organization for evaluating alternative transportation networks. Extrapolations of existing distributions of activities, based on past trends, plans, zoning restrictions, and staff judgments about land-holding potentials are used to project future distributions of activities. This sounds much like a formalization of the methods used by county planners that were discussed earlier. In allocating activities, another simulation model for transportation studies also takes account of their accessibility to other activities.

Urban Growth Models
Other models are more concerned with the effects of urban growth in general, rather than its effects primarily on the desirability of various transportation networks. One is designed to calculate the change in activities, such as housing and employment, resulting from both population growth and intra-regional migrations. Changes are estimated using such factors as the accessibility of subareas within the region to other activities and various amenities such as the amount and quality of municipal services. Another model uses the location of basic employment to determine the pattern of residential location. The location of the resident population is used, in turn, to determine a pattern of location of retail trade and services. This hierarchy of locational decisions is iterated several times to arrive at a stable condition. An extension of this model has prediction as its main purpose.

*M.E.T.R.O.**

Perhaps one of the most ambitious undertakings is M.E.T.-R.O., part of the efforts being made by Richard Duke and his associates at Michigan State to improve the quality of education in urban planning and to advance urban research. M.E.T.R.O. combines simulation and gaming to explore the interrelations between urban change and the political process. A key part is the use of Lansing, Michigan, as a laboratory community. Data on Lansing, collected over a period of time for the simulated parts of the model, will allow the modification and validation of these parts. But although the simulated parts of M.E.T.R.O. are already based on impressive amounts of real data, the designers make no predictive claims at this stage.

A Fundamental Problem in Educational Planning

This discussion has alluded to the fact that housing patterns determine not only the number of students enrolled in school, but also the characteristics of the student population. At the same time, housing, industrial and commercial growth, and other land usage patterns, by and large, determine the tax revenues from which education draws its support; so projections of land use can provide planners with information about both future demand (as generated by enrollment) and future resources (as provided by local taxes). Yet, educational planning is presently carried out almost independently of other planning for land use. It is incongruous that the educational establishment spends almost all of the local tax dollar, yet participates in local planning almost *not at all*. This puts the schools in the position of having to *react* to changes in the urban and suburban areas with which they are so intimately concerned, instead of having a voice in planning the future development of those areas. The problem of projecting enrollments in an environment that can change radically because of changes in land use, as well as the larger problem of sound educational planning in general, are intimately tied up with the

*Richard D. Duke and Richard L. Meier, "Gaming Simulation for Urban Planning," *Journal of the American Institute of Planners,* Vol. 32, No. 1, January 1966, pp. 3-17.

other aspects of environmental planning. Mere coordination may not be sufficient to solve this dilemma. Somehow educators should be able to affect the development of land in ways similar to those in which other concerned institutions can affect it. At present, there is no formal mechanism for doing this. To formalize links with the planners and politicians might permit a more orderly development of the schools within the urban scene.

APPENDIX D

COST-EFFECTIVENESS ANALYSIS FOR EDUCATIONAL PLANNING*

Margaret B. Carpenter and Sue A. Haggart

Introduction

Cost-effectiveness is both a powerful and an often misused technique of analysis. Its misuse stems from its very power, for it gives superficially simple, quantitative "answers" to highly complex problems whose sources and repercussions are very poorly understood. So that the results of cost-effectiveness analysis may be used most wisely in educational planning, it is necessary to know how to structure, conduct and interpret the analysis.

Educational planning is ultimately concerned with achieving a more effective use of educational resources in improving pupil performance. There are several intermediate steps in the realization of this goal. The educational planner must first determine what resources are being used directly to produce specific

*This material was published in *Educational Technology,* October 1970, pp. 26-30. It is included in this volume as an appendix because it draws together in one place many of the points made throughout the book.

educational performance or outcomes. From this base of knowledge, he may then estimate the resources required to make changes in various aspects of the educational process. These changes may range all the way from changes in the objectives of education, per se, to changes in instructional methods. This means he must be armed with an informational framework about his current system that is as complete as possible and with a methodology for estimating the future consequences of proposed changes.

Cost-effectiveness analysis is a tool that can assist the planner in relating the resources required by an educational program to its effectiveness, often measured by pupil achievement. For the purpose of analysis, we look at schools as "systems." From this analytical viewpoint, an educational system is perceived as being an arrangement of elements (such as teachers, classrooms and the like) and processes (such as instruction and counseling) that combine to produce student learning. There are factors within the system that influence the relationships between the resources used by the system and the student learning that results; there are also factors external to the system that have impacts on these relationships. Just what these factors are is being widely discussed now and will be for some time to come. We will not directly explore the many facets of this question here. (Their consideration is, of course, an integral part of analyzing the educational process.) Our purpose is to look at the problems involved with the use of the technique of cost-effectiveness analysis in educational planning.

We mentioned that cost-effectiveness analysis is concerned with *educational programs.* The term "educational program" can have many meanings, such as *the in-service teacher training program.* From this point on, we shall restrict the term to apply to *a set of activities and resources that, taken together, bring about a specific kind of student learning.* A program must be described in terms of certain basic characteristics—its effectiveness, its cost, its resource requirements, and the way it is carried out.

Cost-effectiveness analysis is, quite frankly, a technique for comparing programs, and may be used:

- to help assess the relative worth of several innovative programs with the same educational outcome (such as improvement in reading achievement);
- to determine whether a single program is becoming more or less effective as time passes so that steps may be taken to improve it, if necessary;
- to help assess the relative worth of the same program for different student populations (such as those with differing socioeconomic backgrounds) or in different school settings.

The goal of the analysis is not to provide the planner with the alternative that "maximizes" or "minimizes" specific characteristics; the goal is to provide information which together with the judgment of the planner permits a compromise among the characteristics of the alternatives within the various environmental constraints, such as budget level or political atmosphere.

The term *cost-effectiveness* should be broadened to *resource-effectiveness* for reasons which will be made clear shortly. *Resource* will be used in the common way to mean *a source of supply*. The way in which the resource requirements of a program are analyzed is inseparable from the purpose of the analysis—to relate the resources used by the program to program effectiveness. Ideally, program cost should include only those resources that can be directly related to program effectiveness.

Problems concerning resource-effectiveness analysis can be broken into two largely parallel sets, one focusing on resource analysis and the other on the analysis of effectiveness. Common problems are those of definition—of the misleading nature of single measures, and of the lack of well-developed methodologies for analysis. We shall discuss these two sets of problems in turn and then conclude by addressing problems concerning resource-effectiveness analysis itself.

Resource-Oriented Problems

In order to be able to choose among alternative programs as applied to different educational situations, the planner must have techniques for comparing and evaluating estimates of the resources required by the programs throughout the time span of interest.

Determining the Resources Required by a Program

In the past, educational institutions have accounted for the cost of doing business primarily for the purpose of financial control. Funds for different purposes have come from different sources and may not be traded from one account to another. Keeping track of these accounts in terms of end-items of expenditure was the major task of the budgeting and accounting activity.

When cost is used for choosing among alternative programs, however, the source of funds is of secondary significance. Rather, it is necessary to know what each alternative will require in terms of personnel, facilities, equipment, training activities, dollars, and the like, not only at present but throughout the foreseeable life of the program. Few school systems can describe the resources that go into existing programs, let alone estimate what existing programs or alternative programs will require in the future.

This is not, however, an insurmountable problem. It is possible to draw up a set of variables describing the resource requirements of alternative programs that is sufficiently broad to encompass the major variables in each program and, at the same time, sufficiently compact to be manageable. This must be undertaken at the outset if cost-effectiveness analysis is to be carried out.

There is a more subtle problem, however, whose solution may not be so easily reached. This is the problem of definition of the "real" resources in education, that is, the resources that actually are the *source of supply* of learning. Many attempts are now being made to identify such resources, and some small progress has been made, viz., teacher verbal ability appears to have a positive effect on student learning. The amount of time a student participates actively in some learning process may well be another resource, but there seems to be no easy way to measure this at present. The amount of time that a teacher devotes to the subject in the classroom is only a proxy measure. Much work in this area will be necessary before it is possible to identify the real resources in education.

The Misleading Nature of a Single Measure

Resource analysis has a seductive quality engendered by the availability of a single measure, the dollar, by which most resources can be measured. Given this, it is a natural step to add all of the dollars to obtain a single indicator of resource requirements—the "cost of the program." Although in some cases such a number might be quite sufficient for resource-effectiveness analysis, in most instances the single measure buries many characteristics of the program of which the planner should be aware in making his choice.

One significant aspect concerns the timing of the expenditures; are they required in a lump sum, can they be spread over several years or will they recur as long as the program is in existence? Thus, projections of expenditures over the expected life of the program are required to provide a true picture of dollar needs. A display of the expenditures required over several years contrasts with the usual practice of assessing the cost of a program solely in terms of the initial research, development, and implementation costs.

Another significant aspect is that in general the resources required are of very different kinds, and dollar measures do not reflect these differences adequately for decisionmaking. For example, a program may require that a certain percentage of the teachers belong to a particular minority group, but these teachers will receive the same salary as any teachers with similar background and experience.

Thus, the cost-effectiveness analysis should always display the major resources required for each year of program life, along with their associated dollar costs, and should particularly note items which may be difficult to obtain (but whose scarcity may not be reflected adequately in their dollar costs). The problem is to identify and estimate the major, crucial, or scarce resources that will be required for full implementation of the programs.

*The Lack of a Fully Developed Methodology
for Resource and Cost Analysis*

Some of the methodology required for the analysis of cost within cost-effectiveness analysis has already been developed, although it is not in general use in educational institutions. Much of the methodology can be developed in a rather straightforward fashion simply by using techniques that have been developed elsewhere to identify and cost those resources that contribute directly to a given program. Several pitfalls exist, however, of which the analyst should be wary.

The objective of cost-effectiveness analysis is to facilitate choice among alternative programs. Therefore, costs which actually will remain fixed regardless of which programs are implemented (within limits) should not be "allocated" to particular programs. For example, a school district with enrollment in a particular size range will require a relatively fixed administrative staff to run it, with concomitant facilities to house and supply the administrative function. If all of the cost of central administration were to be allocated to instructional programs, it would have to be done by largely arbitrary rules (except in some special cases where curriculum experts work in specific subject areas, for example). Worse, if such allocations are made, changes in the direct cost of a program will appear to generate corresponding changes in the indirect, or allocated, cost, when in fact such changes would not actually follow. The key to realistic cost analysis in these instances is to identify those resources that will not change in response to program changes and to set them aside under *unallocated* functional categories such as *administration* or *student services*. The question of which costs to allocate to which programs is of very real importance and will have to be resolved for cost-effectiveness analysis to be carried out.

Special problems of resource allocation are also posed by "core" programs, programs that teach two or more subjects within a single session. If student achievement on each subject is measured separately, some decision must be made on how resources and activities within the program are apportioned among the subjects. If, however, a single measure of student achievement that encompasses the several subjects has been devised, there is no need to allocate resources within the program.

These problems of resource allocation are most easily, and consistently, handled if a resource/cost model of the district has been developed. The development of a resource/cost model is also an essential step in achieving a workable methodology of analysis for educational planning. This model would comprise a set of mathematical expressions that relate variables describing the district and the programs to estimates of resource requirements and cost. With such a model, the analyst can formulate a description of the district at each future date and simulate the results of conducting each alternative program within the district.

The model must be broad enough that each of the alternative programs can be fully described by the basic variables and relationships that make up the model. For example, requirements for teachers are usually directly related to projected enrollment, but if a program is largely self-paced, the number of teachers required may be more sensitive to the number of points in the learning sequence at which a teacher's assistance is needed than it is to enrollment.

Often analysis will suggest that alternative programs be combined or that parts of programs be used in ways in which they were not used before. The model should be able to accommodate such variations as these, also. At the same time, care should be exercised to keep the model to a manageable size. There are so many aspects of school districts and educational programs that it is very easy for the number of variables included in the model to reach astronomical values. The only way to avoid this is for a skilled model builder who is well informed on the workings of educational institutions to tailor the model to the questions being addressed.

Effectiveness-Oriented Problems

The effectiveness of a program is a set of measures or indicators that describes the learning that the program has brought about. The impact of the program on such groups as parents, teachers, or the community at large may suggest peripheral benefits and can be used to choose among programs of apparently equal teaching effectiveness, but these benefits are not central to the problems surrounding effectiveness.

Measuring Effectiveness

The problems of defining and measuring the effectiveness of educational programs must be dealt with before the cost-effectiveness of alternatives can be analyzed. A central problem is the selection of instruments that measure attainment of program goals validly and reliably. In many academic areas, there are tests of student achievement that may be used with some confidence. But if program goals include such objectives as changes in a child's conception of his own self-worth or improvements in the child's relationships with his peers, it may be more difficult to obtain or devise instruments that are valid and reliable; sometimes very expensive techniques such as individual observation or interview by trained psychologists must be used.

Even if acceptable measuring instruments are at hand, care must be taken to assure that they are administered in a consistent fashion; otherwise, the comparability of scores may be in question. This may require, for example, that a single team of testers administer all pre- and post-tests that are to be used as measures of effectiveness.

Finally, in interpreting measurements, the evaluator must decide which scoring mode is appropriate for the program goals. Grade-equivalent scores show the grade level at which the students are performing, but are not appropriate for inferences about the effect of the program on the rates of growth of children who started at different grade levels. For this purpose, percentile scores, which allow comparison of the relative position of students at different time points, are preferable. But the comparison of percentile scores is misleading as a measure of the *amount* of change, although it is useful as a measure of the *direction* of change in relative standing. A more accurate representation of the amount of change would be given by standard scores.

The Inadequacy of a Single Measure

Because of the complexity of the learning process, a full

analysis of effectiveness should produce a *set* of measures and indicators, rather than a single measure. These measures and indicators should be kept track of for several years in order to determine the effects of specific programs, because temporary spurts in growth may be of little value in the long run.

It is also important to determine the effects of specific programs on student performance in other educational programs, for example, the effect of a reading or mathematics program on those programs that make use of reading and computational skills such as history, science, and the like. Although it seems logical to assume that improved performance in reading would carry over into improved performance in most other areas, some programs may encourage more of such carry-overs than others and some could even have negative effects. These considerations are important. In spite of the fact that they add a considerable burden to the task of analysis, parallel longitudinal testing programs in several subjects should be conducted. This is a potentially more valuable approach than just measuring achievement in a single dimension such as reading or mathematics. This means that setting up a research program specifically designed to test hypotheses about the interdependence of student achievement among academic subjects may be required to obtain a full description of the effectiveness of a single program.

As suggested earlier, educational programs may be directed specifically to goals other than improvement of student achievement in such subjects as reading and mathematics. For example, the program may seek to change the attitudes of the parents toward their children's schooling. Objectives such as these are usually thought of as fostering the attainment of the primary objective of student achievement, but the causal relationship may go in both directions. In any event, if the program devotes resources specifically to attain such ends, some means for determining to what extent the ends have been gained should be set up; and experimental design should include similar programs that do not devote resources to attaining such goals. This is particularly important when questions arise concerning whether to apply a successful program as a "package" or to use only those portions of it that seem to have been most conducive to its success.

If it is accepted that a single number for the dollar cost of a program conceals most of the information needed for decision-making, it should be even clearer that no single measure of program effectiveness will tell the whole story about the worth of the program, because any program promotes several different kinds of change in the student. Because these changes are different in kind, no unit exists by means of which the changes attributable to a particular program can be made commensurate. Thus, the effectiveness of a program can only be presented as a *set* of measures and indicators. In order to choose among alternative programs, the planner must then judge the relative importance of the various aspects of program effectiveness *as they apply to particular schools.* For example, the teaching of reading may be of primary importance in inner city schools but may carry much less weight in schools in upper middle class neighborhoods. One of the major tasks is to decide how to rank measures and indicators of effectiveness vis-a-vis schools in various socioeconomic areas.

The Lack of a Methodology for Estimating the Effectiveness of Future Programs

Many aspects of the effectiveness of past and ongoing programs can be measured by pre- and post-tests of student achievement. The relationships among test results and educational resources of various kinds can also be inferred by using standard techniques of regression analysis. Unfortunately, such analyses can only describe what has happened in the past and cannot be relied upon to predict future program effectiveness if major changes in factors influencing learning (such as the social environment) are likely to take place. In addition, because the "real" resources in education may not yet have been identified, regression analyses may fail to treat the resource-effectiveness relationships that are crucial to the success of the program. Longitudinal studies address just such matters as these. Hopefully, such studies will contribute to the future development of models of program effectiveness that can be used in educational planning in the same way that resource and cost models could be used today.

The Need for Criteria of Effectiveness

Lacking reliable models that relate educational resources to program effectiveness, it is necessary not only to weigh the relative importance of measures and indicators of different aspects of effectiveness but to judge what levels of effectiveness are acceptable. If, for example, growth in reading achievement of one month per month of schooling is acceptable, is a growth rate of .95 month per month unacceptable? What if the latter growth rate is provided by a program that has more evident peripheral benefits than the former? Or what if the latter program reached more students for the same cost?

A rationale for the resolution of issues such as these is an integral part of the analysis; setting criteria, or standards, for judging effectiveness can help to supply this rationale. An important problem is whether different criteria are to be chosen for students with different characteristics, such as socioeconomic background, or whether the same criteria are to be applied to all students. An obvious need is to know what is the average achievement of students with different characteristics under current educational programs. Whatever criteria are chosen, they should only provide general guidelines to the planner, rather than draw fine lines between the acceptable and the unacceptable. This is because the measures available are subject to error and, at the same time, are only proxies for what we would really like to assess—student learning. And this is why peripheral considerations can often tip the balance of decision between one program and another.

Analysis for Educational Planning

From the foregoing it should be clear that a single number purporting to be a cost-effectiveness ratio must hide more than it reveals about the overall value of an educational program. This is because the requirements of a program for resources are multi-dimensional and time-variant; the same may be said for indicators of program effectiveness. The educational planner, whether the analysis is aimed at a modest change in the current way of doing business or whether the analysis addresses the question of incorporating a major innovation, must have adequate information—information about the change and about its impact on the resource requirements of other programs and on the effectiveness of other programs. When the planner is considering the implementation of promising innovations in his district, he will need to know, for example, to what extent the success of the innovations depends on the *characteristics of the schools in which they have been used,* particularly the socioeconomic status of the school population. Because of the great variability among school districts and among schools within a given district, it seems unlikely that any innovation can be replicated in a new school without some modification. For example, the new school may already have some of the equipment needed for the program or may have to add more or fewer specialized personnel. Therefore, the resources required to implement the alternative innovations will have to be estimated for the new school. Ideally, this work should be done by collaboration between people familiar with the original programs and the school district personnel. If each district has information readily available about the resource requirements of its programs it should then be able to estimate the resource requirements of the innovations as alternatives.

In addition, there are characteristics of a school that are related to the effectiveness of an innovation. It is very unlikely that the characteristics of the new school will exactly match those of the school successfully using the innovation. The characteristics of the student populations will differ in some respects; the relationships among the teachers, students, administrators, parents, and community will not be the same; and other educational programs in the schools will also be different. The impacts of these differences on program effectiveness will need to be estimated, through collaboration between people familiar with the original programs and the school district personnel. During the course of this work, a rationale for ranking criteria of effectiveness will be developed that will be tailored to each school in the district.

Because of these problems in comparing programs, the best way to use cost-effectiveness analysis is to construct *equal-cost alternatives,* that is, to adjust the dimensions of each program (such as the number of students enrolled) so that each program will incur approximately the same total cost over some appropriate period of time. In this way, the educational planners will be freed from having to consider cost when choosing among alternatives and can concentrate on the more difficult aspects of effectiveness, the phasing of dollar requirements, and the requirements for scarce resources. Because the use of a single measure of effectiveness (since any program brings about student change of several kinds that are not commensurable) is less defensible than is the use of dollar cost, the reverse of this procedure—to construct *equal-effectiveness alternatives*—is a dubious approach. Moreover, the projection of the estimated cost of a program can be done with a great deal more confidence than can its effectiveness.

In educational planning, one alternative, simply to continue current practice, should be included for baseline data. Although this alternative will usually not incur the same cost as will the innovative programs being compared, it is important to know its projected future cost and effectiveness so that the added resource and cost requirements incurred by the innovative programs may be estimated. Then the *incremental* requirements that are associated with improved effectiveness will be known. (It often turns out that these incremental requirements are small compared with the requirements simply to maintain current practice, even though they might seem large when considered in isolation.) Thus the first step toward cost-effectiveness analysis must be to estimate the future resource requirements and effectiveness of current programs.

There are many instances in which the future resource requirements of an innovative program are quite uncertain. This may arise because of uncertainties in projected enrollments, for example. In such a situation, it is important to know whether the choice among alternative programs would change if the future were different from some "most likely" case. If one program appears desirable under a wide range of future possibilities, it is obviously a good choice. If not, it is possible that the educational planner will want to choose a program that hedges against future change rather than the one that seems best in the most likely case.

The results of all this work will be estimated measures or indicators of resource requirements, cost, and ranked aspects of effectiveness projected over the time period of interest for each program and for alternative futures. The display of these items, along with supporting explanatory text, will provide planners with the information on the resource requirements and effectiveness of alternative innovative programs that they will need for making informed choices. Thus, a carefully designed display and textual presentation is a significant part of the resource-effectiveness analysis. Only in this way can the educational planner guard against the indiscriminate use of a single cost-effectiveness "number" so far removed from its limitations that it is not only useless but dangerous.

SELECTED BIBLIOGRAPHY

Barro, S.M., *Alternatives in California School Finance,* The Rand Corporation, R-633-RC/CC, May 1971.

Baumol, W.J., *Testimony Given Before the Subcommittee on Economy in Government of the Joint Economic Committee,* 90th Cong., 1st Sess., U.S. Government Printing Office, Washington, D.C., September 1967, pp. 152-179.

Becker, Gary S., "Investment in Human Capital: A Theoretical Analysis," *The Journal of Political Economy,* Vol. 70, No. 5, 1962.

Bureau of the Budget, Bulletin No. 68-9, Washington, D.C., April 12, 1968, p. 3.

Carpenter, M.B., *Analysis of Educational Programs,* The Rand Corporation, P-4576, March 1971.

Carpenter, M.B., *Program Budgeting as a Way to Focus on Objectives in Education,* The Rand Corporation, P-4162, September 1969.

Cass, James, "Politics and Education in the Sunshine State," *Saturday Review,* April 20, 1968, pp. 63-65, 76-79.

Coleman, James S., *Measures of School Performance,* The Rand Corporation, R-488-RC, July 1970.

Coleman, James S., *The Evaluation of Educational Opportunity,* The Rand Corporation, P-3911, August 1968.

Coleman, James S., et al., *Equality of Educational Opportunity,*

Office of Education, U.S. Department of Health, Education, and Welfare, Washington, D.C., 1966.

Crecine, J.P., *Computer Simulation in Urban Research,* The Rand Corporation, P-3734, November 1967.

Duke, Richard D., and Richard L. Meier, "Gaming Simulation for Urban Planning," *Journal of the American Institute of Planners,* Vol. 32, No. 1, January 1966, pp. 3-17.

Eastmond, Jefferson, *Quality Measurement Project, Final Report,* New York State Department of Education, Division of Research, 1962.

Ezekiel, M., and K. Fox, *Methods of Correlation and Regression Analysis,* John Wiley & Sons, New York, 1963.

Fisher, Gene H., *Cost Considerations in Systems Analysis,* American Elsevier Publishing Company, Inc., New York, 1971.

Fisher, Gene H., *The World of Program Budgeting,* The Rand Corporation, P-3361, May 1966.

Fisher, Gene H., "The Role of Cost-Utility in Program Budgeting," Chap. 2, in David Novick (ed.), *Program Budgeting: Program Analysis and the Federal Budget,* 2nd ed., Harvard University Press, Cambridge, Massachusetts, 1967.

Golden, L.L.L., "Challenges of the 1970's," *The Public Interest,* Summer 1968, p. 104.

Gorham, William, "Notes of a Practitioner," *The Public Interest,* Summer 1967, pp. 4-5.

Hanushek, Eric, *The Value of Teachers in Teaching,* The Rand Corporation, RM-6362/CC-PR, December 1970.

Hartley, Harry J., *Educational Planning-Programming-Budgeting: A Systems Approach,* Prentice-Hall, Inc., Englewood Cliffs, New Jersey, 1968.

Hirsch, Werner Z., et al., *Inventing Education for the Future,* Chandler Publishing Company, San Francisco, 1967.

Hirsch, Werner Z., and Morton J. Marcus, "Some Benefit-Cost Considerations of Universal Junior College Education," *National Tax Journal,* Vol. 19, March 1966.

Hitch, C.J., and R.N. McKean, *The Economics of Defense in the Nuclear Age,* The Rand Corporation, R-346, March 1960, and Harvard University Press, Cambridge, Massachusetts, 1960.

Jenkins, Robert E., *Educational Equality/Quality. Report No. 1. Program Alternatives,* San Francisco Unified School District,

San Francisco, December 1967.

Johnson, Carroll F., *White Plains Racial Balance Plan*, White Plains Public Schools, White Plains, New York, July 6, 1967.

Kershaw, J.A., and R.N. McKean, *Systems Analysis in Education*, The Rand Corporation, RM-2473-FF, October 30, 1959.

Levien, Roger E., *National Institute of Education: Preliminary Plan for the Proposed Institute*, The Rand Corporation, R-657-HEW, February 1971.

Lindman, Erick, "Resistance to Innovation in American Education," in Werner Z. Hirsch, *et al.*, *Inventing Education for the Future*, Chandler Publishing Company, San Francisco, 1967.

Mager, Robert F., *Preparing Instructional Objectives*, Fearon Publishers, Inc., Palo Alto, California, 1962.

McKean, R.N., *Efficiency in Government Through Systems Analysis*, John Wiley & Sons, Inc., New York, 1958.

Mood, Alex, "The Operations Analysis Program of the U.S. Office of Education," in Werner Z. Hirsch, *et al.*, *Inventing Education for the Future*, Chandler Publishing Company, San Francisco, 1967.

Novick, David (ed.), *Program Budgeting: Program Analysis and the Federal Budget*, 2nd ed., Harvard University Press, Cambridge, Massachusetts, 1967.

Passow, A. Harry, *Toward Better Schools. A Summary of the Findings and Recommendations of a Study of the Schools of Washington, D.C.*, Teachers College, Columbia University, New York, September 1967.

Petruschell, R.L., *Some Curve-Fitting Fundamentals*, The Rand Corporation, RM-5766-SA, December 1968.

Planning-Programming-Budgeting: Guidance for Program and Financial Plan, U.S. Department of Health, Education, and Welfare, Washington, D.C., April 12, 1967.

"Programs and Practices in Compensatory Education for Disadvantaged Children," *Review of Educational Research*, Vol. 35, No. 5, December 1965.

Quade, E.S., *Systems Analysis Techniques for Planning-Programming-Budgeting*, The Rand Corporation, P-3322, March 1966.

Quade, E.S., (ed.), *Analysis for Military Decisions*, The Rand Corporation, R-387, November 1967.

Quality Measurement Project, Final Report, Division of Research,

New York State Department of Education, New York, 1960.
Rapp, M.L., et al., *An Education Design for San Jose Unified School District's Compensatory Education Program*, The Rand Corporation, RM-5903-SJS, May 1969.
Rapp, M.L., M.B. Carpenter, S.A. Haggart, S.H. Landa, G.C. Sumner, *Evaluation of Results and Development of a Cost Model*, The Rand Corporation, R-672-SJS, March 1971.
State-Local Finances Project, *Planning for Educational Development in a Planning, Programming, Budgeting System*, The George Washington University, Washington, D.C., 1968.
State-Local Finances Project, *PPB Notes 1-8: Planning, Programming, Budgeting for City, State, County Objectives*, The George Washington University, Washington, D.C., June 1968.
"Testing and Evaluation/Two Views," *The Urban Review*, Vol. 2, No. 3, December 1967.
U.S. Congress, Subcommittee on Economy in Government of the Joint Economic Committee, *The Analysis and Evaluation on Public Expenditures: The PPB System*, Vols. 1-3, 91st Cong., 1st Sess., U.S. Government Printing Office, Washington, D.C., 1969.
Weisbrod, Burton A., "Preventing High School Dropouts," in Robert Dorfman (ed.), *Measuring Benefits of Government Investments*, Brookings Institution, 1965, pp. 117-149.
Wildavsky, Aaron, "The Political Economy of Efficiency: Cost-Benefit Analysis, Systems Analysis, and Program Budgeting," *Public Administration Review*, Vol. 26, No. 4, December 1966, pp. 292-310.

INDEX

Ability levels, 143
Academic achievement, 164, 165 (fig.)
Accuracy, reasonable degree of, 105
Achievement
    actual, 131
    changes in growth, 180
    indirect effects, 178
    see also Tests
Achievement-related variables, 193-194
Activities
    administrative, 22
    cross-classified by attributes, 30
    overhead, 33
    re-examination of established, 31
    support, 33
    two-way interaction between, 29
ADA, see Average daily attendance
Administration
    continuity of, 13
    and general support, 93
Administrative activities, see Activities
Administrative costs, see Costs
Adult education program, 216
A fortiori analysis, 158
Allocated costs, see Costs
Allocation
    artificial, 54
    efficient, 139
    of resources, 141-142
    of students, 242-251, 248 (fig.)
Alternative(s), 86, 95, 100, 154
    comparison of, 120, 133
    definition of, 69
    developing, 156
    differences among, 120
    evaluation and selection of, 229
    generation of, 158
    generation of equal-cost, 167
    preferred, 17
    rank, 155
    selection of the preferred, 121
    specified, 99
    systematic examination of, 17
    translating actions into, 96-99, 97 (table)
    see also Equal-cost alternatives; Effectiveness of alternatives
Analysis
    assumptions of, 157
    characteristics of, 156
    contingency, 158
    of an educational program, 161
    identification of qualitative considerations, 157
    limitations of, 157
    for planning, 167
    process of, 155 (fig.)

role of, 155-156
techniques of, 157-159
see also Cost analysis
Analyst, role of, 17-18
Analytical aspects of program budgeting, 9, 13-17
Areas of choice, 232
Assessment measures, 190
see also Tests
Assumptions, 169, 176
Attitude Change, 189
Automation, 118-119
Average daily attendance (ADA), 111-116, 113 (table), 114 (fig.)

Base case total cost, 120-123, 122 (table)
Behavioral objectives, *see* Objectives
Benefit-minus-cost, 148-149
Benefits, major, 151
Berkeley School District, 214
Budget(s)
appropriation, 50
capital, 93
current, 93
definition of, 49
expenditure side, 49
level, 238
see also Traditional budget(s); Program budget(s)
Bussing, 214

California Achievement Test (CAT), *see* Tests
California State Advisory Commission on School District Budgeting and Accounting, 3
California State Department of Compensatory Education, 242
Capital budget, *see* Budget(s)
Capital construction, 91
Capital cost, 91
Capital outlay account, 54
CAT, *see* Tests
Categorization
by academic field, 38
by levels, 43
by scope of action, 218 (table)
by subject area, 43, 46
by type of student, 40, 42 (table), 43
Causal relationships, 151
CERs, *see* Cost estimating relationships
Classification
by level, 46
multidimensional, 46
scheme, 45
three-way, 46, 48
Communication, device for, 11
Comparability, 151
Compensatory education, 211, 215, 250
evaluating, 252
Contingency analysis, *see* Analysis
Control aspect, 9
Core programs, 28, 275
Cost(s)
administrative, 54
allocated, 52-54
classroom-related, 169-173, 171 (table)
comparison of five-year, 122 (fig.)
increased, 4
increment, 120
minimize, 18
student-related, 172 (table)
support, 170 (table)
Cost analysis, 95, 100, 102, 116
methodology, 103
Cost and effectiveness, 16, 82, 137, 164, 212
Cost and resource implications, 102
Cost-benefit analysis, 148, 149 (fig.)
Cost-effectiveness, 18
Cost-effectiveness, 9, 271, 282
problems, 271
purposes of, 157
relating resources to effectiveness, 271
technique for comparing programs, 282
Cost element, 106
definition of, 104, 107 (table), 109 (table)
Cost estimate, 99, 120
Cost-estimating relationships (CERs), 110

Index

Cost models, 103, 117
  ad hoc considerations, 119
  basic goals, 117
  characteristics, 117
  degree of automation, 117
  degree of formality, 117
  ease of calculation, 118
  errors in internal logic, 118
  level of mathematical sophistication, 117
  responsiveness, 118
  role of in cost analysis, 118
  specific application of, 117
  see also Models
Cost structure, 106
Criteria, 154
  for achievement, 143
  overuse of, 143
  see also Effectiveness
Criterion-referenced tests, *see* Tests
Crosswalk, 50-54, 51 (table), 57
Crosswalking
  basic logic, 50-54, 51 (table)
  example, 238, 240 (fig.)
  general guidelines, 52
Curriculum composition, 78-87, 79 (table)
Curve fitting, 259-263, 260 (fig.), 262 (fig.)

Data, 224
  grade progression, 263
  and information aspect, 9
Data file of student characteristics, 12
Data-related problems, 222, 224, 226-227
Decisionmakers, 15-16, 71, 73, 123
Decisionmaking, 15-16, 232-233
  levels of, 6
Decision matrix, 173
Decision variables, 93, 100
Diagnosis, continuous, 145
Direct instructional programs, 54-57, 56 (table)
Disadvantaged students, 46
Disaggregation, 120
Discount rate, 121
Documentation, 9-10

Durrell Reading Test, *see* Tests
DYNAMOD, *see* Model(s)

Economic effectiveness of education, 148
  see also Effectiveness
Education
  economics of, 148
  goal of, 237
  multi-faceted nature of, 204
Educational effectiveness, 101, 134
  see also Effectiveness
Educational objectives, 23, 27 (fig.)
  formulation of, 23, 31
  hierarchy of, 26, 27 (fig.)
  "philosophical," 24
  socially oriented, 24
  see also Objectives
Educational planning, 280
Educational programs
  demand for, 4
  diversity in, 4
  three-way categorization of, 34 (fig.)
Educational system analysis, 38
Effectiveness, 100, 124-125, 149, 164
  of alternatives, 181 (fig.), 193
  analysis of, 91, 95, 100, 124
  comparing, 173
  criteria of, 16, 135, 142
  of current programs, 282
  dimensions of, 125
  district-wide, 137, 140 (fig.)
  district-wide testing, 125
  indicator, 134
  program, 93
  of program elements, 125-131, 138 (fig.)
  rationale for ranking criteria of, 281
  and resources, relationship between, 136 (fig.)
  use of measurements, 125
  see Measures of effectiveness; Tests
Efficient allocation, *see* Allocation
Enrollment projection, 257-269
  current techniques for, 258-265

by programs, 76-78, 92 (table)
by student characteristics, 76-78
see also Model(s)
Equal-cost alternatives, 99, 173, 180, 281
comparing effectiveness of, 175
effectiveness of, 180
generation of, 173
see also Alternatives; Effectiveness
Estimating relationships, 108, 116
see also Cost estimating relationships (CERs); Model(s)
Evaluating alternatives, 6, 16, 116, 152
basic techniques of, 152
see also Alternatives
Evaluating educational innovation, 12
see also Innovation
Evaluation
functions of, 186
long-term, 191
planning, 186
short-term, 197
Evaluation data, 201
see also Criteria; Data
Evaluation of innovation, 12
Expenditure consequences, 17
over time, 9, 230
Experimental controls, non-interactive, 191
Experimental design, 190
example of, 199

Feedback, 254
Financial impact, time horizons of, 60
Fixed charges account, 54
Food service and community service accounts, 54
Fundamental intellectual skills
language and communication skills, 35
learning how to learn, 37
quantitative skills, 35
study skills, 35
Future alternative courses of action, 49
Future utility cost, 110

Gaming, see Simulation
General support costs, 52
Gifted students, 46
Goal-oriented, 236
Goals, see Objectives
Grade equivalents, 195
Grade-equivalent scores, 277
Grade-point averages, 147
Grade progression, 263-265
Grade progression data, see Data

Health account, 54
Hedges against future change, 282
Hierarchy of objectives, see Objectives
Hypothesis, 112
reasonableness of, 113

Increment cost, see Cost(s)
Indirect costs
allocation of, 53
definition of, 53
see also Cost(s)
Information, organized, 230
Informational support, 232
Information base, organized, 11
Information system, 188
Innovation, 281
change in quality of output, 190
change in utilization of resources, 190
goal of, 196
resource requirements of, 281
Innovative program, 186, 188, 199
evaluating, 190
Input requirements, 117
Inputs, specification of, 193
Inputs and outputs, 11, 154
Instruction, vertical organization of, 75
Instructional
activities, 22
description of method, 94
design, 80-85, 84 (table)
support programs and auxiliary services, 85

Judgments

Index

objective, 189
subjective, 189

Learning objectives, 32
   activities indirectly related to, 33
   generally, 33
   in specific subject areas, 32
   student-type categories, 33
   subject-oriented, 33
   see also Objectives
Least squares, method of, 113-115
Level of detail, 50
Life objectives
   career-related activities, 32
   family and community
      involvement, 32
   participation in cultural
      affairs, 32
   see also Objectives
Lifetime income, 150
Linear relationship, 113
Long-range educational
   objectives, 195
Long-range planning, 23, 222
Long-run requirements, 257
Long-term objective, 201
Long-term program assessment,
   197-198
Long-term sense, 198

Maximize outcome, 18
Maximizes or minimizes, 272
Measurements, interpreting, 277
Measures, sets of, 279
Measures of effectiveness, 25, 125,
   146, 177
   ability level grouping, 130
   attitude change, 183 (fig.), 184
   growth rate, 183 (fig.), 184
   misuse by overuse, 135
   socioeconomic level grouping,
      130-131, 131 (table)
   uses of, 131-140
   see also Effectiveness; Tests
Measuring devices, 189
   see also Tests
Measuring instruments, 194, 277
   see also Tests

M.E.T.R.O., see Model(s)
Minimize cost, see Cost
Model(s), 82, 100, 103, 154
   complexity of, 187
   computer simulation, 267-268
   definition of in historical
      context, 68
   grade progression
      (DYNAMOD), 258
   M.E.T.R.O., 268
   Office of Education enrollment
      projection, 258
   population, 258
   of transportation, 267
   of urban growth, 267
   variables in school district,
      100 (table)
   see also Cost models
Modeling
   analytical, 68
   methodology of effectiveness, 68
   methodology of resource and cost,
      68
   school district program, 100-101
Multidimensional, 280
Multiple objectives, 254
   incommensurable, 129
   see also Objectives
Multi-year planning, 70, 103

Net-benefit approach, 149
Nonallocated programs, 214
Noncost factors, 105
Nondollar resource requirements, 9
Nonquantifiable, 156
Norm-referenced, 146
Norm-referenced tests, see Tests

Objectives
   abstract, 25
   activities related to, 23
   affective, 38
   behavioral, 24-25
   choice of, 154
   define, 23
   examine, 23
   formulate, 23
   hierarchy of, 146

higher-level, 128
identify, 23
instructional, 25
lower-order, 129
measurable, 189
measuring progress, 189
multiple, 29
not operational, 25
observable, 189
philosophical, 25
of program elements, 127-128, 236-237
program level, 26
setting of, 8 (fig.), 9
specification of, 189
statement of, 13-14
student-oriented, 126 (table)
subprogram level, 26
synthesis, 30
Occupational training, 38
Operation and maintenance, 22, 93
accounts, 54
costs, 54
Operational characteristics, 104
Options, 169
Output-oriented programs, 232

Pearl River, see Program structure
People-related problems, 222-227
Percentile scores, 277
Performance capabilities, specific, 117
Planning
adequacy of, 254
definition of, 49
Political
atmosphere, 282
considerations, 213
Population model, see Model(s)
Predetermined variables, 100
Present value, 121
Problems categorized by scope of action, 210-219, 218 (table)
Problems in public education, 205
Process-oriented evaluation, 256
Program, 45
analysis, 93
definition of, 50

differentiation, 75
and financial plan, 9-13
objective-oriented, 238
Program budget, 49-50
array of program categories, 46
categories of, 52
contents, 57
example of, 63 (table), 239 (fig.), 240 (fig.)
format of, 45-48, 47 (table), 238, 239 (fig.)
set of resource and cost categories, 46
structures, 58
see also Crosswalk; Traditional budget
Program budgeting, 3
activities of, 8 (fig.), 223 (fig.)
activity areas in developing a system, 227-229, 228 (fig.)
allocating the data to cost categories, 50
components of, 8 (fig.)
definition of, 221
description of, 7, 8 (fig.)
documentation of, 8 (fig.)
impact of features, 223 (fig.)
major components of, 7, 8 (fig.)
nature of, 6-7, 8 (fig.), 9
problems of, 222-226
system-analytical aspect of, 14 (fig.)
uses of, 10-12
see also Allocation
Program categories, 35-43, 36 (table)
design of, 28
Program categorization, 30-31, 35-43
by academic field, 38
descriptive, 31
iterative, 31
by level, 43, 44 (table)
prescriptive, 31
rationale for, 31
by subject-oriented learning objectives, 35-40, 36 (table)
by type of student, 40-43, 42 (table)

Index

Program characteristics, 101
Program development and
  evaluation, 39
Program differentiation, 91
Program effectiveness, *see*
  Effectiveness
Program element(s), 17, 22, 25, 45
  definition of, 50
  district-wide effectiveness, 137
  effectiveness, 125, 146
  effectiveness of nonprimary, 135
  examples of, 50
  goals must be specified, 127
  multiple objectives, 127
  objectives of, 128
  realignment of, 23
  relationships among, 143
  structuring of, 236
Program memorandum, 10
Program 6, assessment, guidance,
  and counseling, 144
Program structure, 20, 43-45,
    237 (fig.)
  characteristics of, 232, 233
  definition of, 21
  hierarchical classification scheme,
    22
  illustration of for state
    department
      of education, 234 (fig.)
  level-of-education categories, 33
  multidimensional, 22, 30
  nature of, 230-232, 231 (fig.)
  Pearl River, 235-236
  role of, 230-232
  stable, 23
  three-dimensional nature of, 35
Programs, 22
Project R-3, 242-251
  description of, 168
  primary objectives, 177 (fig.)
Projecting
  enrollments, 75
  by planning departments, 259
  see also Model(s)

Racial mix and student
  achievement, 215

Raw scores, 195
Regression analysis, 279
Relationship, two-way, 30
Resource allocation, 3, 25, 68, 275
  see also Allocation
Resource analysis, 101
Resource and cost analysis, 91
Resource and cost model, 98, 101,
    222, 276
  see also Cost model(s); Model(s)
Resource and effectiveness
  relationships, 153
Resource-effectiveness analysis,
  single measure, 276
Resource-effectiveness
  relationships, 134
Resource implications, 86
Resource input
  ratios, 82-83
  specifications, 83, 87
Resource requirements, 15-16, 83,
    93
  calculation of, 87
  and cost, 81, 100
  translation into financial
    requirements, 88
Resources, 4
  allocation of, 6, 158
  alternative uses of, 69
  availability of, 4
  cost of, 4
  future requirements for, 15
  shifted, 142
Resources and effectiveness, 154
Results, presentation of, 157
Retarded students, 46
R-3, *see* Project R-3

Sampling, 133
San Jose Unified School District,
  Project R-3, *see* Compensatory
    education; Project R-3
SAT, *see* Tests
Scholastic Aptitude Test (SAT),
  see Tests
Scholastic capability, 139
School board, policymaking role
  of, 18-19

School bond issues, 4
School district configuration, 90-91, 92 (table)
School integration, 214
School system, 71-73
 decisions and programs, 74 (fig.)
 resource requirements and budgets, 88-90, 89 (fig.)
Scope of action, 206
Scoring mode, 195
Sensitivity analysis, 116, 158
 see also Cost estimating relationships (CERs)
Shortcoming, 258
Short-term objective, 201
Short-term program assessment, 197-198
Simulation, 163, 168, 176, 180, 184
Socioeconomic, 162, 261, 280-281
 environment, 130, 139
 strata, 143
 variables, 250
Special studies report, 10
Standard scores, 277
Standardized achievement test, see Tests
Structural aspects, 7
Subobjectives, 146
 operational, 30
Subprograms, 22, 45
Success, definition of, 142
Sunk costs, 103
Superintendent, decisionmaking role of, 18-19
Support functions, 22
Support program resource requirements, 54-57, 91
Support-type programs, 214
System-analytical aspect of program budgeting, 14 (fig.)
System-analytical studies, 86
System of analysis, 13
System variables, 86, 93-96

Tax overrides, 4
Teacher types, 106
Teaching, 213
Team, 213

Tests
 assessment, 216
 California achievement test (CAT), 162, 165 (fig.), 243
 criterion-referenced, 133, 142, 146
 Durrell Reading Test, 162
 norm-referenced, 132, 143
 Scholastic Aptitude Test (SAT), 147
 standardized achievement test, 143
 see also Measures of effectiveness
Time horizon, 103, 120
Time period, 102
Time-variant, 280
Timing, 197
Tracking, 162, 213, 242
Tracks, 130
Trade-off analysis, 235
Traditional budget, 49, 238, 239 (fig.), 240 (fig.)
 accounts, 52
 summary of, 52, 62 (table)
 see also Crosswalk; Program budget
Translating program budget to traditional budget, 50
Transportation account, 54
Transportation models, 267
Try-out period, 188

Uncertainty about the future, 158
Urban growth models, see Model(s)
Utilization of facilities, 53

Value judgments, 129
Variables, 80, 86
 compactness, 70
 decision, 71, 73
 generality, 70
 internal, 73
 policy, 71
 predetermined, 71
 selection of, 70
 target, 73
Visibility, 66
Vocational college preparatory programs, 46
Vocational programs, 216

SELECTED LIST OF RAND BOOKS

Arrow, Kenneth J., and Marvin Hoffenberg, *A Time Series Analysis of Interindustry Demands,* North-Holland Publishing Company, Amsterdam, The Netherlands, 1959.
Bagdikian, Ben H., *The Information Machines: Their Impact on Men and the Media,* Harper & Row, New York, 1971.
Bellman, Richard E., and Stuart E. Dreyfus, *Applied Dynamic Programming,* Princeton University Press, Princeton, New Jersey, 1962.
Bretz, Rudy, *A Taxonomy of Communication Media,* Educational Technology Publications, Englewood Cliffs, New Jersey, 1971.
Buchheim, Robert W., and the staff of The Rand Corporation, *Space Handbook: Astronautics and Its Applications,* Random House, Inc., New York, 1959.
Dorfman, Robert, Paul A. Samuelson, and Robert M. Solow, *Linear Programming and Economic Analysis,* McGraw-Hill Book Company, Inc., New York, 1958.
Downs, Anthony, *Inside Bureaucracy,* Little Brown and Company, Boston, Massachusetts, 1967.
Dresher, Melvin, *Games of Strategy: Theory and Applications,* Prentice-Hall, Inc., Englewood Cliffs, New Jersey, 1961.
Fisher, Gene H., *Cost Considerations in Systems Analysis,* American Elsevier Publishing Company, New York, 1970.
Hastings, Cecil, Jr., *Approximations for Digital Computers,* Princeton University Press, Princeton, New Jersey, 1955.

Hearle, Edward F.R., and Raymond J. Mason, *A Data Processing System for State and Local Governments,* Prentice-Hall, Inc., Englewood Cliffs, New Jersey, 1963.

Hirshleifer, Jack, James C. DeHaven, and Jerome W. Milliman, *Water Supply: Economics, Technology, and Policy,* The University of Chicago, Chicago, Illinois, 1960.

Hitch, Charles J., and Roland McKean, *The Economics of Defense in the Nuclear Age,* Harvard University Press, Cambridge, Massachusetts, 1960.

Kershaw, Joseph A., and Roland N. McKean, *Teacher Shortages and Salary Schedules,* McGraw-Hill Book Company, Inc., New York, 1962.

McKean, Roland N., *Efficiency in Government Through Systems Analysis: With Emphasis on Water Resource Development,* John Wiley & Sons, Inc., New York, 1958.

McKinsey, J.C.C., *Introduction to the Theory of Games,* McGraw-Hill Book Company, Inc., New York, 1952.

Nelson, Richard R., Merton J. Peck, and Edward D. Kalachek, *Technology, Economic Growth and Public Policy,* The Brookings Institution, Washington D.C., 1967.

Novick, David (ed.), *Program Budgeting: Program Analysis and the Federal Budget,* Harvard University Press, Cambridge, Massachusetts, 1965.

Pascal, Anthony, *Thinking About Cities: New Perspectives on Urban Problems,* Dickenson Publishing Company, Belmont, California, 1970.

Quade, E.S. (ed.), *Analysis for Military Decisions,* North-Holland Publishing Company, Amsterdam, The Netherlands, 1964.

Quade, E.S., and W.I. Boucher, *Systems Analysis and Policy Planning. Applications in Defense,* American Elsevier Publishing Company, Inc., New York, 1968.

Sharpe, William F., *The Economics of Computers,* Columbia University Press, New York, 1969.

Sheppard, J.J., *Human Color Perception,* American Elsevier Publishing Company, Inc., New York, 1968.

The Rand Corporation, *A Million Random Digits with 100,000 Normal Deviates,* The Free Press, Glencoe, Illinois, 1955.

Williams, J.D., *The Compleat Strategyst: Being a Primer on the Theory of Games of Strategy,* McGraw-Hill Book Company, Inc., New York, 1954.